Eagle Shadow

by

Shelly Greenhalgh-Davis

1stBooks - rev. 12/20/01

Prologue
Nebraska Territory
1864

The sun was beginning to set on the quiet Nebraska plain. A glowing fire lit the tepee from within while three Cheyenne braves stood watching as their old friend lay dying.

"As the sun grows cold and night covers our tepees, so the warmth of my life escapes this day. It will rob my heart of another morning fire." His wrinkled face hid the guilt that filled his heart. Raising a withered hand and signaling one of the braves to kneel beside him, he confided, "Beartooth, remember my young son who died many moons ago?"

"Yes," replied Beartooth. "But the brave who killed him was banished from our people. He paid for his crime."

"No," the old one objected, "it was because of my grief that I blamed him. But he was innocent. No one killed my son. He drowned. Do you know the Sacred Mountain many sleeps to the north?" Beartooth nodded. "At the place where the water flows over a rock is where my son drowned. The rock and the forest around it are filled with evil spirits, and the water runs with death. It is forbidden ground."

"We will not go there," said Beartooth.

"And the brave who was banished from the people, you must find him and bring him back. If he no longer lives, then find his family and bring them to us."

"But it has been many moons. What if they do not come?"

"They must come. They are our people. Tell them I am sorry. Tell them I have suffered for the shame I brought to their family. Go now, and only come back when you have found them."

Without hesitation the Indian obeyed. He left the tepee, gathered up minimal provisions, mounted his horse, and turned westward. The sound of galloping hooves soon faded as the rider vanished into the darkening night.

Chapter 1
Montana Territory
1865

A brief afternoon rain had left the grasses on the Broken Bow Ranch fragrant and glistening. The air had cooled, rejuvenating the sweaty cowboys and causing them to quicken their pace at branding calves. The crackle of a dying branding fire mingled with the pained bellow of calves, the swish of ropes, and the shouts of cowboys to create a familiar cacophony of sound in this high Montana valley.

Nathaniel Hunter, known to everyone as Nate, released a calf to run bawling back to its mother with its still-sizzling brand. He wondered if the mother cows remembered going through this same experience when they were calves.

He coiled his rope, mounted his horse and headed back into the herd to cut out the last calf for the day. The mother cow saw him coming and dug in, prepared to protect her offspring from being taken away. But under Nate's guidance, his horse bore down on the pair, chasing off the mother and facing the calf head-on. The horse matched the flustered calf's every move, darting first right, then left, then right again until Nate saw his opportunity to run his horse in behind the calf and drive it away from the herd. Then the chase was on as the horse quickly closed the distance between itself and the running calf. With his legs clenched around the horse's belly, Nate leaned down, almost parallel to the ground, and tossed his lariat neatly around the calf's neck. The horse skidded to a stop, sending dirt clods flying and tightening the rope, slamming the calf on the ground nearly senseless.

In a flash Nate was on the ground too, holding the calf's legs down with both hands and one foot while another cowboy burned the distinctive Broken Bow brand, a B shielded on the left by a broken half circle, into its hip. Nate performed this whole task with masterful skill. He was eighteen years old but he'd been doing this for four years.

The half-Indian Nate had a tall, muscular build, tan skin, and dark eyes that always looked deep into those of the person to whom he was talking. His wavy black hair almost covered his ears and he never wore a hat. His buckskin pants, lined with fringe, were tucked inside leather moccasin boots. He sported a fringed buckskin jacket held together at the waist by a wide rawhide belt from which hung a knife. A Colt .45 single-action revolver was slung low on his hip, the handle conspicuously notched thirteen times. Fitted snugly about his neck was a string of Cheyenne tribal beads.

The air still smelled of burnt hide as Nate helped douse the branding fire, then mounted his horse and began coiling his rope.

He was a little mystifying to his fellow cowhands. His expression would never reveal his thoughts, but his ability to perceive other people's characters shortly after meeting them was almost eerie. He was rarely roused to anger, but any slur against his heritage warranted a fight. His pride in the Cheyenne was instilled in him by his father, and those who knew Nate knew better than to raise his ire. He held his head high and it seemed he feared nothing.

There were close to thirty workers on the Broken Bow. Most were bachelors and some were temporary hands, but there were a few families, such as the Hunters. They had once worked on a farm on the Platte River in Nebraska Territory. Word spread about a huge, new ranch up north that needed people, so they decided to try their hand at herding cattle.

Buck Hunter was a full-blooded Cheyenne Indian; his name had been shortened from his Indian name, Wild Buck Hunter. His wife Lydia was a white woman and they had two children, Nate and Lena. Buck and his son were both cowhands on the Broken Bow. Lydia and Lena were employed to do the washing, clean bunkhouses, and serve three meals a day in the dining hall.

Nate and Lena were close to their father who had taught them all about Indians—the language, the customs, the meaning of age-old traditions such as the Sun Dance and the Four Sacred Arrows, the honor acquired by counting coups on an enemy in battle. He had proudly told them of the well-organized government of the Northern Cheyenne nation and its famed ruling body, the Council of Forty-four. Nate had learned from his father how to track game and hunt as if he were one with the animal. Nate possessed the keen senses of his blood brothers, and although he and Lena had never seen a Cheyenne Indian aside from their father, they were not strangers to the red man.

Nate was reluctant to ride back just yet. He loved the feeling of a job well-done and he wanted to survey his work a moment longer. He was proud to be a hand on the Broken Bow. The ranch had grown substantially in the four years his family had been there. The owner, Boss Sinclair, was a fair man and seemed to Nate like he'd been a rancher all his life although Nate knew he had not been so.

Nate thought of the Indians again and a twinge of dread festered in the pit of his stomach. His father said an Indian named Beartooth had visited one day while Nate was out mending fences. Beartooth brought a message for the Hunters direct from the deathbed of a brave. The Hunters were wanted back at the band of their ancestors, and Beartooth seemed intent on carrying out the mission with which he'd been charged. He had told Buck that the soul of the dead brave could not rest until the Hunters allowed the Cheyenne to beg their forgiveness for the wrong that had been done and had taken up their rightful place among their people.

Nate knew his family wouldn't return to the people, but still, the whole thing gave him a bad feeling. He knew everything about his people, but they had always been far away, nameless and faceless. Now one of those people had come here. He had a name. And he was trying to shake up Nate's perfect world.

"Caught ya daydreamin', eh?" said a voice beside him. It was Gus, the ranch foreman, a man with an easy manner yet firm enough to keep the hands in line.

"Say, Nate, I think the boys need to have a little fun," said Gus, one cheek bulging with a chaw of tobacco.

There was taunting in his voice and Nate narrowed his eyes suspiciously. "Something tells me I'm not gonna like your idea of fun."

Gus smiled out of the corner of his mouth. "Well, you were kinda braggin' yesterday that you could ride Daredevil."

Nate shifted in the saddle uneasily. Where had his presence of mind been when he made such a statement?

"You ain't gonna chicken out, are ya?"

"No," Nate quickly answered.

Gus' smile grew wider. "Then you'll do it?"

"Yeah, I'll do it."

Gus gave a loud whoop and Nate couldn't help but smile.

*   *   *

It was a springlike afternoon in Timber Fork and the little town buzzed with activity. There seemed to be more immigrant wagons than usual, and a freight caravan was just pulling onto Main Street after a long trip from a point farther east. The rattle of wagons and clink of harness chains mingled with the sound of cracking whips and barking dogs, and the smell of new wood wafted through the air from the nearby lumber mill.

The sight of the pretty young woman stood out on the dusty street as Tara Sinclair rode her spirited black horse Molly. Tara wore a tan riding skirt, brown gingham blouse, and riding boots. The sixteen-year-old looked charming in whatever she wore, and her slender frame and striking beauty were the envy of the other town girls. Her long, light brown hair was a glory to her and fell gracefully over her shoulders in a wavy mass. She had eyes as blue as the sky on a cloudless day and they were deep-set in her prim, fair-skinned face.

Her family was considerably wealthy, certainly by Timber Fork's standards, the burgeoning settlement in western Montana Territory at the foot of the Lewis and Clark range. Tara dressed fashionably as women from the city usually did. She didn't appear as one who was born to the pioneer life but as a displaced lady trying to maintain as cultured an existence as possible in this remote frontier town.

The Sinclair family's roots were in Chicago where Tara's grandfather, John Edward Sinclair, had educated himself in the science of iron smelting and founded the Sinclair Iron Works, the city's premier foundry. He achieved such a knack for the iron business that within three years he had people in St. Louis and Detroit starting foundries in those cities. He spent his later years traveling in high style on the new railroad, visiting his factories and amassing a sizeable fortune.

Tara had heard how John Sinclair's wife Maeve, an auburn-haired Irish beauty, had stunned Chicago with her lavish parties and a guest list boasting captains of industry, politicians, and visiting New York actors. She had talked often of her home in County Meath, Ireland, of the dances at Kilbaillie, of sneaking away from her parents' house at night to visit the local pub to hear the tenant farmers spontaneously break into song. She danced to their spirited jigs and was moved by their sad ballads. A great three-masted ship had borne her adventurous soul away to the New World, never to return. But Ireland was never far from her heart, and Tara had been named for the Hill of Tara, the place in County Meath where the ancient kings had been crowned.

John Sinclair's sons had not followed him into iron work but they had acquired his business prowess and applied it to their chosen fields. Tara's father, Edward Sinclair, owned Timber Fork's only store, as well as the Split Timber Ranch just east of town. His brother, the elder Jerome Sinclair, owned the Broken Bow a few miles west of town, and that's where Tara was headed now. The Broken Bow was a hundred-and-fifty-thousand-acre spread and a cattle empire at its greatest. The name Sinclair was highly respected throughout the Territory. Tara's presence on the street commanded attention from passersby, and many a cowboy, miner, and townsman tipped his hat as she rode by.

She rode from the noise of the town into the quiet countryside. The rain clouds were moving eastward and the sun had come out again. The song of unseen birds could be heard in the distance, and the only other sound was the clap of Molly's hooves as they struck against the packed earth. Clumps of bitterroot and other flowers grew beside the still-wet, wheel-rutted road.

Tara had been at school all day and she had homework to be done, but she was glad her father had a message for her to take to Uncle Jerome. The ride to the Broken Bow was relaxing and pleasant, and Molly seemed to enjoy getting out as well.

She came to Elkhorn Creek, the eastern border of the ranch. She crossed over on a wooden bridge, then followed the road under a cedar arch that bore the name of the ranch, and on to the top of the next rise where she reined in her horse.

At the bottom of the hill were spread out the main buildings—barns, bunkhouses, and a dining hall. To the south, apart from the other buildings, stood the mansion. This prominent white structure with a porch extending across the front was centered in a five-acre yard shaded by huge cottonwoods and pines and was the home of Boss Jerome Sinclair and his wife.

A crowd was gathered around one of the corrals, and Tara's heart lept at the prospect of some excitement. She kicked her horse into a gallop and sped down the hill. A short time later, with her horse tied to a hitching post, Tara was headed towards the cheering cowboys. Through openings in the crowd, she could see that someone was being jerked about on top of a bucking bronco. She stopped short. It was Nate Hunter, that half-breed. And he was on Daredevil. She made her way to the fence to watch as Nate tried to ride one of the toughest broncs on the ranch, a good-for-nothing beast only kept around for those who accepted dares to try and ride him.

Surprisingly, Tara was the only town girl who did not think Nate was utterly good-looking. To the rest, his sincere, staring eyes, sharply defined features, and attractive though rare smile held an alluring, masculine charm. But to Tara, he was an odd one. All the other cowhands admired and respected her. They treated her like a boss's niece should be treated, like a Sinclair should be treated. But Nate wasn't impressed in the least by such things as social position, and he was the only person in the world from whom she could not command respect. While everyone around her whooped and yelled for Nate, Tara secretly hoped to see Daredevil toss him unceremoniously into the dirt.

The wild black horse jumped high in the air and twisted and jerked, trying his savage best to throw the rider from his back. But Nate stayed on as if glued there, holding the rope with one hand while his other arm flailed the air. Finally Daredevil quit bucking and began running in confused circles. Nate swung a leg over and slid off the horse triumphantly. The cowboys broke into cheers and applause, and some pulled out money to settle bets while others vaulted over the fence and gathered around to give Nate a congratulatory slap on the back.

Tara was not going to congratulate him. She moved away from the crowd as subtly as she could and headed for the mansion, trying to remember what the message was that she was supposed to tell her uncle.

When Tara exited the mansion and walked to the hitching post where Molly was tied, she was surprised to find Lena Hunter waiting for her. Lena said nothing and Tara went about untying her horse, but she was conscious of Lena watching her. "Hello," Tara said finally.

"Hi," said Lena with a bright smile. "I saw you at the corrals earlier. What'd you think of Nate's ride?"

Tara mounted her horse and gathered up the reins. "Well, Daredevil is getting old. He was bound to wear down sooner or later."

"You're not leaving already, are you?"

"Yes, why?"

Lena hesitated a moment. "I have something to show you."

Tara couldn't imagine what Lena had that would interest her. "I really haven't time, Lena. I should get home."

"Oh, it'll only take a minute. It's just down in our barn."

"Way out th—" Tara looked down at Lena's excited, eager face and smiled. "Well, all right." She extended an arm down and Lena took hold and climbed onto Molly behind Tara.

Lena was a year younger than Tara. Her smoky dark eyes conveyed an inner strength that belied her small, willowy frame. She had pretty Indian features including smooth tan skin and straight black hair that reached to the back of her waist. Unrestrained by ties or hairpins, it fluttered freely in the wind. She was dressed in a riding skirt, boots, and a red flannel shirt drawn in at her slender waist with a strip of rawhide. A rabbit's-foot charm dangled on a string of leather about her neck.

Seldom did she ever dress differently as living on a ranch and being around cowboys made her a bit wild and carefree herself. Though her mother would rather her to have been more ladylike as town girls were, Lena would have no part of it. There was too much of her father in her for that.

They rode for a mile across the fields south of the Sinclair mansion till they came to the Hunters' barn situated about fifty yards from their small cabin. Lena vaulted off the horse and waited for Tara to dismount.

"Go ahead," said Lena, motioning to the barn door. "It's just right in there."

Tara headed for the door. She turned to see if Lena was with her and was startled when Lena almost ran into her. Tara pulled open the barn door and entered. She walked into the center of the barn, peeking into stalls, expecting to find perhaps a new foal or some puppies.

"Lena, where is—"

Suddenly the atmosphere exploded in bursts of color, Indian whoops, and falling hay.

Tara screamed in terror as Nate landed in the hay in front of her. His bare chest and face were decorated in garish designs with black, red, yellow, and white war paint, and he held a tomahawk in one hand. He collapsed in laughter as Tara clutched her throat and glanced up at the loft to see if anything else was coming. She felt the blood rushing to her cheeks, and her forehead and palms became uncomfortably hot.

As she watched Nate hold his stomach and laugh so hard he couldn't speak, her momentary thoughts of terror transformed into unbridled fury. She clenched her fists and spoke through gritted teeth, "You're not funny." She averted her eyes, adding, "And put on a shirt."

It seemed stifling hot in here. She must get outside and get some fresh air. She caught a glimpse of Lena's smirking face as she brushed past the girl on her way to the door. She slammed the barn door behind her, trying to shut off their laughter which resounded in her ears.

She walked two steps and gasped. In front of her, three Indian braves sat bareback on spotted horses.

Chapter 2

Nate's stomach hurt from laughing as he picked himself up from the hay. He hadn't had this much fun in a while. And all she could think of to say was 'Put on a shirt'? He'd have to think of a way to return Lena's favor of getting Tara to come out here.

"Nate," he heard Lena call from outside, "come out here now."

There was a note of urgency in her voice. Nate tossed his tomahawk aside, donned his shirt leaving the buttons undone, and joined Lena and Tara outside. He gulped when he saw the braves. They were Cheyenne. Without a moment's delay, he ran around the side of the barn and toward his cabin. "Pa!" he shouted. "Come out here!"

Buck Hunter emerged from the cabin. He was a tall, wiry Indian with black hair just beginning to gray. He wore it shoulder-length and kept it out of his face by a red bandana tied around his forehead. He followed Nate back to the barn and stood looking warily up at the visitors.

The braves were clad in buckskin leggings and breastplates made of bone, and various shapes and sizes of feathers and beads accented their attire. They sat solemn and straight on their horses, obviously the finest representatives of a proud people.

The middle brave eyed Buck briefly, then his gaze focused on Nate. Nate was suddenly conscious of the homemade greasepaint on his face. He bowed his head sheepishly and used both hands to rub it off as best he could.

The brave's face registered a flicker of amusement, then his eyes switched back to Buck. "I have brought others of our people with me," the brave said, indicating his companions on either side. "We know you will return with us to our people."

"I will not, Beartooth," replied Buck.

Nate's interest was piqued. So this was Beartooth, with whom his father had spoken before.

"We are your people," stated Beartooth emphatically. "Among us you would be welcome."

"My father was not welcome among you," said Buck. "Now he's dead. It's too late to make amends with him. Here on the Broken Bow we are welcome and we are needed. Boss Sinclair has much land and many cattle. We work for him."

Beartooth's austere eyes reflected disgust. "You have been corrupted by white man's ways, Buck. But you are Cheyenne and you cannot pretend that you are not."

7

"I am proud to be Cheyenne," Buck firmly replied. "But my place is here. My wife is a white woman, and my children are as much a part of her people as they are mine."

Beartooth swung one leg over his horse's head, slid off, and handed his rein to the brave on his left. He was almost as tall as Buck, had broad, sinewy shoulders, and appeared to be about the same age. "The time will come when we will have to fight the white man to take back lands which he has stolen from us these many moons. If you stand with the white man, there will be no mercy for you."

"And if you stand against the white man, you stand against my family as well, and there will be no mercy for you."

At this, Tara ran to untie her horse. The Cheyenne paid little attention to her as she mounted up and kicked her horse into a gallop. She soon disappeared across the fields.

"You would stand with our enemies and fight against our people, against our chief, Red Feather?" Beartooth's question came as a challenge. "You would fight against me?"

"I would fight anyone who threatened my family's freedom," replied Buck evenly. "And that includes you."

"Then fight me now," said Beartooth as he unsheathed his knife.

Nate drew in a breath and took a step back. He stared at the knife and his heart began to pound.

"Oh, Pa, please don't fight him," pleaded Lena, "please."

"Go on in the house, Lena," said Buck, never taking his eyes off Beartooth. Lena didn't move. "Go on now. It'll be all right."

Lena obeyed and Beartooth assumed a fighting stance. "You say you are proud to be Cheyenne, Buck. We will see what kind of brave you are."

Buck felt around his waist but his knife wasn't on him. Still watching Beartooth, he held out a hand towards his son. "Nate."

Nate dutifully pulled his own knife, ran forward to pass it to his father's waiting hand, and took his place back against the barn wall.

Beartooth and Buck hunched over and began circling, trying to size up each other's abilities in advance and anticipate weaknesses. It became obvious within moments that Beartooth was an accomplished fighter, but Nate watched, unflinching, knowing that his father's courage matched any Cheyenne's and that Buck would never be bested by this brave who seemed to have some personal point to prove.

Beartooth took the first swipes. Buck dodged the blade as it passed near his heart and returned some jabs of his own. The circling continued and Beartooth kept on with swipes in various directions to throw Buck off guard. Like a flash of lightning, Beartooth grabbed Buck's free arm and twisted it behind his back. Beartooth's knife came around in a direct line for Buck's chest, but Buck

8

dropped his own knife and caught Beartooth's wrist, stopping it with the force of a brick wall stopping a bullet. In the next instant, Buck was bending over, flipping the brave over his back. Beartooth landed in a heap on the ground, and Buck scrambled to retrieve his knife before his foe could arise. Beartooth regained his footing a fraction of a second late. Buck's knife sliced the brave's cheek open from the corner of his left eye to his chin, sending tiny rivers of blood down his face and neck.

Beartooth's hand covered the wound and he gritted his teeth against the pain. There was fury and a thirst for revenge in his eyes. One second of slowness could kill, and Beartooth wouldn't make that mistake again.

Two horses came galloping across the fields towards them and one of the braves on horseback pulled his rifle from a sheath beside him and rested it across his horse's withers. Buck and Beartooth stopped to watch as Tara and Jerome Sinclair reined in their horses and dismounted. Boss Sinclair was a heavy-set man with an authoritative air about him. His thick white hair and mustache aged his fiftyish face.

The boss took in the situation in an instant, then trained his rifle on Beartooth. "Be glad your face is all that's bleeding. Now get off my land." Beartooth defiantly stood still and Jerome cocked the hammer back. "I said get off my land." At that moment the brave on horseback pointed his rifle at Jerome. Jerome swung his rifle around and pulled the trigger. The blast knocked the brave off of his horse with a grunt.

Tara covered her mouth with a trembling hand as she cowered behind her uncle, who reached behind him to shield her.

They all watched the brave struggling to rise as blood streamed down his chest from the wound in his shoulder. Beartooth and the third brave helped him up and lifted him onto his horse. Then they remounted, dug their heels in the horse's sides, and galloped away, leading the injured brave's horse by the rein.

Jerome relaxed his posture. "Buck, Nate, are you all right?" The Hunters nodded. "I'm sorry, Buck," said Jerome. I didn't mean to hurt anyone. I only meant to warn them."

"I know," replied Buck. "But I think it's safe to say we'll be seeing them again."

Jerome put his big arm around Tara's shoulder and gave it a squeeze. "Let's go back and tie up Molly behind the wagon, Tara. I'll drive you home."

Chapter 3

It was dark by the time Tara's uncle had dropped her off in front of the Sinclair store and home. Her nerves had calmed, but the sight of the Indian being shot off his horse pervaded her thoughts. If only she hadn't gone for her uncle. If only she hadn't gone with Lena out to their barn in the first place. No, she told herself, that wouldn't have made a difference. Somebody still would've been hurt.

She waved goodbye to her uncle, led Molly along the storefront past the neat window display of boots and suspenders, and around the side of the two-story structure that looked like many other buildings in town except that its wood boasted a fresh coat of white paint. After stabling her horse in the barn, she ascended the steps to the back door of her home. She heard voices in the parlor and hurried in to see who they were.

Silence settled on the room when she entered. There sat her white-haired, spectacled father, her petite, brown-haired, blue-eyed mother with her younger brother and sister, a man, a woman, and three small children. But across the room was a girl about Tara's age and her older brother. The girl wore a faded calico dress and two short blond braids.

Tara's face lit up. "Julie!" The girls ran to each other and hugged. "What on earth are you doing here? I thought you were in Oregon."

"We were, but we're back again."

"You mean to stay?"

"Of course!"

Julie had the same big blue eyes, freckled face, and cheerful nature characteristic of all of the Curtis clan.

"Oh, you haven't changed a bit," said Tara.

"What about me, Tara?" asked Mark, her brother. "You remember me, don't you?" He looked like his sister but his hair was a lighter sandy blond.

Tara seemed oblivious to anyone else while she smiled warmly and took his hands into hers.

"Of course I remember you, Mark, and I can't tell you how happy I am to see you."

Mark arose from his seat laughing. He was almost a foot taller than Tara. "It's been a long time," and he gave her a bear hug.

"Two years!" exclaimed Tara. "That's long enough."

Tara's mother spoke. "They came in just a half hour ago, Tara. We couldn't wait for you to come home."

Tara took a seat between her friends and conversation resumed. But Tara was not listening. She was remembering her girlhood in Chicago. There the

Curtises had become close friends of the Sinclairs, and Julie and Tara grew up together. So when the Sinclairs made the move West in 1860, the Curtises came along too. There in the flourishing town of Timber Fork, Tara's uncle founded the Broken Bow and her father founded the Split Timber and built the store.

By this time Tara was becoming a young woman, and before long she and Mark Curtis fell in love. He was sixteen. She was fourteen, and for months she floated on air. It was wonderful to have a tall, handsome beau, and he consumed her thoughts every waking moment.

But, unlike the Sinclairs, Hiram Curtis was not to be tied down, and so, just three years after they had come West, he moved his family again, this time to Oregon. Mark was eager for adventure, and his sadness at the thought of leaving Tara, though genuine, was short-lived. Tara always knew the break was hardest on her, and it took a long time for her to be convinced that life without Mark was possible. She had gotten used to the fact that she would never see them again, but here they were, and her mind was exploding with questions.

Her father, Edward, summed them all up for her when he inquired, "So what's happened to all of you since you pulled out with that wagon train in '63?"

Hiram Curtis recounted the story to his wide-eyed listeners. "Well, we made the trip all right and settled in the Big Sandy Valley near Fort Brooks. We built us a nice house and barn and did a little farming. Everything was going along pretty well until last year when we started having trouble with the Indians. They didn't take too well to us settlin' up their valley and huntin' in their woods. So they started raiding the fort. The army was afraid that they would massacre all of the white settlers so they moved us into the fort. In the last raid they set fire to our crops and tried to burn the fort too."

Edward's wife, Margaret, shook her head, "Oh, how horrible!"

"It was, Margaret," said Hiram's wife, Polly. "Mark had to fight Indians with his father, and the other children and I carried buckets of water to put out the fire. Imagine, children having to risk their lives like that!"

"Aw, Ma," Mark protested. "We made the Indians run, didn't we?"

"But just the same, that was the last straw," said Polly. "That's when I told Hiram we were coming back here, and if he didn't take us I would take the children and go myself."

"So I thought I'd better do as she said, otherwise I'd be fightin' more than Indians," Hiram added, drawing everyone's laughter.

"He wanted us to go on down to California," said Mark apologetically, "but Ma wouldn't allow it."

The conversation ranged to the town and things that had happened there since the Curtises left. Following dinner with their hosts, the Curtises accepted the Sinclairs' offer to stay with them until they had a place to live.

That evening Tara and Mark met on the back porch, alone for the first time in two years.

"I've been waiting for this," said Mark, a gleam in his eye.

Tara smiled. "I just can't believe you're really here."

There was a moment of quiet contemplation, then Mark spoke softly. "I was hoping we'd have another chance."

Tara bowed her head. "I was hoping the same thing."

"Tara, all during our trip back I worried that you'd have nothing to do with me. I wasn't sure I could even face you, but I see now that you don't hate me."

"I tried to forget about you but I couldn't," replied Tara. "I feel the same about you now as before you left."

Mark took her hand, entwined his fingers with hers, and leaned forward to kiss her.

Tara backed away. "You only just came back, Mark. We've hardly spent any time together."

"I thought nothing had changed," he laughed. "It was never that hard to steal a kiss from you before." He paused. "You've really grown into a beautiful woman in the last two years." He attempted the kiss again, and this time, her resolve weakened, she accepted it and kissed him back.

They were slow to break away from each other, but when they did he followed her to the porch railing where their gaze was lured to the mountains a few miles away to the northwest.

"Just think, this isn't Nebraska Territory anymore," Tara proclaimed. "It's now Montana Territory."

"That's right. And someday it's going to be a state."

"Oh, I don't know about that."

"You just wait and see. But by then I may not be here. I still want to go to California."

Tara's heart plunged but she concealed her dismay. "California! What's there?"

"Gold!"

Tara did not share his enthusiasm.

"Well, that's not all, of course. There's land and—"

"There's land here."

"But don't you see? It's just the idea of going somewhere I haven't been." He looked at her sidewise and his voice softened. "I hope we could go there together someday."

"Oh, Mark," she sighed. "I hope you're not too different from before."

"I don't think so. But if I am, I know one thing that's the same. I still love you."

"And I you," she answered with a squeeze of his hand. "It's getting late. I'd better go in now."

* * *

"We'll have to go riding on the Broken Bow, Julie," said Tara as she stood bent over in her bedroom, brushing her hair over her head. "You always loved that." She stood up straight, flipping her hair back in place. Julie, in her nightgown, sat on the bed facing her, blissfully grinning. "What?" asked Tara.

"The Hunters are still here, aren't they?"

In her mind's eye, Tara saw Nate again, falling from the rafters and yelling like a madman.

"Yes. I don't think they'll ever leave."

Julie laughed. "I see you still feel the same way about them."

"I don't think I could bear to see you take up with that uncivilized hired hand, Nathaniel," said Tara.

"Oh, you misjudge him. Nate's as civilized as you or I."

"Well, I heard that his father used to be a wanderer before he was married, never attaching himself to a worthwhile trade, just aimlessly moving about."

"What difference could that possibly make to me?" laughed Julie.

"It's just not a respectable background." Tara figured she was overreacting just a little, but she was fond of Julie and the thought of her getting mixed up with Nate made Tara shudder. She slipped behind a folding screen and changed into her nightgown. "And do you think he's ever seen the inside of a schoolhouse? No, he'd rather chase cows than get an education."

"And I happen to know," said Julie, "that Mrs. Hunter was once a schoolmarm and is capable of educating Nate and Lena herself."

"Well, it doesn't show, not in Nathaniel anyway." She came out from behind the screen. "Let me tell you what he did after you moved away. His father told him that when he turned sixteen he could buy a gun. So he worked and saved up his money. On his birthday he came in the store and bought a Colt .45. And do you know what he did? He took that nice, expensive gun and carved thirteen notches in the handle. And he never even killed anybody!"

Julie broke into laughter. "You can hardly blame him for that."

Tara gave a hopeless sigh. "Love truly is blind." She smiled and patted one of the pillows. "Here, you can have the side next to the window."

Chapter 4

The Hunter cabin was a humble place but very homey because of Lydia's handmade red-checked tablecloth and matching curtains, and the vase of wildflowers on the mantle of the stone fireplace. Besides the main room, there was Buck and Lydia's bedroom, and Nate and Lena's bedroom divided in half by a curtain.

Day normally began at five a.m. for the Hunters, so it was still dark outside as Lydia poured coffee into tin cups as the family sat down to a breakfast of biscuits and gravy.

"Gus told me last night that he wants me to come along this fall when you all drive the cattle to the railhead," said Nate with a grin. "That means extra money, you know."

"That's good," Buck replied. Then glancing at Lydia, "Let's just hope it'll be safe enough to leave your ma and Lena here alone."

Nate frowned. "Surely this Indian mess will be cleared up by then, don't you think? I mean, you taught that Beartooth a lesson. You're not afraid of him, are you?"

"No," said Buck, "but I'm concerned."

"Why? He's only one Indian."

"But he's got a whole band of Cheyenne to back him. And the first blood has been drawn. Now that Boss Sinclair shot one of theirs, they'll want revenge."

"Your father thinks they won't give up on us very easily," said Lydia.

Nate sopped up the last of the gravy in his bowl with a biscuit. "But it's been nearly three weeks since that happened and we haven't seen hide nor hair of 'em since."

"That's what makes me nervous," said Buck. "I've been thinking, it might end up that we'd have to move away from here and go someplace where they can't find us."

This remark drew shocked looks from the others. Never before had the suggestion come up to leave the Broken Bow.

"Oh, Pa," sighed Lena, "we just couldn't do that."

"I hope we don't have to," replied Buck.

*   *   *

An hour later Nate was immersed in his work, counting cows and calves as they were driven one by one through a chute into a corral. He sat on his patient horse, tying knots in a rope to represent each group of twenty-five. The count was going to exceed last year's by several dozen. It would be a good year for the Broken Bow.

He looked up during a break in the counting and spied Tara Sinclair and two others walking towards him in the breaking light of dawn. What was the queen bee doing up so early, he wondered. He started to look away but took a double-take. "Well, if it isn't a couple of Curtises!" he exclaimed. He tossed the rope to the boy manning the chute. "Take my place a minute, Andrew."

He dismounted and jogged to meet the group. "I heard you were back from the Oregon country," he said as he shook hands with his old friend Mark.

"Yep," Mark replied. "We just moved into the last house on Main Street up in town, bought it off old Mr. Coleman. Pa and I are working at the lumber mill."

Julie couldn't mask her impatience. "How've you been doing, Nate?"

Julie had always brought out the coyness in Nate and two years didn't seem to have changed that. He stood a moment, unsure of what to do, before he shook hands with her. "Hello, Julie, I've been doing fine. I heard you had trouble with Indians out there."

"How'd you know that?" asked Mark.

"The Indians told me," replied Nate matter-of-factly.

The visitors stared at him a moment before Julie, realizing it was a joke, burst into laughter. She turned to see Tara's reaction, but Tara simply watched Julie and shook her head. Julie could find humor in the oddest of things.

"So tell me what happened," said Nate, folding his arms. He leaned against a corral fence and looked from one Curtis to the other as they took turns filling him in on their experiences in the Oregon fort. He shook his head in dismay upon hearing of the devastation of the last raid. "'Bout how many Indians were there?" he asked.

"I'd say close to seventy-five," guessed Mark. "And mean bastards, every one. They used some kind of poison arrows. If one of 'em hit you, you'd be dead within a minute, if not from the wound, then from the poison. I saw one soldier shot off the wall, and the worst thing that happened to him was he fell on the outside of the wall and he didn't die right away. They scalped him alive."

Tara put a hand over her heart and moaned. "How horrible. I'm glad you got away from there."

Nate was equally appalled. That familiar feeling of dread crept into his soul again as he recalled Beartooth and the other Cheyennes. Indians were fierce fighters and they could be cruel. The Curtises had been lucky. Nate had been trying to take his own family's situation lightly, but his father must know what they were dealing with, and that's why he was thinking of taking the family and leaving the Broken Bow.

"Nate!" yelled Gus the foreman, causing Nate to jump. "We ain't payin' you to stand around jawin' all day!"

*   *   *

Most of the hands had gone to dinner when Tara, Julie, and Mark found a quiet place to stroll near the corrals where in one, some mares and foals had been turned out for exercise, and in another, four orphan calves stood watching the frisky foals. Mark seized his first opportunity to give Julie a subtle nod.

"Tara, I've enjoyed this so much," said Julie. "But I really must get home and help Ma unpack."

Tara was left staring after Julie as she rode away, then she turned to Mark and narrowed her eyebrows. "You made her leave, didn't you?"

Mark's only reply was a chuckle laced with guilt.

"All right, what is it?" Tara questioned.

Mark shifted his gaze to the calves, took a deep breath, and scratched his neck. "I want you to marry me, Tara," he blurted out. Tara's mouth fell open, but before she had a chance to respond, Mark hurriedly continued. "Marry me and come with me to California. What do you say?"

Such a proposal gave Tara mixed feelings and twice she opened her mouth to reply only to change her mind. "Mark, I don't want to go to California or anyplace else," she said finally. "You know that's not for me, nor for you either. You belong here where your family is, and you need to be in a stable business."

"Oh, Tara, you can't be so narrow-minded. Wouldn't you like to live on a place as big as this ranch?"

"Of course, but we don't need to go to California for that." She looked blissfully at the horses in the corral. "I could never leave this place. This ranch and Timber Fork are tied to the Sinclair name. And I am a Sinclair!"

"But I'm asking you to be a Curtis. Tara, you're not bound to this place. If we're married we're free to go anywhere and do anything we want. And I promise you that we could do fine in California."

Tara longed to break away from the powerful grip of his independence. She turned away and began walking towards the barn. "That sounds familiar. I believe your father said that to your mother about Oregon. And look what happened. You lost your crops and nearly your lives to the dreadful Indians."

"Well, I'm not going to let one bad thing back me down," said Mark, persistently following her. "And besides, that was Oregon."

Tara stopped and faced him. "You really are different than when you went away. What has happened to you, Mark? I don't feel like I'm talking to the same person."

Mark laid a sympathetic hand on her shoulder. "Aw, Tara, I'm sorry. I just want so badly for you to see what I've seen. There's such a big world out there. I know you're hesitant but we can make it on our own. You'll see. We don't need your family's name to get by."

Tara was becoming irritated, but Mark must have known for he changed his approach drastically. "Listen, I've heard so much about the gold down there. Can you imagine? We could have so much money!"

"I don't need money."

"There you go again, settling for what you get from your family. But that's too easy. I want us to make our own money."

"Mark, you don't understand. My mind is made up. I would consider marrying you but I won't go to California with you."

"It's unbelievable," Mark grumbled. "If your family was to move, you wouldn't hesitate to go, but you don't trust me enough to ride five miles out of town with me. Face it, Tara, you're being childish."

"Childish! How dare you say that! Let me tell you a thing or two..." She was interrupted by the sound of chuckling and turned to see Nate in the barn doorway, bent over to inspect his horse's hoof. By his grin, it was obvious that he was entertained by this spectacle, but upon receiving Tara's glare he tried his best to erase the smirk.

Tara strove to hide her embarrassment. He must have appeared in that doorway only within the last minute. "And just what are you doing here?"

He pointed down with a piece of wood he was using to wedge a rock out of his horse's shoe. "Horse picked up a rock."

She looked down at the hoof and back up at him. "I can see that. Does that have to be done right here?"

"Tara, don't," whispered Mark.

"You stay out of this!"

"No, I will not!" he fired back.

Tara forgot about Nate. "You listen to me, Mark Curtis. You were gone two years and I never expected to see you again. And you can be sure there were plenty of other boys who came to court me. Now you show up, the next thing to a complete stranger, and expect me to do anything in the world for you."

Mark was taken aback by this scolding. "I'm sorry, Tara," he said after a pause. "I didn't think of it that way."

But Tara searched his eyes and could tell that they were only words. His heart was not in it. He had indeed changed from the agreeable young man, content wherever he was, whom Tara had known. She could feel the mounting pressure of their differences and the hopelessness of the situation. "If I don't go with you, will you still go to California anyway?"

"Don't question me that way, Tara."

But Tara waited for a more specific reply.

"I really want to go," he said in one last, weak plea.

There was an uneasy pause during which Mark sensed that his future hung in the balance.

17

She spoke very calmly. "Then go, it's all right with me. Go to California and look for your treasure at the end of the rainbow. I want you to be happy, Mark, and if that's what will do it then go on, but it will be without me."

"No, please, Tara," he begged, "don't do this—"

"It's too late now. You made your feelings clear. There are things more important to you than me. Now that you don't have me to stop you, you can go and chase whatever suits your fancy."

"Wait a minute. Give me a chance to—"

"Oh, I'll give you a chance, as soon as you dig up enough gold to buy the Broken Bow!" She spun on her heel and began to stomp away but stopped when she saw Nate watching her from the barn doorway. His uncaring look following such a momentous event infuriated her. She looked him up and down in disgust and continued on her way.

Mark looked down at the ground and sadly shook his head, not even looking up when Nate came over.

"Don't let it get you down, Mark. She ain't worth it." On seeing Mark's glare, he went on, "I'm telling you, Mark, give her up. It takes a lot of gold to buy the Broken Bow."

Mark couldn't listen to Nate's good intentions any longer. "I wish I'd never come back from Oregon," he muttered as he walked away.

Nate tried to figure out what it was about love that led people to such funny behavior.

*   *   *

Late that afternoon Tara rode alone on the Broken Bow. Here on the vastness of the ranch, she could always find rest from her problems, and as she came upon beautiful Elkhorn Creek, she could already feel the memory of the argument with Mark easing its hold on her mind. She left her horse to graze then walked down the bank and sat in the cool grass in solitude amidst the weeping willows swaying in a gentle breeze. As she lazily leaned against the trunk of one of them, she watched the water glide over the rocks, making its way south to a lake somewhere miles away. That water, Tara thought, had come all the way from a spring in the mountains north of town. She wondered how long it took one drop of water to make the complete trip. Her thoughts were interrupted by the slow thumping of a horse's hooves coming closer. She fixed her eyes on the path and waited to see who would appear. Nate walked down leading his tired horse. He ignored her as he tied his horse, knelt by the creek for a much-needed drink of water, and sat under a tree across from her. He heaved a great sigh and closed his eyes to rest.

Tara fought to hide her embarrassment after her earlier confrontation with him. "A ranch this big and you always seem to end up where I am."

18

Nate opened his eyes. "Or maybe the other way around? I'm the one who lives here you know."

"Keep in mind to whom you're speaking," said Tara. "It is my uncle who owns this ranch. You only work here."

Nate reached out to pet his horse's muzzle. "It's really amazing. The boss is such a nice man. Who'd guess that you were related to him?"

Tara knew he was congratulating himself for his cleverness with words. She was going to rail on him but restrained herself. She figured she probably deserved that barb and now they were even. "I'm sorry for the way I spoke to you earlier. My anger should not have been directed at you."

"That's okay. Don't lose sleep over it."

"You know, Nathaniel, you're very lucky to work here. There are a lot of people who would envy your position."

He always hated it when she called him by his given name. Every single time. Just something about the way she said it. "I know. But the Broken Bow is lucky to have the Hunters too. I wonder what the boss would do if we went away."

"What do you mean by that?"

"I mean the Indians want our family to go back to them."

"Really? And that's what that fiasco was about at your barn when my uncle shot the Indian?"

"Yeah."

Her interest aroused, Tara scooted closer to him. "So then you're going back to the Indians?"

"Course not. My ma's already made that clear, especially since Lena and I were raised among white men."

"And what does your father think?"

"He does what's best for us. That's why we might have to move away."

"How come your father left his people in the first place?"

"It wasn't my father. It was his father. My pa was about ten or eleven when it happened."

"Happened?" Tara was curious. "Sounds like something big. What was it?"

"About thirty years ago, a Cheyenne brave blamed my grandfather for killing his son. But my grandfather didn't do it."

"How do you know he didn't?"

Nate answered her distrust in a firm voice. "Because he said so. Anyway, my grandfather and his family were banished from the people."

Tara tried to conceal a pleased smile. So even Indians hadn't wanted to be around his family. She made a mental note to tell this news to Julie.

But Nate was not finished. "About a year ago, that brave died, and on his deathbed he confessed that he'd lied and my grandfather was innocent. So they aren't mad at us anymore."

19

"Well, I guess your grandparents will want to go back to them."

"Oh no, they won't be going. They both died, even before my parents met each other."

"Well, if your family hasn't had any contact with the Indians, how did they find out where you were? Aren't the Cheyenne down in the Nebraska Territory?"

"An Indian named Beartooth was sent to find us. He spent a year tracing us. He heard that my grandparents had died somewhere in the Territory and that my father had gone looking for work. He followed the same trail my father took till he ended up in northwestern Missouri. That's where my parents met and married and where me and Lena were born. Then from the farm family that Pa worked for, he learned that after five years there we moved to the Platte River in Nebraska. So he went there and found some more people who knew us. And that led him here."

Quite a persistent Indian, this Beartooth, thought Tara. But such a shame that the Hunters didn't want to return to their own kind. She arose from the grass and started up the bank to where she'd left Molly. As an afterthought, she stopped and turned to face Nate again. "I hope the Indian my uncle shot is all right," she said, feeling a bit awkward.

A momentary flicker of surprise crossed Nate's face, then vanished. "Me too," he replied.

*   *   *

It was dusk that evening when Nate finished his work and returned to his home in the fields. Buck sat on a bench by the door, tediously twisting long strands of horsehair into a rope. His wife Lydia was sitting in her rocking chair in front of the fireplace mending a shirt, and Lena sat at the table with an open book in front of her. But no one seemed too involved in their tasks.

"Why the long faces?" asked Nate as he hung his holster on a nail and took off his jacket.

Lydia looked up from her mending. Her light brown hair was twisted into a bun in the back and a few loose, curly strands framed her blue eyes and gentle face. "We were just talking about where we might go if we leave here."

Nate sat down opposite Lena. "It looks like we're really going, aren't we?" He couldn't conceal his disappointment.

Lydia, too, didn't want to think about it. "I saw that the boss's niece was here today."

Nate rolled his eyes. "I think it would do us good to see less of her."

His father chuckled. "Do I sense a bit of dislike?"

"You sure do. All I have to do is see her coming and it's enough to make me turn and go the opposite way."

Lydia smiled. "Come now, Nate, it's not that bad, is it?"

"Oh, it's worse." Nate began a comical imitation of Tara's arrogant voice. "It's my uncle who owns this ranch. You only work here." Then back in his usual voice, "She wouldn't recognize work if it stepped up and said hello."

"Surely it doesn't bother you that you do something for your money," Lydia replied.

"Course not, I'm proud of it. It's just that she can't stand anybody who's not her kind."

"And her kind being?" asked Buck.

"Prestigious, rich." Nate hesitated a moment. "And not dark-skinned."

A teasing grin broke on Lena's face. "I wouldn't think you would talk that way about her seeing as how she's the one who brings Julie here."

"And you, Lena, should mind your own business," Nate retorted.

Lena laughed. "You needn't be so shy about it, Nate. Everyone knows you have a crush on Julie."

"Is that true, son?" Buck said, smiling. "I thought I'd never see the day."

"You haven't seen it." But he saw Lena's look and knew he couldn't tell a lie. "So what if I do? What should it matter to you?"

Lena flashed a satisfied grin.

"All right, it's time to get back to studying," said Lydia. She pulled a book from the shelf and set it in front of Nate.

"History," groaned Nate, staring at the cover. "Surely there are more important things to study if I'm going to be a ranch foreman."

"You'll be a ranch foreman if you want to be and you'll make a fine one," said Lydia. "But you will also be an educated one. I want you and Lena both to remember that you can never learn too much no matter how long the good Lord lets you live."

This kind of statement was typical for Lydia. Though her son and daughter did not attend school as their friends in town did, she was determined that they should never feel the difference. So she spent the evenings drilling them in complicated ciphers that would have made the other cowboys' heads spin. She carefully instructed them in the rudiments of grammar and Latin, and introduced them to the classics of literature and the great American and English poets. It was not uncommon for her to request an impromptu recitation at the dinner table during which their father listened with admiration. He was appreciative of his wife's knowledge and her desire to pass it along to the next generation.

Though Nate often teased his mother about never letting him out of school because of his age, he knew very well what her views were, that studying and learning should be a lifelong pursuit. And so, after spending an hour reading about the War of 1812, Nate closed the book and went to bed. The coming of sleep was welcomed after a busy day.

The Broken Bow was silent now except for the lowing of cattle far away. It was the perfect ending to a day much like many others on the ranch, calm and peaceful, almost like the lull that comes before a storm.

Chapter 5

It was late in the month of June and the days were growing longer and warmer. A month of no rain had dried out pastures and, as Buck Hunter put it, left the rocks thirsty. Ranch work had slowed up some and the Hunters were eating dinner together for the first time in weeks. The mood was somber and Nate and Lena both noticed when Buck and Lydia exchanged uneasy glances.

Finally Lydia lowered her fork and looked squarely at Nate and Lena. Her voice was calm and gentle as always. "You know how we feel about what the Indians are trying to do. I just want you both to remember one thing. Should anything happen to your father and me, we don't want either of you to ever give in and go to live with Indians. You are Hunters and you were well-raised. It would not be fitting for you to take on their uncivilized ways. Never forget that, hear?"

This kind of talk worried Lena. "Ma, nothing's going to happen to you."

"We're not counting on anything to happen," said Buck. "Just remember what we've told you."

Nate smiled. "You know we wouldn't go with the Indians, Ma. So put your mind at rest."

Buck finished his dinner and pushed his plate back. "It's time for me to go up to see the boss."

"What's he want with you?" asked Nate.

"I don't know. I just got a message saying he would hand me our week's pay personally."

The others looked at each other in dread but their thoughts remained unspoken.

After Buck was gone, Nate excused himself from the table and went outside. Lydia later found him on the front porch, gazing at the range where dusk was gathering and an evening breeze was gently swaying the grasses. Just above the horizon the sinking sun was arraying the sky with orange and rose, which gave way to blue higher up.

His mother approached him and put a hand on his shoulder. "What is it that's bothering you, Nate?"

"Let's not fool ourselves," said Nate. "We all know why Pa was called to the boss's house. He's going to fire us."

"Come now, Nate, you can be more optimistic than that. You know that Boss Sinclair counts us as friends."

Nate knew that his mother, too, was afraid for their jobs. He looked pleadingly into her mild countenance that reflected the sienna glow of the sunset. "Please, Ma, don't hide anything from me. I know all about what's going on.

You've got to be honest with me. You're afraid that Boss is going to make us leave, aren't you?" For a while she didn't answer and Nate thought he had said too much.

"Yes, I am. Now, Nate, you must listen to me. I'm sorry you've felt left out. I guess we have tried to keep you and Lena sheltered from this, but there's a reason. All your lives, all you've ever known of the Cheyenne is what your father has told you. It's true that he told you much about their life and customs. But being that you haven't seen the living proof of these stories, the Cheyenne are still a foreign people to you and Lena. I tell you, I'm glad for that. But now that their existence is becoming more real to us, we're trying to keep them from involving you. You both have your lives ahead of you and we want the best for you. I hope you understand that, son."

"I do understand, Ma. But we're a family. We should go through this together. If things get worse we'll need each other to lean on."

She smiled tenderly and pushed a few stray locks of his hair back. "You show wisdom in making that statement, Nate. And I'll admit you're right." She regarded him thoughtfully. "You really like Boss Sinclair, don't you?"

"Yes, I do," replied Nate. "I mean, to think he carved all of this out of nothing." He shook his head in amazement. "He has no idea how much I watch him and try to learn from him."

Lydia walked to the edge of the porch and gazed across the range. Her face took on a gloomy expression. "I don't know where we'll go when we leave here. Whenever we moved before we always knew where to go. But now there isn't anyplace."

"It's not right," said Nate. "It's just not right at all that we should leave because of the Indians. We didn't do anything." He paused. "If this was our land, the boss couldn't tell us to go."

Lydia turned to look at him. "I never knew you to be resentful of the fact that we don't own the land we live on."

"I never was. I never had reason to be."

"You don't have reason to be now. The Lord sometimes causes a bad thing to turn into a blessing later on. Perhaps that's what he'll do for us."

"Maybe, but it's still hard. This ranch is my home. I was going to work up and be the foreman someday."

Lydia smiled. "Don't give up hope. It could be that you'll make a good foreman elsewhere."

"Yeah, maybe."

*   *   *

Buck sat in the mansion's lavish parlor where he was waiting for the boss to show himself. It was a spacious room with a deep red rug and matching velvet

24

draperies over four huge windows. A European tapestry adorned the south wall above the organ, and plush furniture, vases, and figurines filled the room. Buck felt out-of-place sitting in a cushioned, high-backed chair in his worn buckskin leathers and he was eager to return to his comfortable cabin.

Soon Jerome Sinclair emerged from his study. Wearing a black vested suit with a gold watch chain and smoking a pipe, he cut a stately looking figure. But his mode of dress only served to deepen Buck's anxiety. The boss must have considered this to be an important meeting.

After he had greeted his guest, Jerome sat down opposite Buck. "I am aware of your predicament with the Indians," he began, "and my sympathies lie with you. My brother informs me on what townspeople think, and I suppose you know most of them are on your side."

Buck nodded. "I do."

"Well, I wanted to say that it worries me to think perhaps you consider it a burden to us here at the ranch."

"I'm sorry if it's been a burden, sir. I sure don't want to—"

"No, no, please. You are not to blame. In fact, I called you here because I heard there were rumors around the ranch about you being fired. It would be unfair of me to let a good man go because of matters which aren't in his hands. I wouldn't do that."

Buck smiled his relief. "It's good to know that when we leave it won't be on your account."

"Leave? What are you talking about?"

"I'm afraid it's come to that. Blood has been drawn. I'm an enemy to Beartooth now. I've got my family's safety to look out for, and quite frankly, Boss, I'm worried about you and everyone else here. The Indians will see you as accomplices since it's the influence of your white civilization that keeps us here. It might be best if I move out at the end of the week."

"I'm real sorry to hear that," said Jerome, and he meant it.

Buck took a deep breath. "And I'm afraid there's more, Boss. The brave that you shot and wounded, we got word today that he died a couple weeks ago after a long illness related to the wound. And it turns out he was of the chief's family, younger brother I believe."

"Oh, no." Jerome shook his head. "Buck, I didn't mean to hurt anyone. He was going to shoot me."

"I understand, Boss. But the Cheyenne won't. They're gonna want payment in blood. You watch your back."

"Thanks for the warning."

Buck stood and walked to the door. "I appreciate everything you've done for us, Boss."

"No, Hunter, you're the one to be thanked," Jerome said, following him. "You've been with us almost from the beginning of this ranch and that's more than I can say for a lot of others. Your wife is a wonderful woman and it's a fine set of children you have. We'll miss all of you. And wherever you decide to go, none of us will tell the Indians where you went."

"Thank you, Boss. And please be careful."

*　*　*

Late that night Nate returned from night guard duty, the job where the cowboys rode around the herd, keeping an eye out for rustlers and predators. It was usually uneventful, but Nate didn't mind the once-a-week assignment because of the peace and serenity he found under a big Montana sky full of stars. Sometimes he played the harmonica that he always kept in his pocket and at which he had become quite proficient. It did make for an extra-long day because he had gotten up at five o'clock that morning. Luckily he would be able to sleep later the next morning.

He stabled his horse and trudged to his house. Inside, everyone was asleep. He hung his holster on a nail by the door, plodded to his room, and lay on the bed a moment before getting undressed.

He was in a good mood. He knew he wasn't going to be fired, and although he would be leaving the Broken Bow, he was determined to enjoy his last days there. He meant to get undressed but he fell asleep before his plans were carried through.

There was a frantic pounding on the door and shouting. Buck quickly dressed and rushed to the door, and Lydia followed with a lantern. They were met by a boy of about sixteen.

"It's Indians, Mr. Hunter, must be dozens of 'em! My pa was on the night watch and saw their fires about six miles north."

By now Nate and Lena had come into the room.

"They're singing war cries!" the boy continued.

Buck grabbed his gunbelt from its hook. "They're going to massacre!"

Terror flooded Lydia's eyes and Lena clutched her brother's arm.

"They'll reach Boss Sinclair's house first," the boy said. "My pa sent me to tell everyone to get their guns and meet there. We'll try to run them off before they get out this way."

"Okay, Andrew," said Buck, "you go tell the others."

The boy left and Buck strapped on his gunbelt. Then he took Nate's and handed it to him.

"No, not Nate!" cried Lydia, gripping her son's shoulders.

"He has to, Lydia. We'll need all the help we can get."

"But he's just a boy."

"He can handle a gun. Now don't worry, he'll be with me."

Lydia watched helplessly as Nate buckled his holster.

"What about Ma and me?" asked Lena. "What are we going to do, Pa?"

"You stay inside and keep that door bolted shut." He handed a rifle to Lydia. "Hang onto this and use it if you have to."

"Be careful," said Lydia.

Buck and Nate ran to the barn and bridled their horses. They climbed up bareback and galloped into the night. Minutes later, they were tying their horses behind the Sinclair home.

On the front porch, lanterns shed their light, making a circle of visibility thirty feet wide beyond which the darkness loomed, concealing in it the approaching threat. The situation was chaotic. Horses were impatiently stamping their hooves, and on the porch, Gus the foreman was trying to shout orders to men arriving from all directions. When he eyed Buck, he stepped down and ran to meet him.

"I'm glad you're here, Hunter. We've never had anything like this before. What do we do?"

"We'll have to surprise them by being ready for the attack. From what I hear, their numbers outweigh us heavily."

"You're damn right," said Gus. "But we've got to drive them back before they get to the women and children. You think we can do that?"

"We're sure going to try," replied Buck. He began to take charge and give orders like a general. "Nate, you round up those horses and tie them out of sight in back." Nate ran to carry out the instructions and his father turned to Gus. "We need everyone to spread out across the yard, one behind every tree and bush. We'll hold our fire till the last minute. And for heaven's sake, put out these lanterns!"

With these directions, things began to take shape. The men dispersed in the yard and found cover underneath the foliage. Moments later, there came a rider from the north, galloping through the yard and shouting as he went, "Get ready, they're coming and they're coming fast!"

Nate joined his father beneath the low-hanging branches of a pine tree. They lay flat on their stomachs, pulled their guns, and pointed them at the hill over which the Indians would ride.

"You're not scared, are you, son?" asked Buck.

Nate's eyes remained steadfast on the hill. "No, Pa."

The house was dark and the yard silent. About twenty guns were pointed at the hill, and the men of the Broken Bow were confident that no Indian could overrun their defense.

Two minutes went by. The tension was building. Then the faint sound of war cries floated across the fields on a chill wind. Nate's heart pounded rapidly. The reality of what was about to happen hit him. He was glad his father was there.

The war cries grew louder, and before long the first Indians topped the hill. All that was visible were the flaming torches the braves held in their hands, but their eerie, blood-curdling yells evidenced their zeal for battle. More torches appeared on the hill. Ten grew to fifty and then a hundred until they formed a half circle around the main buildings. Chills shot up Nate's spine and he swallowed hard. Never had he dreamed he would face such a deadly foe. It was a scene that would be burned into his memory for the rest of his life. He felt Buck's strong grip on his shoulder.

"Son, I want you to get out of here while you can."

"But I don't want to leave you, Pa."

The war cries were blocked from Nate's mind as he took in Buck's heart-shattering words. "This is going to be the end, Nate. Tonight you'll see the Broken Bow die around you. They'll kill us all. But I have to stay. It's my duty to fight for Boss Sinclair."

Nate was afraid of the Indians but more so of leaving his father alone. He was too loyal for that. "Pa, if you die, I'll die with you."

For a moment there seemed to be a hint of a proud smile on Buck's face. "No, I want my son to live. And you've got your ma and your sister to look after." He gave Nate's shoulder a meaningful squeeze. "Now go before it's too late."

The Indians were charging down the hill. As Nate watched them, he thought of his mother and Lena alone in the cabin. He holstered his gun and crawled out from under the tree. "Be careful, Pa," he said. He was confident his father would be all right. He always was.

But Buck felt differently. While with moist eyes he watched Nate disappear into the dark beyond the tree, he knew in his heart that that would be the last time he ever saw his son.

Nate darted toward the house. Looking over his shoulder at the approaching Indians, he knew he wouldn't have time to get his horse and ride out. His heart beat wildly for he couldn't see or hear anyone he knew. He raced up the steps to the front door and found it was locked. "Boss Sinclair, somebody, let me in, it's Nate!" he shouted as he beat on the door. The Indian yells were so deafening now he could hardly hear his own voice. Then the door opened and a flustered Mrs. Sinclair pulled him inside.

"Lord have mercy," gasped the boss's wife, slamming the door and locking it. "What were you doing out there, Nate? You could've been killed!"

Nate just breathed heavily, half from running and half from nervous fear.

Everyone in the house was still, thankful to be protected by four walls. Mrs. Sinclair, in her blue satin robe with gray-streaked brown hair falling to the middle of her back, grasped Nate's shoulders in a motherly fashion. Sitting on the sofa was a housemaid, the terror written on her face. Boss Jerome Sinclair stood ready by the window with rifle in hand.

They heard the men outside open fire on the Indians. The battle was on! Immediately there came the sound of dying and wounded men, yet the Indians' yells seemed to increase. Those in the house were paralyzed with fear as they listened. The enemy was very brutal.

The boss cautiously held open the curtain and looked out. "My barns!" he shouted. "They're burning my barns!" With the butt of his rifle he broke out the lower window panes. He knelt down, aimed the weapon, and cocked the trigger. "Charlotte, you and the others get upstairs!"

Mrs. Sinclair ushered Nate and the maid up the steps to her bedroom where Nate posted himself by the window.

The scene in the yard below was terrifying. The ranch hands and Indians were engaged in man-to-man combat and the Indians were advancing closer. Nate cringed every time he saw a warrior pull back his bowstring or aim his rifle. The bodies of fallen men were strewn across the yard. To the north, the barns were going up in flames like dried kindling, and he beheld every sickening detail of the battle in their smoky, hellish glow.

Nate knew he was watching the realization of his father's prediction. The Broken Bow was fast falling from its pedestal of prestige to die a painful death in the dust, and with it was dissolving Nate's home. His heartfelt pride in being a part of the greatest ranch in the Territory was being dashed to the ground and he was helpless to do anything.

He turned to see how Mrs. Sinclair and the maid were holding up. In the dark room he could barely make out the faces of the women as they huddled together on the bed. Mrs. Sinclair's eyes were closed and only her lips moved in earnest prayer, but he couldn't hear her for the gunfire, Indian whoops, and whinnying horses.

He turned back to the window. The Indians were casting torches into the trees and grass. He began to worry. Until now he had not doubted his father's ability to handle the attackers, but when the bushes had all burned, there would be no more hiding places and the ranch hands would be at the Indians' mercy. He fixed his eyes on the tree where he'd left his father and held his breath. To his horror, an errant flame began licking its way up the trunk of the tree, gaining momentum and strength as it ascended. He stared, clenching the curtain until his hand was hot. But surely his father had found a safer place by now, Nate thought.

A painful yell downstairs startled him. The boss was in trouble. Nate and the women ran back down to the parlor and found him on the floor by the window, holding a wounded shoulder. Instantly Mrs. Sinclair was at his side. "He's been shot! Sarah, get the medicine and bandages."

"Now, Charlotte, calm down," said Jerome in his usual husky voice. "It's just a scratch."

"But it still needs to be tended to." She sighed anxiously. "I wish we could get out to reach a doctor."

Nate thought of his father who knew a little about doctoring wounds. "I'll go find my pa. He'll know what to do."

"You can't do that," said Mrs. Sinclair. "There's a battle going on out there!"

"I know how to fight," replied Nate as he headed for the back door. Mrs. Sinclair hollered after him but to no avail.

Once outside, Nate acted with caution. The horses he had tied up earlier were excited by the noise and jerked at their ropes, but he couldn't see anyone. He pulled his gun and made his way to the west edge of the house. He checked to see if it was safe before turning the corner. Keeping his back against the wall, he sidestepped toward the front of the house. He had gone only halfway when the sight of a body by the porch stopped him short. The fringed buckskin pants told him it was an Indian. Then he saw the arrow in the chest. He must have been killed by one of his own, Nate thought. He barely made out the face; there was no war paint on it. Nate felt a sick feeling deep inside. "Pa?" he called softly.

He jumped when a hand covered his eyes. He was pulled back a few steps while a man's voice spoke in his ear. "Don't look there, Nate."

The hand moved away and Nate recognized him as a fellow ranch hand. "That's not my pa, is it?" he asked with a tremor in his voice. "Listen, I have to find my pa. The boss has been shot!"

"Your pa's dead, Nate."

The shock stabbed Nate's heart like a knife and he thought he would faint. He stared at the man, his expression blank. "He can't be. I don't believe you."

"Heaven knows I hate to be the one to tell you, Nate. I was with him. We were running to the porch to escape the fire. The arrow just came from nowhere. I'm really sorry."

Nate was silent, unable to display any emotion. He turned to look once more at his father but the man stopped him. "Don't remember him like that, Nate. Now get in the house before they get you too."

Nate had no concern for his own safety. He couldn't feel anything; he couldn't think. Finally he slipped his gun into the holster and ran blindly around the house and in the back door.

When he appeared in the parlor dazed, Mrs. Sinclair asked, "Well, did you see your father?"

The very question triggered the scene in Nate's mind all over again—the arrow in the body, the blood on the chest. At last the impact hit him, and he hid his face in his hands.

Jerome boosted himself up on one elbow to see him. "Oh no," he whispered, for he knew what had happened.

All of a sudden Nate knew what he felt. He felt hate for every Cheyenne Indian that existed. He shouted like a madman at the top of his mournful voice. "I hate 'em, I hate 'em all!" He picked up a vase from the coffee table and hurled it through the window, shattering both into hundreds of pieces. Mrs. Sinclair hurried over to calm him but he jerked away from her.

He soon quieted down, realizing that his outburst hadn't driven the attackers away. He dropped down beside the sofa with his head in the crook of his arm. Mrs. Sinclair knelt by him and squeezed his shoulder with an understanding hand. This time he didn't fight her.

A moment later he raised his head. He had almost forgotten about his mother and sister at home alone. "I've got to get home," he whispered.

"You will," replied Mrs. Sinclair, "but not now."

He rose to his feet. "No, I've got to go now. And you all have to come too. The Indians will burn the house."

"No, Nate," said Mrs. Sinclair, "the house is safe."

"It's not! We're losing the battle, and when we do the Indians will set fire to this place. You won't be able to escape."

Jerome was on his feet now and holding his wounded shoulder. "Don't you set foot out that door! You're one of the Indians' prime targets. You know that."

"So are my mother and sister, and so are you, Boss. And if you don't leave here with me you'll die, all of you! This will be your last chance, Boss."

The Sinclairs and the maid stared at him. Their expressions reflected their fear but they chose to remain with Jerome rather than listen to Nate.

"I tried to warn you," he said softly, the tears streaming down his face. He turned and ran to the back door before they could stop him.

Outside, Nate was surprised by the sight of two braves cutting the horses loose. They could easily have seen him, but they were too busy with their task. He scrambled into the corner beside the doorstep, sat down, and hugged his knees to his chin. He watched helplessly as all of the horses were driven away. He would have to run all the way home, a dangerous risk if he was found by Indians on horseback. But he needed his mother and sister as much as they needed him and he would take his chances.

When the horses were gone, the two braves sneaked around the house out of Nate's view. He heard them break one of the large parlor windows. They were going inside. His first instinct was to go back and defend the Sinclairs, but he knew every minute counted, and his family came first.

Making sure he was alone, he ran into the open away from the house. He stopped by a clump of cottonwood trees and looked back to see if anyone was following. The slow, hollow thump of a horse's hooves behind him startled him and he spun around ready to go for his gun. Out of the darkness emerged the horse carrying Gus the foreman, hunched over and bleeding with two arrows protruding from his rib cage. He knew that the foreman was beyond help and

Nate needed the horse. So he pulled Gus off, and the foreman fell prostrate on the ground. Nate saw that Gus still clutched his revolver in the palm of his hand. His heart was breaking for what he had to do to the still-conscious man, but instinct took over and he tore the gun from Gus' grip and tucked it into his own belt. Then he took Gus' place on the horse. As he gathered up the reins and looked down at the dying man, he suppressed a lump in his throat. "I'm sorry, Gus." He hoped the foreman would somehow have the capacity to understand.

Nate kicked the horse into a gallop and sped across the fields toward home. He stopped afar off and turned to look at the house one more time. There were flames glowing in the south windows. In his mind, he could hear the doomed victims inside, calling for help and crying in vain for mercy from the Indians. It was in this flaming, ravaged world that he was leaving his father behind, murdered by his own people. Nate turned the horse and headed once again for home.

He was relieved when he saw his house with light shining in the back window. His mother and Lena were still there. But a closer look told him that the light was from a fire. Nate impatiently urged the horse to go faster. When he reached the cabin, he jumped off before the horse could stop and raced to the door. It was locked.

"Ma, Lena, open the door!" he shouted, but it remained closed. A girl's scream sounded from within and he panicked. He threw himself against the door several times before the latch gave way and he could enter.

There in the middle of the room, a hideously painted Cheyenne warrior had Lena in a headlock and was forcing her towards the fire in his parents' bedroom. "You let go of my sister!" he hollered as he made a dive for the Indian.

The brave released Lena to meet Nate's blow, and the impact flung both against the oaken china cabinet. Nate scrambled out from beneath just as it toppled over and crashed on the Indian. The fragile china shattered on the floor and the brave was rendered unconscious.

"Did he hurt you?" asked Nate.

"No, it's Ma!" sobbed Lena.

He heard a footstep and turned to see their mother staggering from the bedroom, a knife wound in her stomach. Her eyes gave an immovable, deathly stare. Nate ran and caught her as she slid to the floor, and Lena rushed to her side. Nate's hands quivered as he tried desperately to think of what to do for his mother.

As Lydia lay in Nate's arms, her face still held that calm expression, even now, when she knew that life was slipping away. She weakly reached up to touch the faces of her children. "I love you," she whispered. "Don't let the Indians take you away.... . You're meant for so much more than that."

"Oh, Ma," cried Lena, "please don't die, please."

Nate strove in vain to hold back his tears so he could see her face clearly and remember its every detail. He took her hand, which rested on his cheek and was wet with his own tears, and squeezed it to let her know he would remember everything she said. A moment later, her hand fell limp and her gentle blue eyes closed forever. "Ma, no!" cried Nate. He knew she hadn't heard him and that he and Lena were alone in the little cabin.

He looked at his sister who was calling to her mother again and again, still believing she could wake her. Behind her, he saw smoke billowing from the bedroom. There was little time to mourn. With a heavy heart, he laid Lydia down and gave her a parting kiss on the forehead.

He stood up and attempted to pull himself together. He knew it was no use fighting the fire. They wouldn't be coming back here. He ran to his and Lena's room and pulled his box of personal belongings from under his bed. After filling his cartridge belt and pockets with bullets, he looked for the rifle and found it on the floor by some drawers where his mother had dropped it. He took it into the front room where on the mantle he found a leather pouch of bullets for it, which he tied to his knife belt.

He looked at Lena, dreading the task of separating her from Lydia. "Come on, Lena, we have to go."

"No, I won't leave her," she protested.

"Lena, please, we can't stay here. There's no more Broken Bow. You know Ma would want us to escape." It was all he could think of but it worked a miracle, for Lena responded to his urges and followed him to the door.

They hurried outside where Nate grabbed the reins of the horse.

"Look!" said Lena, pointing. Coming towards them across the field were several flaming torches, and the gallop of horses could barely be heard.

Nate thought fast. "Hide in the barn!" He shoved Lena in front of him and led the horse while they ran the fifty yards to the barn. Once inside, Nate left the horse in an open stall and followed Lena up the ladder to the loft. Frightened and bereaved, they settled into the hay and waited.

"Nate, they'll find us here," whispered Lena.

"I think they'll go to the house first. When they do, we'll run out the other side of the barn."

"But what about Pa? We have to wait for him."

Nate stared at her. She didn't know about Buck, and to tell her would be the hardest thing he'd ever done. He took her face in his hands. "Lena, Pa's not coming back."

"You mean..." she began. She could not finish and Nate embraced her. "Oh, no, not Pa too!" she cried.

Nate hugged her tighter, and while it did little to ease his heartbreak, he was thankful that he had someone with whom to share the pain. "We'll make it, Lena, somehow," he said, though he didn't believe it himself.

He heard the Indians' horses pull up by the house and knew they must act soon to protect themselves.

"What are we going to do, Nate?" whispered Lena. "Where can we go?"

"I don't know," said Nate, wishing he had not been left with the responsibility of their safety. He certainly didn't feel three years older than her.

The thought came to mind that, since there was only one horse, they would have to split up, a frightening prospect. If his sister was going to be alone, he knew the best thing for her would be to go into Timber Fork where she knew people.

He pulled away from her hug and looked into her glistening eyes. "Go into town, Lena," he whispered. "You'll be all right once you get to town."

"You're going with me, aren't you?" she asked hopefully.

"I can't. There's only one horse and—"

"We can ride double."

"No, it would slow the horse down, and the Indians might chase us." He shuffled across the floor to the hay window and looked towards the house. The Indians were looking around inside and out but had not yet started in the direction of the barn. He turned back to Lena. "The horse is in the first stall. I want you to jump on him and leave from the other side of the barn so they won't see you. Run him all the way into town. Make a wide circle towards the south. Stay out in the open, and don't go near any of the cabins. Now the horse is tired. He's about to give out, but keep pushing him on as long as you can. I don't care if he drops dead, just *get to the town somehow*." He pulled Gus' gun from his waist and opened the chamber. He filled the empty slots with bullets and clicked it back into place. "Take this with you," he said, handing it to Lena. "You've got six shots in here."

She tucked it into her belt. "Oh, Nate, how are you going to get away?"

"I don't know, but I will." He had not given any thought to where he would go. He only knew he must go somewhere alone and come to grips with this tragedy. The town was actually the last place where he wanted to be.

"I wish I could stay with you," said Lena.

"I wish too," said Nate, "but the town is the safest place for you. Besides, it's up to you to tell them what happened. There's no one else to tell them."

Lena started to crawl towards the ladder, then stopped and turned around. New tears were forming in her eyes, but she bravely kept her chin up. "Nate, what if something happens? We might never see each other again."

Nate fought back tears as he laid a hand aside of her cheek. "If it's meant to be, we will. But no matter what, always remember our promise to Ma and Pa. Never let the Indians capture you."

Lena nodded; she would remember.

In his haste to get her on her way, Nate had almost forgotten the most important thing he wanted her to know. "Lena, I love you." He kissed her cheek and hugged her one last time.

"I love you, too," she replied. "Goodbye, Nate."

She crawled to the ladder and began to climb down. Nate lay on his stomach by the ladder and stretched his hand to meet hers. He held her hand until it slipped from his reach, then watched until her feet touched the ground. He went back to the hay window, picked up the rifle, and pointed it at the house. He soon heard the horse exit the barn and gallop away. When the sound of the horse's hooves faded in the distance, he breathed his relief. She was well on her way and had escaped detection thus far.

Now it was his turn. Rifle in hand, he scrambled down the ladder and headed for the barn door that Lena had left ajar. Once outside, he sprinted up a hill and looked back at the burning structure that had been his home for five years. The cabin had been his last bastion of security, his last tie to a peaceful, contented life which he would know no more. It was too painful to watch.

He saw Indians moving towards the barn. That was all he needed to get him going. He turned north and paced himself at a steady jog. On and on he jogged until he was alone in a large, empty field. He had no idea where he was going. It didn't matter. He was just a vagabond fleeing in the night. He became weak with fatigue but still his feet carried him on. The tall, dew-covered grasses slapped against his legs and the breeze felt cold against the tears on his face. In the distance he could hear the rumble of a stampeding herd. He kept looking over his shoulder for Indians but his limited realm of vision made that a useless effort and added to his anxiety.

He didn't know how long he'd been running, but he was still on Broken Bow ground when he topped a hill, looked back, and saw those familiar torches some distance away. Behind him, the moonlight silhouetted his figure against the sky, making it possible for the Indians to see him, and they did for he heard one holler to the others. Nate reacted abruptly, running as fast as he could down the other side of the hill.

With the Indians on horseback and him on foot, Nate knew he would have to use his wits to escape, and he was in no condition mentally for that. What's more, he could hear the stampede less than a mile away and coming closer. Without slowing his pace, he veered to the east and tried his best to outrun it.

He looked back and saw that the Indians had topped the hill and were gaining on him. He realized his efforts were hopeless now; he was about to fall victim to the massacre just as all the others on the Broken Bow. He figured he'd be able to take down one or two Indians with his rifle, but he could do no better than that before they got him. His heart beat faster, and he wanted to yell but couldn't utter a sound. Suddenly the frenzied horses came into view, dozens of them, and Nate was trapped. At the last possible moment, he dove for the ground, curled up, and covered his head with his hands. Thundering hooves surrounded him and choking dust was kicked up in his face. He felt so small and inconspicuous underneath the giant creatures, which now didn't give a clue that they had ever been tame. He knew that horses naturally jump over obstacles in their way, but in the dark they might not see him. He closed his eyes and waited with dread to feel the sharp cut of a hoof backed by the bone-crushing strength of a thousand pounds of horse.

When he heard the stampede grow fainter, he opened his eyes and found that the herd had passed miraculously over him. Still he did not move, hoping the Indians might think he'd been trampled to death. This possibility was his only chance for survival. He moved his head so he could see what the Indians would do. A few minutes seemed like an hour to Nate as they stood waiting and watching. Finally they gave him up for dead and rode away.

Nate breathed a sigh of relief. His life had been spared, due in part to anonymity. Had the Indians known who he was, they would have taken a closer look to make certain he was dead.

Alone as he had been a few minutes before, Nate rose to his feet, picked up his rifle, and once again headed north.

*   *   *

It was about this time when a sweaty, panting horse came galloping into Timber Fork. It was jerked to a stop in front of the Sinclair home, and a frantic Lena rushed up the steps and banged on the door. Those sleeping within were awakened, and Edward and Margaret Sinclair clambered down the stairs, followed by Tara and the curious younger children.

"The Indians," cried Lena when they had brought her inside, "they massacred everyone at Broken Bow!"

"No, please God, no," whispered Edward, his eyes shut tightly.

"And they killed my ma and pa," Lena went on.

"Oh, Lena," was all Margaret could say as she put her arms around the girl.

The family sprang into action. Edward rushed back upstairs to dress and take up his gun while Tara comforted the young children.

"Did anyone get away, Lena?" asked Margaret, her chin quivering.

"I didn't see anyone on the way here. There just wasn't any warning."

"What about Nathaniel?"

Everyone was watching Lena intently, but she made no reply.

"Lena, what happened to Nathaniel?" Margaret said again. "Why isn't he with you?"

"We had to split up. There was just one horse," Lena answered. "He was all right the last time I saw him, but I don't know where he is now."

Edward appeared again, prepared to leave. "I'll round up the men and ride out to the ranch."

Lena, clutching Margaret's shoulders, called after him. "Please find my brother alive."

"Don't worry, Lena. We'll find him," assured Edward.

When he had gone and the young children were calmed, the family settled down in the dimmed parlor, staring frightfully straight ahead, waiting in silence. The sound of a door swinging open and running footsteps startled them all. Julie Curtis appeared in the doorway of the parlor, breathless from running.

"I just heard," she said, her voice strained. "My pa and Mark went with Mr. Sinclair to the ranch." She rushed to Lena's side. "Will Nate come here, Lena?"

"I don't know," replied Lena. "He was on foot and the Indians had horses."

Julie patted Lena's knee. "I'll wait for him with you." She crossed the room to Tara, sat beside her, and reached to embrace her, bringing her out of her trance.

"Julie, I'm so scared," said Tara. "We haven't had problems with Indians before. Why would they do this?"

"I don't know." Julie hugged her tighter. "Have faith, Tara. I'm sure your aunt and uncle got away."

Tara gleaned comfort from Julie's presence. The Curtises were experienced in this sort of emergency, and for some unknown reason that seemed to make her feel that her aunt and uncle were safer.

The usually cheerful-looking parlor with its pale green striped wallpaper, European rug, plush furniture, and paintings and ceramics, was now overcast with an aura of fear and dread, and Tara's mother, usually smiling and upbeat, now sat in her rocking chair, tense and worried. Her unblinking gaze was fixed on a picture on the wall but her clear blue eyes were not seeing it. Across from her, Tara's brother and sister's frightened faces were intently watching their mother, dependent on her emotional strength. They all sat as composed as they could, each harboring faint hopes for the outcome of this night.

Thus the waiting dragged on. Only the steady tick of the grandfather clock in the corner and the creak of Margaret's rocking chair broke the silence. The clock struck three, then three-thirty, then four. Finally after four, they heard a horse gallop up and stop by the door. Margaret stopped rocking and they all watched for Edward Sinclair to enter. When he did he was very somber. He walked to his desk and sat down with his head in his hands.

"Well, how bad was it?" asked Margaret.

"There's nothing left," he answered just above a whisper, "nothing at all."

There was an unnerving pause. "Did you see any of the horrible savages?" asked Margaret.

"They were gone when we got there." He lifted his head. His face suddenly seemed old and tired. His eyes stared at the rug as the story poured forth. His low voice would crack now and then. "I've never seen anything so terrible in my life. There must have been a hundred or more of them, Margaret. There was no way the Broken Bow could've defended itself. The house, the barns, all burned to the ground. There were bloodied bodies lying all over the place. We couldn't find anyone left alive."

Tara's lower lip quivered. "What about Uncle Jerome and Aunt Charlotte?"

Edward bowed his head. "They didn't escape." His shoulders began to shake, and for the first time, his wife and children saw him cry.

Lena grasped the arm of her chair until her knuckles turned white. She had no tears left to cry.

Julie took her handkerchief from her pocket and covered her eyes. If everyone, even the owners of the Broken Bow, had lost their lives, then Nate must have too, she thought.

*   *   *

But Nate had escaped. He had kept up a steady pace northward and put a good distance between himself and the ranch. The land turned hilly as he went, and before long he found himself in the mountains. There he hiked still further, driven by the fear of someone following. The forest was thick and he could see no more than six feet ahead of him.

He heard the sound of rushing water and followed it until he found a stream. Perhaps it was Elkhorn Creek; he didn't know. But it was water and he was thirsty. He hiked down the steep bank and set aside the cumbersome rifle and holster. After shedding his jacket, he walked across the stones, knelt by the creek, and used a cupped hand to drink of the cool water. He splashed some on his face, then sat down to catch his breath.

A noise sounded from behind and Nate whipped around, expecting to see a fierce animal charging from the woods. Another rustling noise came from the bushes on the other side and he recoiled in alarm. Nothing happened and he realized he was only hearing the usual harmless sounds of the forest. However, he was still dominated by an element of fear greater than he had ever known, and it seemed that it would drive him to insanity.

He stood up and ran to an oak tree on the bank. He felt safer grasping its thick trunk but it didn't diminish his grief. The Broken Bow had been his whole world, his source of pride, and the object of his loyalty. The ranch hands were like family. What was left of his own family had been torn apart the minute Lena rode away. This he was unable and unwilling to accept.

The sadness of his loss preyed on him and ate away at his soul. He lifted his head to the star-studded heavens and shouted, "God, why? Did it have to happen? Was there no way to stop it?" His eyes blurred with tears, but he looked at his belongings on the ground and knew what he wanted to do. He walked over, knelt down, and picked up the gunbelt. He pulled out the loaded gun and went back to the tree. So the Cheyenne wanted payment in blood for the death of the chief's brother? Well, they could have it. He would wipe the slate clean, pay the debt in full.

He knelt down and with trembling hands he put the barrel to his temple, cocked the hammer, and pressed his right forefinger against the trigger. The barrel felt cold against his head and awakened him to the finality of what he was about to do. Several times his finger let up on the trigger, then pressed down again. He tilted his head back, closed his eyes, and determined to count to five. He got that far and decided to go to ten. As the sweat rolled from his brow he slowly counted to nine and stopped. All he needed was one fleeting second of courage and it would be finished. No, was it courage? He had saved himself from death so many times on the ranch this night, and now it had all come down to this moment, when the simple pulling of the Colt .45 trigger would give the Indians final victory and bring dishonor to his family name of which his father had always been so proud.

Nate released the hammer, lowered the gun, and let it fall on the ground beside him. He threw himself down on the stones and wept bitterly. The fear, the exasperation—all had gotten the best of him and he felt like he'd been abandoned by what little force had been with him a few minutes earlier. And now, his desire to take his own life had left him racked with shame. He could only be glad that no one had witnessed his act of cowardice.

Still, he so desperately wanted to die. Why had he bothered to escape the besieged ranch? What was it besides instinct that made him run? He couldn't remember what had gone through his mind then. Maybe it was just the lonely atmosphere of these woods that affected him. He kept thinking that perhaps he would wake up in his bed at home to another ordinary day, but no, this was real. He had fallen into a cruel trap, trapped into life because he'd been barred from the peace of death. As he contemplated the coming days and weeks, they seemed to be an eternity blacked with sorrow, but somehow he would find a way to pull through; he must.

And so it was, on some big, lonely mountainside as the stars began to fade and an early morning fog rolled in, that an exhausted Nate lay with his head in the crook of his arm and cried himself to sleep.

Chapter 6

Nate slowly opened his eyes. For a second he thought he was in his bed, but the feel of the hard stones beneath startled him and he sat up. Then he remembered the night before and that sad, empty feeling swept over him again.

His dirt-smudged face had lighter streaks where the previous night's tears had dried, and his tousled hair hung limp in his sleepy eyes. He tossed it aside with a shake of his head and looked around at the clearing. It had all the same features as the night before yet seemed less threatening in the daylight.

It seemed like it was about midmorning but the sun's position told him it was really an hour past noon. With half a day left, he sat back and tried to decide what to do.

An hour later found him sitting on a rock near the top of an aspen-covered ridge with his face washed, jacket and holster on, and rifle in hand. He was overlooking Timber Fork in the valley below. He had wandered southeastward, stopping on hilltops to get his bearings, and finally had reached one from which he could view the town. He had started traveling there but somehow felt that's not where he wanted to go. People would swarm on him for details of the massacre since he figured he was one of the only survivors, and he wasn't ready for that. After some more thought, he came to the shocking realization that his friends in town might turn against him, blaming his family for the massacre.

He wondered what it would be like for Lena whom he hoped was staying somewhere in that clump of buildings he was watching. Would the people hate her? There hadn't been time for him to think about these things the night before and now it was too late. Surely no one could do anything to her, he thought. She was only fifteen, and besides, she was a girl. In a few minutes he convinced himself she would be all right.

Now he had only himself to worry about. He wanted so badly to go into town, to be around people and be accepted by them. But did he dare take the risk? His feelings against it grew, and finally, having made a decision, he stood up and looked one last time at the town. Then he turned and faced the wilderness before him. He didn't know where he would go or what would happen to him, and neither did he know that his choice would affect his life for a long time. He only knew that he had left the Broken Bow with the clothes he was wearing, a harmonica, and a small arsenal of weapons, which consisted of a hunting knife, the Colt .45, and a Henry .44 lever-action repeating rifle with which he'd hunted before. He was hungry now and he must hunt for his meal. So he hoisted the rifle to his shoulder and started up the ridge in search of game.

*   *   *

It was Monday, three days after the massacre, and all of Timber Fork attended the funeral, which took place at the cemetery on a hill northwest of town. It was a cloudy, dismal day, but even darker was the cloud of gloom hanging over the black-clothed gathering. It was quiet save for the muffled sobs of a few. Even the weeping willow trees were still, but the calm, steady voice of the minister carried down the hillside as he read a psalm. Behind him lay a row of coffins, and beside each one was a mound of earth from a freshly dug grave and a marker to be placed on it. The plain, fast-made markers didn't seem like enough to honor the nineteen lives that had been snuffed out, but the respect paid by the townspeople was sincere.

For Tara there were no tears. She had cried enough in the days before the funeral, and now she stood beside her family, hardly noticing them or the minister. It was Lena Hunter, standing a ways off by herself, on whom her attention focused. Edward and Margaret Sinclair had allowed the girl to stay with them until a permanent place was found for her to live. But to Tara, Lena represented her greatest challenge of the moment—how to forgive the Indian girl for something for which she wasn't even responsible. She couldn't look at Lena without being reminded of the tragedy at the Broken Bow. She searched her heart for the compassion she knew Lena needed and she was polite, but the inner struggle was tearing her apart.

Lena worked through her grief stoically. She asked nothing of the Sinclairs. For her, all that existed was her hope for news of Nate for his body had not been found among the dead. One afternoon Mark Curtis visited Lena with the news she had waited to hear.

"Lena, your brother's alive."

The first smile in days broke on Lena's face. "Oh, Mark, really? Where is he? I've got to see him." She expected to see Nate walk into the room any minute.

"Well, we didn't actually see him. We only know that he's alive and that the Indians don't have him. I was out searching with my pa and some others and we found his tracks leading into the Lewis and Clark range. We saw a couple places where he's camped and built a fire."

"Then he's safe."

"We're confused about something though. I thought you could help us out."

"What is it?"

"We're wondering why he's staying out there and not coming here."

Lena thought a minute. "Sometimes when he's upset he likes to be alone."

"That could be. But it still doesn't make sense. You two are pretty close. It seems he'd want to be with you. It would be easier for him."

Lena was clearly bewildered too. "I don't know, Mark. I wish I did." The gladness in her voice was gone.

Mark gave her a reassuring pat on the shoulder. "Don't worry, we'll find him."

* * *

Coming into the parlor from the store one day, Tara walked up on Lena unexpectedly as Lena stood before a shelf of family pictures. Tara stopped abruptly and stood watching in silence a moment. She softly cleared her throat and Lena turned at the sound. Tara caught a quick glimpse of her eyes in a rare, vulnerable moment before Lena forced a brief smile. As Tara moved up beside her, Lena pointed to a picture of a thin-boned woman with clear eyes.

"Who's this?"

"That's my Grandma Sinclair."

Tara watched Lena's eyes as she admired the picture, then, in a voice sounding like it wasn't directed at anyone, Lena said, "I wish I had a picture of my mother."

Her face had a strange look and a moment later she left the room and Tara heard the back door swing shut behind her. Tara took her grandmother's picture from the shelf and sat in the rocking chair. She was ashamed that she couldn't remember the last time she'd looked at it. She looked up in the direction Lena had taken and tears filled her eyes. For all that the Sinclairs had lost in the massacre, Lena had lost everything. Not even a picture was left to cherish. She had the Indians to blame but what could she do about that? Since living with the Sinclairs, Lena had never shown any sign of a vengeful spirit, yet Tara knew it was there. And it always would be because she'd never be able to satisfy it. She was, Tara decided, accepting her plight rather well, despite no help from Tara.

Besieged with guilt, Tara blotted her eyes with her handkerchief, replaced the picture on the shelf, and went in search of Lena. She found her in the stable raking out a stall. Lena saw her but kept on with her work.

"You don't have to do that," said Tara.

"I don't mind. I have to make myself useful."

"Well, then I suppose I'll help."

Lena appeared surprised when Tara located another rake and began working beside her.

"Is it true your mother was a schoolteacher once?" asked Tara.

"Yes. The farm family my pa worked for sent him to her to learn to read. That's how they met."

Tara smiled. "And that was in Missouri?"

Lena nodded. "Up till then that was the longest my pa had ever stayed in one place. He always said he needed to stay to finish his schooling." She smiled, a gesture which Tara returned. "Also, that farm family, the Marshalls, were good to him," Lena continued.

"Do you remember anything about them?"

Lena cupped both hands over the rake handle and rested her chin on them while she searched the far reaches of childhood memory. "Mrs. Marshall was tall. I mean, I can picture her right now and she seems eight feet tall." She looked over at Tara's wide eyes. "Of course, I was only three years old at the time."

Tara burst into laughter as she resumed raking.

Lena watched her for a moment, then her own smile transformed into a look of puzzlement. "Tara, you're raking back the straw I just raked out."

Tara stopped and looked at the task to which she'd been giving no thought and a sheepish grin broke on her face. Shaking her head, she reached for Lena's rake and said, "Let's not do this now." She leaned the rakes against the wall, sat down on a bale of hay and indicated for Lena to sit beside her. "So why did you eventually leave Missouri?"

"There were those who didn't think well of my ma marrying an Indian. Ma didn't care for herself, but she couldn't stand to see Nate and me shunned by other children."

Contempt was markedly absent from Lena's demeanor. It was sobering to Tara to realize that living as a victim of prejudice, a concept foreign to her, was commonplace for Lena. In fact, Tara couldn't imagine anything of Lena's life, but she could now sense that Lena had a deeper knowledge than she of humanity's failings, and that she had learned to rise above it with her dignity intact.

"I'm glad you ended up here in Montana," said Tara, and she meant it.

*　*　*

In the mountains north of Timber Fork, Nate was still existing. Food was no problem. He was already a skilled hunter and there were plenty of rabbits, grouse, and other small game to provide meals as well as wild berries and roots. He never had much appetite; he only ate to stay alive. His days were occupied with evading searchers sent by the town to find him. With his cleverly devised ploys, he always kept a safe distance between him and his pursuers and made it impossible for him to be seen, much less caught. In only two weeks he had become familiar with every ridge, ravine, meadow, creek, and stretch of woods in a region five miles square.

Physically he was a survivor. It was the nights that were hard on him, when the loneliness set in to do its destruction. He would sit leaned against a fallen log, tensely clutching his rifle with both hands and staring blankly into the flickering flames of his campfire. From deep in those flames emerged the images of his mother and father, and thus were triggered countless memories.

He saw a small covered wagon crossing a desolate prairie on its way to the Platte River in Nebraska. It was filled with the young family's possessions as, for the first time, Nate and Lena were leaving the place of their birth in Missouri. He remembered the sod house they settled into on the Nebraska farm where his father found work. He recalled the time his father sacrificed hours of his time to help with his son's ridiculous notion of making a wolf trap in the back yard. They dug a deep hole and camouflaged it with branches and grass only to have Nate's mother fall in it. He saw again the time when his sister had accidentally broken a window while they played ball and had cried so hard that Nate confessed to the crime and got a whipping. He could hear plainly the Indian stories his father told and the Bible stories his mother read while her children sat on the floor at her feet.

Then there was a second wagon journey to a big ranch in the north that was just getting started. His memory stopped there and he was afraid to think any further.

Still, when he snapped out of his daydream and saw the campfire again, he found there were big tears rolling down his cheeks. He didn't try to stop them. He knew it was not good to look back, but what else was there to occupy his mind? He could see no future ahead of him, just emptiness—nothing to look forward to, nothing for which to strive. Life was simply a huge, open void that he must cross, somehow without sinking below his present state. He felt he would always live in seclusion, thwarting the attempts of searchers while having no one to go home to afterwards.

When it had grown dark, he would lie down under the protection of the log and gaze at the fire until the warmth dried his tears and put him to sleep.

*   *   *

At the Sinclairs' request, a group of volunteers continued to search for Nate. Edward Sinclair joined them occasionally as did Mark Curtis. But the unfruitful results led the men to widen their search range, thus driving Nate deeper into the wilderness.

The search held a particular interest for young Tara Sinclair. Having Lena around made any news of Nate more personal to her. There were many unanswered questions and Tara gave much thought to them. What was it in this obscure young man that enabled him to foil a search party so smoothly? Even more puzzling was, why would he do it? Had the horrible experience of the massacre affected his mind? Shouldn't avoiding loneliness and being with his sister take priority over everything else? The fact that Lena had no answers made it more of a mystery.

Finally Tara decided to visit those mountains herself. She knew if the searchers couldn't find Nate neither could she, at least not by using their means.

She spoke to the head of the search party and asked permission to ride along on a Saturday. She wouldn't be any bother, she told him, and would ride home on her own when she'd had enough. And no, she wouldn't get lost; she had gone trail riding there many times before and she knew how to use a gun. The man consented. Tara Sinclair always got what she wanted.

When Saturday came, Tara arose early, put on her riding clothes, packed a lunch, and saddled Molly. By the time the sun was peeking over the eastern horizon, she was riding behind three men, headed northward. Within an hour they were on the edge of the Lewis and Clark range, the beautiful but rugged wilderness, several of whose summits were lost in the clouds on this day.

Throughout the morning and early afternoon, the group trekked through woods, ascended and descended mountains, and forded streams, finding nothing more than Nate's worn-out tracks or a days-old campsite. When it seemed it would be a wasted day, the leader signaled a halt to inspect some new tracks. The men all looked and declared that the tracks were indeed fresh, made only hours before.

Tara's excitement grew; it was time to make her move. After announcing that she was going home and convincing her reluctant companions that she didn't need an escort, she struck out on her own search.

For almost two hours she circled the area where the tracks had been found, frequenting open spaces, making herself visible. She felt she was being watched but supposed that her anticipation caused her to imagine it. She came to a deep, clear mountain spring and dismounted for a rest. While her horse drank of the cool water, Tara took in the wild beauty around her.

"You lookin' for me?" a voice sounded from behind.

Tara uttered a gasp and whirled around to find Nate standing only yards away in the clearing.

"I wasn't that hard to track down, was I?" said Nate, amused by the look on her face.

Tara replied, "Oh, I know better than that. You knew I was here. If it were that easy to find you, you would've been caught a long time ago. You've been pulling it off well, I'll say that for you."

"Do you know what happened to my sister?" Nate asked.

"Yes, I do. She's staying with us. She's fine."

Nate breathed his relief.

"She's waiting until my father finds a family willing to take her in," said Tara. "And she wants to know as much as I do, why are you doing this, Nathaniel? Why are you running from people who are trying to help you?"

"Because I don't need help. What they're doing for Lena is good but it's not for me. I won't subject myself to other people's pity."

So it was his pride that stood in the way, Tara thought, just like always.

"Was there anyone else who escaped the massacre?" Nate inquired.

"Just six others besides you and Lena. One was a woman, and two children escaped with her. They've all left the Territory by now and gone back East."

"I'm sorry about your aunt and uncle."

"Thank you."

"I wish I could've helped them." Nate sadly shook his head. "All those people. So what's Timber Fork doing about it? Will they retaliate?"

Tara was ashamed to answer. "There are not enough settlers to go up against the Cheyenne. They've sent word to the cavalry at Fort Mason, but no one thinks they'll be of much help. With the war in the East just barely ended, not many troops have been posted to the frontier yet. And nobody knows who the Indians were who attacked the ranch or where they are." Then as an afterthought, "Do you know anything?"

Nate searched his memory. "The only one I know by name is Beartooth. He was a messenger sent to talk to my father."

"Would you know where he is?"

Nate could see the mounting hopelessness of the situation. "No," he said with a shake of his head.

His look was one of resignation. Tara knew he wanted revenge just as Lena did, but that would remain a fleeting dream that dissipated with the first signs of wakefulness.

"So the men look for me instead and try to take me back against my will. Now that's what I call senseless." He walked over to an oak tree, sat down, and leaned against its trunk, his rifle laid across his lap.

As Tara watched him she had pity on him. He was very different from when she had last seen him. He seemed so tired and withdrawn. He took deep breaths as if trying to quell a lump in his throat. His listless eyes were full of anxiety and an insatiable longing for something. She was in the presence of the most-talked-about person among the customers in her father's store, only they spoke of him with admiration and astonishment at how he ran trackers in endless circles. But she had discovered something no one else knew. What he had taken upon himself to do wasn't easy. The pressure was taking its toll.

"Why don't you come back to town?" asked Tara. "You could end up dying out here."

"I can't go back. I'd just end up living in a shack in town, working at the lumber mill. I couldn't give Lena any respectable kind of life. No, that's not for me, not like it used to be."

"But it won't be like it used to be ever again. You have to settle for something else."

"But is that all? Is there nothing more for me?"

She had caught him in an unguarded moment, when he had revealed more of his inner self to her than he ever had before. But he quickly threw up the barrier again.

"Anyway, I'm doing fine on my own. I don't need help."

"I'm not so sure about that. You're not going to make it much longer, Nathaniel. Just look at you. You're tired out already. You keep looking on either side to see if anyone is around, and you're holding onto that rifle until your knuckles turn white because it's the only thing that makes you feel safe. What would your parents say if they saw you like this?"

"You shut up about my parents!" Nate lashed out so suddenly it made Tara jump. "It was people just like you who tried to get my parents to do something they didn't want to do that drove them to their graves!" His voice grew soft and strained. "I know I don't look like I'll make it long but I will, as long as I think I'm doing what's right for me. Your friends from town may track me a long time, but they won't outlast me. I'll do what I have to to survive out here."

To discuss it any further would be hopeless, Tara knew. He saw her as the enemy too. She went to Molly and picked up the reins.

Nate stood up. "Don't you tell a soul about this."

"But, Nathaniel—"

"Promise me."

Tara sighed and gave in. "Okay, I promise. But what about Lena? She wants to know how you're doing."

Nate's hardened look melted at the mention of his sister. "Just tell her I'm fine and not to worry. I hope she understands why I can't be with her right now."

"I'll tell her." Tara mounted her horse. "Can I meet you again, next Saturday afternoon right here?

"Okay, but you still won't change my mind if that's why you want to come."

Tara didn't care if he changed his mind or not. She only wanted to see if he was still as sure of himself after another week.

She rode away from the spring the way she had come. When she looked back across the clearing, Nate had disappeared into the woods as swiftly and silently as a shadow.

"I've got some news for you," Tara said as Lena walked into the stable where she was unsaddling Molly.

"And I've got some for you." Lena did not seem enthusiastic. "I'll be leaving here Thursday morning to go to Minnesota."

"Minnesota," Tara echoed. She hadn't expected Lena to go so far away.

"The Madisons here in town have relatives in St. Paul, the Taylors. They have three sons. They heard about the massacre from the Madisons and they wanted to do something to help. They offered to let me stay with them for a year or two if I would like. I accepted. Mr. Taylor's a lawyer and they're very wealthy. I'll be able to go to a real school. Ma would like that."

"Oh, Lena, the city will be so exciting for you," Tara said, smiling. "And three sons—" She narrowed her eyes. "—my, aren't you lucky."

47

Lena bowed her head and grinned. "I think they see this as some sort of cultural exchange thing. Anyway, I'm sure they'll be nice. I just wish I could've seen Nate again and that we didn't have to be split up."

"Well, I have some news you'll want to hear. Today when I was riding in the mountains I saw Nathaniel and spoke with him."

A glazed look came over Lena's face, and Tara couldn't tell whether she would laugh or cry. "Tell me, how is he?" Lena urgently asked. "What did he say?"

Tara glanced to see if anyone was near. "He's well. You must keep it a secret. He doesn't want to come back to town and get pity from anyone. He wants to be left alone for now. He hoped you'd understand."

Lena sat on a bale of hay and looked through the open stable door at the mountains. "I do understand," she replied. "Nate is his own person. The only ones who could ever tell him what to do were Ma and Pa and the boss." She looked at Tara, her eyes pleading for a solution Tara couldn't provide. "I know he wouldn't be happy at all where I'm going, but I still can't help wishing we could be together."

"I know," said Tara. "He told me to tell you not to worry."

Lena smiled. "There's no need to. He knows what he's doing in those mountains."

"I'm to see him again next week," said Tara. "I'll tell him of your plans."

"Would you do me a favor?" Lena took the rabbit's-foot charm and its string from her neck and handed it to Tara. "Give him this for me. It's the only thing I saved from the massacre. It's supposed to be for good luck. He needs it now more than me."

"He'll get it," Tara assured her.

*   *   *

That evening when Mark Curtis stopped by to discuss the search for Nate with Edward Sinclair, he was surprised and pleased when Tara wanted to talk to him too. Alone with her on the porch, it reminded him of the day he'd returned from Oregon and they had met in the same place.

"No luck with the search yet?" asked Tara.

"Afraid not," sighed Mark. "I've thought this over again and again, and I can't figure out why Nate's running from us."

"Well, if he doesn't want to come back to town, why make him?"

"That's a rough country out there, Tara," said Mark, pointing to the dark silhouettes of the mountains. "He could get himself killed."

"But can you help him by making him do something against his will?"

"I think we have to if we're sure that what he's doing isn't good for him. That's what bothers me about Nate. I know he's making a mistake but nobody can get near to talk to him." His eyes met Tara's and he didn't try to hide his frustration. "A friend of mine might die out there and there's nothing I can do about it."

"You mean if you found him you would take him by force?"

Mark looked away from her and hesitated, uncomfortable with the question. "I wouldn't want to do that, but yes, I would. I just wish he'd give us a chance to help him."

Tara smiled and changed the subject, afraid he would grow suspicious of her concern. "Tell me something, Mark. How come you haven't talked about going to California since that day on the Broken Bow?"

"It's not as important anymore, I suppose," said Mark with a shrug. "It was a foolish sacrifice I made that day, and after making it I lost interest in adventure. I don't even care what's over the next hill."

"But Mark, you wanted it so badly."

"There were things I should've wanted more. Tara, there hasn't a day gone by that I haven't regretted what I did to you. I wish we could turn the whole thing back around. But I guess it's too late for that now."

A short silence followed and Tara felt awkward.

Finally Mark looked away from her and sighed. "I'm just a damn fool."

"Oh, Mark, that's not true," said Tara. "You have to follow your heart, and if your heart was in California then, it will be again. But no matter what, we'll always be friends, you know that."

Mark smiled. Tara's forgiving and amiable attitude was what he had always liked about her.

*   *   *

Mark had no idea how his talk with Tara had disturbed her. She wondered if she should tell the search party that she had seen Nate. There was no doubt that if they found out about her visit with him by other means, she would anger a lot of people. Then again, to break her promise to Nate would be considered an unforgivable act by him. But of course, he had never liked her before and she hadn't lost sleep over it then. By early Monday morning she had made her decision.

Chapter 7

Thursday morning the Sinclair family stood on the loading platform at the stage depot. Lena stood with them, not giving any outward indication of the turmoil she felt inside while she waited for the eight o'clock stage to be loaded. She awaited this trip with dread for it would be a long, arduous one. She would be traveling with strangers and be met by more strangers when she reached St. Paul.

The Sinclairs had done everything they could to bolster her courage and excite her about the journey. Margaret had sewn the dress she now wore, a white calico with a strawberry pattern, and packed a basket of sandwiches for her. Lena felt that her few words of thanks were inadequate in the face of their generosity, yet they said that they would welcome her back if Minnesota didn't suit her.

The driver gave the boarding call. Lena said goodbye to Edward and Margaret Sinclair, then stood before Tara.

"Don't forget to write," said Tara.

"I won't." Lena gave her a hug. "Goodbye, Tara." She took her basket from Margaret and began to move toward the stage, then stopped and turned to Tara. "I will see Nate again, won't I?"

"Of course you will," replied Tara as cheerfully as she could.

Lena forced a smile and climbed into the stagecoach. As the horses started into a trot and the stage rolled away, she reached her arm out and waved.

*   *   *

One day the following week Nate stood on a rock overlook on the east side of Mount Defiance, where he spent the majority of his time, scanning the valley below for searchers as he had done many times before. But this time his sharp eyes picked out something he did not expect—Indians, three of them on horseback about a mile away in the brush. He wondered from which people they came. Suddenly his heart beat faster as he realized that he had trodden the same path only the day before. They were Cheyenne Indians and they were tracking him. How had they known where he was, or even that he was alive? One thing was certain; the Indians wanted him, and that was going to make Nate's life more difficult. In order to stay free of the Indians he would have to match wits with them. That would be no simple task, considering that the strategies he used to outsmart the town men were of Indian origin and the Indians wouldn't be fooled so easily by them. He knew only too well the persistence of the Cheyenne. They would not give up until he was captured or dead. But Nate would not allow them either option. He would stay out of the hands of the Cheyenne, even if it meant being on the run indefinitely. He must use every skill he possessed and develop yet more skills, but he was determined to succeed, if only to deny the Indians the satisfaction of overpowering another of the Hunter family.

*   *   *

Another Saturday came and Tara visited the spring, hoping Nate would show himself again. Maybe now he would be ready to surrender himself. She waited more than an hour. He wasn't coming, she decided. Of course he wouldn't, after what she'd done. She was getting ready to leave when Nate emerged from the woods. His look and his voice were harsh.

"Something told me I might find you here," he said.

Tara smiled and walked closer to him. "You weren't here last week."

"You're damn right I wasn't here," said Nate. "I agreed to meet you, not representatives from Timber Fork that you send in your place."

"What are you talking about?"

"Don't play ignorant with me. You told the men where to find me. You broke a promise and betrayed me." He narrowed his eyes at her. "Of course, I expected as much from you, and so they were unsuccessful."

Tara's smile was gone in an instant. "All right, so I did that! You think you're so clever because they didn't catch you. How do you know that I didn't bring anyone this time who's hiding in the woods?"

"Because I know you wouldn't risk being embarrassed by a second failure."

"Listen, Nathaniel, I did that for your own good. Even your friend Mark said you should be brought back to town."

"And naturally you would listen to Mark. Does Mark know that the Indians are looking for me?"

"Indians!" Tara's eyes widened.

"Yes, Cheyenne Indians, here in these mountains."

A chill slithered up Tara's spine as she thought of the Indians being so near.

"You see, I couldn't go back to town if I wanted to," said Nate. "The Indians might do anything to capture me, even attack Timber Fork if that's where I was. So you'd better stop conniving to get me caught because I'm doing this for the good of all your friends in town. But mind you, if they were all like you, I couldn't care less what happened to them."

Tara was too concerned about Indians to hear Nate insult her. She even missed the next thing he said. "What?" she asked.

"How's Lena getting along?" asked Nate.

Tara gathered her thoughts to give Nate the news she knew he wouldn't like. "She's not staying with us anymore. She left Thursday a week ago."

Nate's expression softened. "Where did she go?"

51

"St. Paul, Minnesota."

Nate stared at her, trying, though not wanting, to fully comprehend the fact that Lena was no longer safely sheltered nearby. Then, gazing at the spring, he finally asked, "So who are the people?"

Tara told him all that she knew about Lena's new home and assured him that she would be fine, but nothing she said could ease Nate's sadness.

"I knew it seemed impossible," he said, "but I'd hoped there'd be some way I could see her before she left."

"I'm so sorry," said Tara. She circled around in front of him. "I know this is hard for you, with Lena gone and the Indians after you and all. If I could be of assistance in any way—"

"Since when were you ever of any assistance to me? Last week when you sent your friends to pick me up?"

"They weren't my friends. I was only—"

"You were just trying to make yourself look good by telling them what they wanted to know. Well, I won't have anybody, especially some vain rich girl, pitying me."

"For heaven's sakes, you're so swallowed up in your foolish pride that you can't even recognize a chance to save yourself. You know I never liked you, Nathaniel Hunter, but at least I can put away my dislikes in favor of helping others. Tell me, what's it going to take to bring you down?"

"Listen, what I need most is company, somebody to talk to. Why'd it have to be you? Why couldn't it have been Julie?" Immediately Nate was embarrassed for saying it. The fact that Tara didn't answer made him feel even more awkward. "I'm sorry," he muttered, looking away from her.

"It's okay," said Tara. "Julie probably wishes it would've been her too."

"Look, there is one thing you could do for me."

"What is it?"

"I need ammunition to hunt with."

It thrilled Tara to have Nate finally ask something of her, to admit a need. She began to pace back and forth in front of him, jerking her chin at him as she talked. "So it's ammunition you want, is it? And you expect me to get it for you. That costs money, you know."

"I know, which is why I'll pay back every cent as soon as I can."

"As soon as you can? That's putting it in vague terms."

"You have my word."

"How do I know that your word can be trusted?"

"Hunter credit's always been good in your store, you know that. Now are you going to get it for me or not?"

"I don't know. I'll think about it."

"Never mind then. I'll find another way to get it."

Tara knew what he meant and refrained from antagonizing him. "Well, I can't let you turn to thievery. I'll bring you bullets for the rifle and the gun too. Don't worry about paying for it. You'll probably get killed before you get a chance to."

"You're too kind. But I don't take charity—"

"I'm not about to give you any. If I keep paperwork on your debts my father might see it. I'll buy ammunition for you, and you pay me back as soon as you can."

"All right then," said Nate. "Bring a batch next Saturday afternoon. Go up to Mount Defiance. On the south side where Elkhorn Creek flows down, there's a little waterfall. Meet me there."

"Why not here?"

"Too wide open. It's not safe anymore. There's a hollow, like a small cave in the rock behind the waterfall. It's well-hidden. That's where I'll be."

"Wait a minute. What about the Indians? What if I run into them?"

Nate remained aloof. "Make sure they don't get the ammo."

Tara rolled her eyes as she stomped over and picked up the reins of her horse. But Nate was not finished with her.

"If you tell anyone I will know."

"*I know!*" Tara threw her hands in the air in frustration. She'd had enough of this ungrateful lout and she would show up the next Saturday only if she darn well felt like it.

Just then she remembered the rabbit's-foot charm in her saddlebag and took it out. "I almost forgot," she said, handing it to Nate. "Lena wanted you to have this."

Nate didn't say anything while he fingered the rabbit's foot in his palm, but Tara knew he was appreciative.

"Till next Saturday then," she said, "if I come."

*　　*　　*

The Sinclair store was the usual place for the town men to gather to exchange news of their families, work, rumors of Indian unrest and faraway gold strikes. Most of those who had searched for Nate had given up and opted to leave him be on his own. He could obviously take care of himself, and if he wanted to live as a recluse, they wouldn't stop him. But only recently had they heard of the Cheyenne warriors dogging Nate's trail.

"I don't know about you fellas," said one man, "but I feel uneasy knowin' that some of those murderous redskins are ridin' so close to Timber Fork."

"I know what you mean," said another. "I certainly don't want to have a run-in with 'em."

"Well, boys," drawled a big, heavy man with a dark red mustache and beard, "what the Indians want is Nate and that's none of our concern. They can have him. We never knew him that well anyway."

"Speak for yourself, Jed," said a boisterous voice. "You're just a drifter who drops into town once in a while. It's true many of us didn't know Nate well. He stuck to himself a lot. But he's still one of ours and we can't forget about him so easily."

"I agree with Collins," said the man who had spoken first. "We can't forget him. On the other hand, we've got ourselves to think about."

"So what are you saying?" asked Hiram Curtis.

"Those Indians want him bad or they wouldn't have sent braves all the way here to fetch him. I say we keep looking for him, and if we capture him first, we should turn him over to the Cheyenne."

"No, that's out of the question," said Edward Sinclair.

Tara had been dusting behind the counter, listening all the while. She slowed down when she heard her father join in the discussion.

"I knew Nate a bit better than some of you perhaps. He never bothered anybody, and he doesn't deserve to have us turn against him."

"It ain't really turnin' against him," one man said. "We never said he did anything wrong."

Mark Curtis, the youngest of the group, who usually kept quiet, spoke up. "But you want to turn him over to his own enemies, and that's not right no matter how you look at it. He's innocent."

"Oh sure, he's a good kid," said the man who seemed to be leader, "but he's too dangerous to have around. The Cheyenne might start threatening Timber Fork. If we turn Nate over to them, they'll pull their braves outta here. We can all rest easier."

Three other men nodded in agreement.

"What's the matter with all of you?" said Edward. "Don't you have any backbone? Don't you understand what a cowardly decision like that means for Nate? You don't have the right to take his freedom."

"But he's only one person," the man answered. "We're talkin' about protectin' the lives of a couple hundred settlers. One solitary kid isn't worth what Timber Fork could lose in a massacre. Now some of the men here are with me on this. You can't change our minds, Sinclair, but nobody said you had to go with us. But if you don't come in with us, I know the Curtises will side with you. And we really need your help."

"No, I cannot support that decision."

"I won't help you either," said Hiram.

"Nor I," said Mark.

Tara continued her dusting as if she hadn't heard a word, but secretly she was glad her father, Hiram, and Mark had taken a stand for Nate.

*   *   *

The next Saturday as planned, Tara rode to Mount Defiance. She followed the twisting Elkhorn Creek and almost lost it when she was forced to detour because of heavy brush. It was difficult to navigate her horse through some spots, but Tara wasn't about to tie her and continue on foot. She felt like she'd left all signs of civilization and safety, and she needed Molly for company. She began to think that maybe Nate had lied about this meeting place. But then, what purpose would that serve? No, she decided, even he wouldn't stoop that low.

She guided Molly up yet another steep, bushy incline, then halted her at the top. Here, surrounded by rugged terrain and large boulders that could easily conceal a dangerous animal, or worse, an Indian brave, she stopped to consider what she was doing. She figured she did feel somewhat sorry for Nate, but why in heaven's name was she going to all this trouble to help him? Well, this would be the last time, she determined. She had already tried to talk sense into him to no avail; Lena was far away and Tara wouldn't have to answer to her. So she would give him the ammunition today and leave him to it. She had no more obligation to him.

She was filled with hope when she heard the sound of the waterfall. She rode on, then minutes later the trees gave way to a clearing and her eyes beheld it. Its breathtaking beauty dared her to come closer, but when she did she felt like she was intruding on a secret spot. She dismounted and walked across a large, flat rock to the edge of the creek beside the waterfall.

To her right about five feet above her head, the creek's rocky floor came to an abrupt end and spilled its shiny white threads of water into the clear, rippling pool a foot below her feet. There it lingered awhile before flowing back into the mountains. Standing only yards away from the cascade, Tara could faintly see the colors of a rainbow just above the water's surface and could feel the cool mist from the falls tingling her skin. On either side of the falls smooth and jagged rocks were embedded in the earthen wall with an abundance of ferns growing between. All around the pool the clearing was green with foliage, and one huge willow tree leaned far out over the water with its graceful bows almost touching the surface.

Tara hadn't known that the rough and difficult trail would lead to such a glorious, hidden place. The power of its striking features and sacred silence generated a warm, mellow feeling in her. It was an enchanted place, a place where pure and majestic beauty knew no time. It had existed in all its natural grandeur for hundreds of years, yet Tara felt as if she had been the first to see it.

That feeling quickly faded when she looked across the pool and saw Nate appear from behind the sweeping boughs of the willow tree. Another intruder.

"Hello there," she called to him.

Nate returned the greeting.

"I'm on the wrong side of the creek," said Tara.

"No, you're not," replied Nate. He walked to the waterfall, disappeared behind it and, to Tara's surprise, came out on her side. "So you actually came to meet me," he said.

"You thought I wouldn't?"

Nate shrugged.

"I do have some bad news," said Tara.

"First the ammunition."

Tara went to her saddlebag, took out the box of bullets, and set them on the rock at his feet.

"Thank you so much," said Nate after inspecting the goods. "This will do fine. Now, what's the bad news?"

"The town men know about the Indians who are looking for you. They're afraid of the Cheyenne, and some of the men intend to catch you and turn you over to them. I know of eleven that are in on it so far."

Nate gave her a long, serious look, but he didn't seem surprised. "It's hard to believe those back-stabbing fools were ever friends of mine," he said.

"My father and Mark were against them and tried to stop them."

"Good for your father and Mark, but not so good for me."

Tara could sense desperation beneath his deep concern. Indians and white men alike were out to get him, but Nate was alone on his side. There was no one in whom to place his trust. He wouldn't even trust Tara, and she now wanted to prove to him that he could.

"I don't know," sighed Nate, "maybe I ought to clear out of the Territory and start over again somewhere else."

"You do and you'll lose the only contact you have with your sister."

Such a sacrifice was out of the question. Nate dismissed the thought.

"You're fighting a losing battle," Tara continued. "You must give in while you're still alive. I'm sure the men could be persuaded to change their minds about turning you over—"

"No! They won't change their minds and neither will I. You think that giving in can solve everything but it can't."

"Nathaniel, there's no other way."

"You damn well better stay out of it," he said, pointing his finger in her face. "This is my business, not yours."

"And I suppose if you get killed that's your business too?"

"Yeah, as a matter of fact it is."

"You're a fool, Nathaniel Hunter."

"If I am at least I only have myself to blame. And anyway, I never asked for your advice, just ammunition."

"You watch how you speak to me or you won't get that."

"Listen, if you think my life depends completely on you and your father's store you got another thought coming."

"Likewise, you Indian. My father's store is respectable and doesn't need to deal with the likes of you."

Nate was growing tired of the insults being hurled back and forth. It all seemed pointless. Their longstanding hostility paled in comparison to the problems he now faced. He needed someone on his side. "Look, every time we're around each other we argue. If you're going to be coming here often we're going to have to try to be friends." He was a little embarrassed for making the suggestion, and by the way she folded her arms and looked at him, he knew it was a lost cause anyway.

"Are you saying that just to get your ammunition?"

"All right, if you're going to be that way, just forget it."

"No!" Tara blurted out, surprising herself and Nate. "No, let's not." Nate was watching her, waiting. "I agree that we... we need to be friends. I will if you'll stop insulting me. No matter what you think, I don't think I'm better than you." She paused. "Just more sensible."

"You had to get that last bit in, didn't you?"

"No, I'm sorry. I didn't mean that." The words came out in a rush. "I can do this. I know I can." She stepped forward and offered her hand for a handshake.

"Friends then," said Nate as they shook hands. "Maybe now you can call me Nate?"

Such familiarity was uncomfortable for Tara. "But Nathaniel is your name. I've called you that for four years." He made no reply but under his piercing gaze Tara knew that giving in to his wish would have to be part of the package. "All right, if you prefer."

Silence followed. Now that they couldn't argue, it was difficult for either to think of anything to say.

"Such a beautiful place this is," said Tara finally. "It's real hard to get to."

"I know. I figured if you made it here without turning back it would be worth it to show you my hiding place."

"Your hiding place?"

"Yep. Come on, I'll show you the cave." He motioned for her to follow him.

They walked to the falls where there was a space of about three feet between the water and the rock over which it fell. The rock curved out at the top where the water flowed off, thus making this space.

"Hold your breath," said Nate as he started making his way along the rock behind the falls.

Tara followed, trying in vain to avoid the hundreds of tiny, cold sprinkles that dampened her face and clothing. A few steps later the rock wall opened into a hollow. She walked into the middle and stood marveling at this discovery.

The hollow was big and roomy. It extended into the rock about eight feet, and the ceiling was about four feet above Tara's head. The light was dim but the rock walls shone with threads of water trickling down. Here and there grew clumps of plants, which thrived on the moisture in the cave.

Tara had to raise her voice over the crashing sound of the waterfall. "This is amazing. I suppose no one knows about it. How did you know it was here?"

"I've always known," replied Nate. "Even when we still lived in Nebraska I knew that a place like this existed 'cause my pa told me about it. The Indians, they know it's here. But they won't set foot in this place, which is why I do."

"Why don't they come here?"

"It's forbidden ground to them. They believe it's full of evil spirits."

Tara shot him a sharp glance, then turned and left the cave the way she had come.

Wondering what he had done, Nate came after her. "What's the matter with you?"

She stopped and faced him. "Are you going to try to scare me with your Indian ghost stories?"

Nate beheld her like she'd lost all semblance of sanity. "Absolutely not. If you're scared it's your own fault."

"Well, I'm not scared." She sat down on the big, flat rock and lightly dipped her fingers in the water. "So your father was here before, was he?"

"Yes, a long time ago." He sat down across from her. "You remember I told you about the brave's son who drowned? This is where it happened."

Tara withdrew her hand from the water. "Right here?"

"Yes. The Indians hold Mount Defiance to be very sacred. Before the white settlers came, the Indians would come here every year before buffalo-hunting season to perform ceremonies and pray to the spirits to give them good hunting. My pa came here with the people a few times when he was a boy. It was on one of those trips that the brave's son died. Only the brave knew how it happened, so when he accused my grandfather, nobody could go against his word. He had never liked my grandfather."

"And that's really why you're here now," said Tara, thinking of the chain of events which brought Nate to this forbidden place.

"Yep. My grandfather's so-called crime drove my family away from this place. And fate brought us back when we heard about the Broken Bow getting started." He shook his head. "No, I don't believe there's any ghosts here. It's just a place where I can rest. As long as I'm in these woods the Indians can't touch me. I just have the white settlers to worry about."

Tara smiled. "I think you've been handling them pretty well." She stood and went to her horse. "I'd best be going before Papa wonders what's keeping me. I told him I was going to the Split Timber."

"You told a lie to your father?" Nate asked in mock surprise.

"No I didn't. I'll stop out there on the way home. There's nothing dishonest about that."

Nate smiled and shook his head as she rode away.

Chapter 8

Weeks passed by and summer changed into autumn. The new season took hold on the wilderness and transformed its dark green into striking yellow, scarlet, and crimson—the Moon of Falling Leaves the Indians called it. The valley grasses turned golden brown and there was a nip in the air. Winter snows weren't far away.

Just as the season changed, so did Nate. He had lived in the mountains over three months now and learned invaluable lessons in survival. He knew a portion of the Lewis and Clark range like the back of his hand and that knowledge served him well. No Indian had been able to track him down for Nate knew the Cheyenne tactics as well as they did and used them cunningly. Occasionally a brave had picked up his trail and come so close to catching him that Nate had been forced to run recklessly through the woods, relying solely, not on tactics, but on quickness and surefootedness to get him free. Some braves had even seen him a couple of times when his path took him into the open, but without fail he would throw them off by hiding in the leafy branches of a tree or retreating to the Grotto, as he had come to call it, where Indians wouldn't follow. Indeed he had succeeded at matching wits with this people whose blood he shared.

As for the white settlers, Nate had done more than just manage against them. He had humiliated them by making their efforts look weak. Yet he had earned their respect, for even they saw how the mountains had worn experience on him and proven him until his physical and mental abilities were far greater than theirs.

Nate wasn't sure why so many people wanted him captured or what they intended to do with him when they got him. It almost seemed as if they were enjoying the chase.

The main benefit that Nate had derived from this way of life was to rid him of any doubts he had about himself and give him overpowering confidence. He knew he was clever. He expected his pursuers to know they must try their hardest to catch him. He expected to outsmart them every time they came close to him. It was a hard and lonely life he led, but he was used to it. He was a mountaineer.

There was one person who saw a softer side of Nate and that was Tara. Nate had come to look forward to her visits since she was his only contact with civilization and because she was someone to talk to. He discovered she wasn't really hard to get along with as they learned to accept each other's personalities.

Tara continued to bring him the bullets he needed, bought with money from her allowance. Occasionally she brought him extra things—a woolen blanket, a penknife, a flannel shirt, matches, cookies. He had no idea how she managed to smuggle the luxuries out to him or why, but he gratefully accepted all of it. They reminded him of the settled, secure life he had left behind.

*   *   *

At times, Tara wondered if she was doing the right thing. If anyone found out about the secret meetings with Nate, there would be a terrific scandal. And she had her reputation to consider. Then there were the Cheyenne braves who rode in the mountains. She never saw them and Nate assured her they were only interested in him, nevertheless she always took the most direct route to the Grotto and packed a gun on her saddle.

But in spite of the risks, she kept up the visits for one reason. It made Nate happy and that gratified her. Because of her company over the weeks, she had seen him come through despair, sorrow, and anger, and gradually pull himself together. She had even seen him laugh for the first time since before the massacre.

One mid-October day, Tara rode to the Grotto and found Nate waiting for her as he often did now that he trusted her.

Nate smiled. "Afternoon." He looked the same as the summer before except that his hair had grown a couple of inches and flipped out in little curls at his neck.

After dismounting and saying hello, Tara handed him a small box. She followed him into the hollow behind the waterfall where he knelt down and pushed back a stone to reveal a hand-dug hole containing a leather-lined wooden box which held the goods Tara brought. He added the new item to his stockpile and replaced the stone.

Outside again, Tara talked excitedly. "I have wonderful news for you."

"About Lena?" he asked hopefully. "Is she coming home?"

Tara shook her head.

"I'm invited to dinner then."

"No," Tara laughed. "The men stopped the search for you because of winter coming." The smile that slowly broke on Nate's face seemed to Tara the most genuine he'd ever given her. "I'm so excited for you."

"Are you really?"

He waited for an answer and Tara felt awkward. "Yes."

Nate raised his eyebrows. "Then you'll invite me to dinner now?"

"No, I will not," laughed Tara. She drew her coat around her tighter. "You can't spend the winter here, Nate. You won't survive."

"So you're always telling me, but I have an idea. Out in the northwest section of the Broken Bow there's a dugout by the creek, been there a long time. It faces south and it's shielded from the winds. I can stay there."

"I wouldn't think you'd want to go there after what happened."

61

"The dugout's a long ways from where that happened. I wouldn't have any reason to go there."

"It sounds like a good idea then," Tara said. "The ranch is abandoned now, but if anyone went there I'd know about it and tell you beforehand."

"How would you know?"

"Since my uncle died my father now owns the ranch," Tara explained. "Of course, it's not making any money, but Papa would like to keep it in the family. I think he'd sell though, if someone offered enough."

Nate was uninterested in the monetary value of the ranch. "Why didn't you tell me before that your father owns the ranch now?"

She shrugged. "You didn't ask. As you know, Uncle Jerome and Aunt Charlotte's two sons went back to Chicago a few years ago. Neither of them wanted the ranch, so they signed it over to Papa."

He turned away from her and a long, contemplative silence followed. Only Nate could see the harm in what Tara had just told him. "Tara, I think you shouldn't come here anymore."

Tara was taken by surprise. "Why?"

"The Broken Bow may be out of business but the land is still valuable, and the Cheyenne know that. So if they decide to threaten the white settlers in Timber Fork, it'll be at the expense of the owner of the Broken Bow. Boss Sinclair was their main target before. Now it could be your father, and that could put you in danger too."

"But the Indians haven't threatened us."

"Not yet. But some of the settlers are afraid it will happen, and that's why they want to turn me over to them. And they're right. I can see it coming."

"Well, I don't think I need to stop coming here."

"I'm dead serious, Tara. The Indians may see you riding here sometime and take a notion to capture you. And when they find out who you are—"

"I wouldn't tell them."

"If they flashed a knife in front of you, you would. Tara, I know the Cheyenne. I've seen what they'll do to get what they want. You've got to promise you'll stop coming here."

Tara tried not to show how disappointed she felt. "Okay, I won't come here again."

"I'll still see you," said Nate. "The Indians will leave for the winter. I'll move to that dugout and you can meet me there next time."

*   *   *

The dugout was a large hole in the bank beside Elkhorn Creek. Thick-growing grasses and bushes camouflaged the entrance. In the winter the snowdrifts piled up and blocked the opening, but underground it stayed sufficiently warm. The same week Nate moved, the first snow of the season came and the Indian braves headed for home.

It was in front of this dugout that Tara sat on a rock beside the frozen creek on a crisp Christmas day, wearing a bright red coat with a hood framed in fur, a new Christmas gift. The clean, glittering snow stretched to the horizon where it met with a solid, powder blue sky. A cold, sharp wind whipped against her rosy-cheeked face. Behind her, her father's matched Tennessee Walkers, hitched to the sleigh she'd driven out from town, tossed their heads, the condensation of their breath visible in the air.

Nate stood across from her, wrapped in animal skins, arms folded with one foot resting on a rock. He noticed that her cheeks matched her new coat and the color of her eyes matched the sky, and for the first time he thought she was pretty. "How in the world did you get away?" he asked.

"Oh, it's a madhouse back there," replied Tara, shaking her head. "Jared broke Rachel's new doll already, Mother's cake fell, and the Curtises can't decide what time they'll be able to come for dinner. There are so many people in the house I can't hear myself think. They probably don't know I'm gone." Nate's look of longing for days gone by did not escape Tara's notice and she abruptly changed the subject. "I have a surprise for you." She waved an envelope in her hand. "I got a letter from Lena."

"Really? She finally wrote?" Nate squatted in the snow in front of her.

"It just arrived yesterday." She unfolded the letter and began to read, "'Sorry it has taken a while for me to write but I've been so busy settling in. St. Paul is such a big place. There are so many buildings and people. The women all dress so fancy, and everything is so modern. The school I go to is a big brick building two stories high. The Taylors treat me like a princess. They have three sons—'"

"Oh, I bet she likes that," Nate said with a grin.

"She doesn't say." Tara resumed reading. "'The oldest is Kendall. He's married to Belle, who is my teacher. Then there's Ward and Beau. We live in a great big house with a porch across the front, something like Boss Sinclair had. Their grandmother lives with us too. She and I share the same room. She's the one who's teaching me the proper etiquette for dinner parties and socials. Such things are strange to me but I suppose I have to learn. We get invitations often because Mr. Taylor has a lot of business friends who entertain.'"

Nate was mesmerized by his sister's experiences. He was puzzled when Tara began to laugh. "What's so funny?"

"The look on your face. I could just see you at a formal dinner party."

Nate smiled. "I guess that's why you never invite me to dinner." He waited for Tara's shy laugh, which always followed his joke about a dinner invitation. Then he turned meditative. "Well, the city may be big but it can't be as big as this land is."

63

"She mentions you in here." She looked back down at the letter. "Tell Nate I miss him and to take care. Love, Lena."

Nate thanked Tara for reading the letter but his initial excitement was gone. "It sounds like she's really happy in the city."

"Don't worry," replied Tara. "She'll come back here."

"You really think so?"

Tara nodded. "She has more to bring her back here than to keep her there."

Never taking his eyes off her, Nate reached into his pants pocket and produced a tiny, rough-made wood carving of a rearing horse and handed it to her. "I made this for you."

Tara's eyes brightened as she ran her fingers over the delicate carving. "Why, Nate, it's beautiful. Such fine detail. I didn't know you could carve."

"Me neither actually. I've had time to practice."

"It's the perfect image of Daredevil."

"How'd you know it was Daredevil?"

"I can tell by his powerful muscles and the mean look in his eye. I remember when you rode him that day."

"Oh, that. He was getting old. He was bound to wear down soon."

Tara halted her study of the carving and lifted her eyes to meet his.

Nate grinned. "Well, Lena told me that's what you said." Tara flushed in embarrassment. "It's okay," Nate continued. "You were right. At least he won me some money first." He cocked his head to one side and cast his eyes upward. "I wonder whatever happened to that horse."

"Probably dead of old age by now," replied Tara matter-of-factly. "Food for the buzzards."

Nate chuckled, then thoughtfully stared at her for the longest time, until she began to feel self-conscious.

"Merry Christmas, Tara."

Chapter 9

The winter was long and very cold, and it was well into April before the snows melted in the valley, revealing a green, newborn land. Once again birds burst forth in song, flowers of every color and shape swayed in the soft breeze, and the world was alive again.

No sooner had spring touched the Lewis and Clark range than Nate migrated back to his mountain home. No settlers attempted to track him this year. Though the scar of the massacre was still on the hearts of the people, most had forgotten about the young man who had survived and disappeared into the mountains. And there was no imminent threat of Indian trouble for no Cheyenne had been seen since the year before.

It was easier on Nate not to be chased. He had the woods to himself and could hunt where he pleased. He endured all mountain weathers with ease. During the hot hours of the day he remained in the shade of the forest. When the wind blew across the ridges with the force of a stampede, he moved away from the leeward side of the mountain, and the occasional rainstorms found him watching the changing sky from the shelter of a rock overhang or a small cave.

He spent hours honing his fast-draw skill with his Colt .45. This had once been a fun pastime, but now it had taken on more importance. He had often heard the saying, 'God did not make all men equal. Colonel Colt did.' And so, his prowess with the gun became a pressing goal. He practiced, repeatedly, pulling the gun, cocking the hammer, and firing until he could perform all three steps in one fluid movement. He discovered that cocking the hammer with his left hand as the gun was drawn was quicker and easier. When that skill was sufficiently mastered, he worked on accuracy. Fast-drawing a gun was useless if one had to take time to line up a target in his sights. So he shot many an animal skin to pieces until his aim was dead-on.

He became equal in proficiency with his knife. Time after tedious time he repeated the same move—unsheathing the knife, turning towards an imaginary enemy behind him, and throwing the weapon. He familiarized himself with the weight of the knife and the feel of it in his hand, as if it were part of his body. The target he'd carved on a tree became a ripped-up piece of evidence of his success with this maneuver.

In the evenings in front of the fire he often played his harmonica. He played everything he knew, from the church hymns his mother liked to sing, to the mellow, soothing songs he'd used to calm the cattle at night, to the catchy tunes of the barn dances on the Broken Bow when the cowboys would invite town girls out on summer Saturday evenings. Nate never invited anyone and he never danced, but he didn't get teased since his harmonica and Gus' fiddle made up the entire band.

He loved to observe the constellations in the night sky. His father had told him some of the Indian names for them, but he preferred their Latin names. It made them seem more mysterious. And so he would purposely let the embers of his campfire die down so he could have clear views of the Northern Cross, of the Pleiades, and of his favorite, Orion, a hunter like him. He found that if he closed one eye and held his hunting knife above his head just so, he could match it to the sword in Orion's hand.

He did not keep an exact accounting of the days but he knew when it was August because while camped in a clearing, he was afforded an unobstructed view of the Perseids. He had marveled at the heavens before while guarding cattle on the Broken Bow, but here in the wilderness, accompanied by the occasional howl of a coyote, the stars somehow seemed less distant and more connected to the natural events of the earth.

He was used to his life alone by now and even enjoyed having only himself to answer to. But one thing stayed on his mind and that was the girl whom he had waited for by the waterfall so many times. For his own sake he regretted making Tara promise not to come to the Grotto anymore, though he knew it was best for her. There was more to his reasons that he had not let on to her. Her family lived in a sort of golden existence, a revered place where his kind never visited, and despite her being a contact with his sister, despite her supplying him with ammunition, even despite her being a friend, she was, when it all boiled down, a Sinclair, and he mustn't let himself get too close.

Tara still got ammunition to Nate by hiding it in a predetermined place in the valley north of town, but she, too, missed the visits. She had begun to be drawn to his unique character, the fierce independence, the strong yet gentle way of speaking, and the light, jocular remarks that made her laugh. She had developed a genuine concern for his plight. She ached in a way that surprised her to see him free to live among people and not have to hide like an outlaw.

It wasn't until the spring and summer of that year had passed that the tide suddenly turned and posed a threat more serious than ever to Nate's freedom. The Cheyenne band of his ancestors had spent the months enlisting the help of other Cheyennes, and now in late September, the Moon of Drying Grass, dozens of warriors with their women and children poured into the Territory and made their encampments around Mount Defiance, the Sacred Mountain. Following their ancient custom, they danced around their campfires at night and sang chants. But it wasn't just for the sake of good hunting. They knew that their young rebel Indian brother still lived. They knew, too, that he had proven himself to be equal to a brave, and they wanted him to be joined with them. They knew if they could gain Nate as an ally that their collective power would be strengthened, both for the hunt and in battle.

The town of Timber Fork feared the worst. Every night until the first light of dawn they heard the Indian drums beating monotonously and saw their fires glowing on the horizon. Once before bands of Cheyenne had joined together and it had ended in mass slaughter. Determined not to see a repetition of that tragedy, the town leaders sent for the United States Cavalry at Fort Mason over fifty miles to the east.

It was at a dance one Friday evening in the schoolhouse where townspeople of all ages were trying to forget the drums and the fires that a young captain in uniform entered and stepped onto the platform in front of the room.

"Could I have your attention please?" he began in a loud, husky voice. The room hushed and every eye turned to him. "As you all know, the Cheyenne are camped all around Mount Defiance. I hate to spoil the evening for you folks, but we don't know what the Indians have in mind. I have to ask you all to leave now and return to your homes."

Some in the crowd murmured their displeasure while others expressed fear at the thought of Indian trouble.

"Now there's no reason at all to panic," said the captain. "Major Elliot and I are here to keep things under control and I assure you we will. We just want to be sure everyone is safe at nighttime, so please go straight home and make sure every lady has an escort."

* * *

Tara was standing under a tree on a hill by the schoolhouse, gazing anxiously at Mount Defiance, her lacy and ruffled dancing dress fluttering in the breeze, when Julie Curtis found her.

"Tara, what are you doing here? The captain said we should go straight home."

"I heard him. Julie, the town is not what the Indians are after. I know what they want but I can't tell anybody." Tara nervously looked back at Mount Defiance. "Nate Hunter's on that mountain."

"How do you know? He could be on any mountain."

"No, he stays on Mount Defiance. He's completely surrounded. What'll I do?" She could see Julie was confused, and she gave no thought now to spilling the secret she'd kept for over a year. "I met with him quite often since shortly after the massacre, until last spring. I supply him with ammunition."

"What?" whispered Julie.

"You won't tell anyone, will you?"

Julie seemed not to hear her. "Do you know what you're doing, Tara?"

"What else could I do? Some of the town men wanted to capture him and turn him over to the Indians. I couldn't let that happen, and he has to have ammunition." Julie looked at her for what seemed to Tara a very long time. Suddenly Tara realized she was trembling. She wondered if Julie had noticed.

"Is it possible that you're in love with him?" asked Julie.

Fear seized Tara's heart. She didn't know why Julie would think that. "Just because I helped him out doesn't mean—"

"It's okay if you don't want to tell me, Tara. But don't try to fool yourself."

The impact of Julie's words hit Tara hard as she realized that maybe she was blind to something Julie could see. "I don't know what to think. I'm just so worried about him. Oh, Julie, I'm afraid to say any more."

Julie knew for sure now what Tara couldn't say. "I'm afraid for you, Tara. Do you dare have any kind of relationship with him? If the town knew—"

"I know. If the town knew I'd be in trouble. But what am I to do?"

Julie looked towards the glow of the Indian campfires around the mountain where Nate was trapped and thought hard. "I have an idea. Some town men are starting a committee with some soldiers from Fort Mason to discuss relations with the Indians."

"I know that. My father's on it," said Tara as if she expected Julie to have known.

"Well, so is Mark. Talk to him about it and he can tell the committee. He won't use your name. If nothing else it will dispel fears of a massacre when they know what the Indians really want."

"But what will Mark say about this?"

"Does it matter more to you what Mark will say than what will happen to Nate?"

Tara realized Julie's suggestion was the best course to take. "I'll speak to him tonight."

* * *

Mark saw her first. "Tara, what are you doing by yourself?"

"Would you like to walk me home?" She slipped her arm into his.

Mark always felt honored when Tara passed up other men in favor of him. They started down the board sidewalk under the specter of the wooden buildings, now darkened and quiet for the night.

"I need your help, Mark," she said. "I hope you'll give it to me."

"All you have to do is name what you want. You know that."

"I'm afraid it isn't so simple." Tara looked to be sure no one was within hearing distance, then she began. "Nate Hunter is up there on Mount Defiance. He's surrounded by Indian camps."

Mark stopped walking, looked first in the direction of the mountain, then at Tara. "Are you sure?"

Tara nodded.

"How do you know this?"

His eyes bore deep into hers, and Tara found she had to look away from him. "I used to visit him almost every week. I keep him supplied with ammunition for hunting."

"What? How long has this gone on?"

"Since July a year ago."

"Good grief, that's ever since he disappeared!"

"It's been nearly six months since he went back to the mountains and I haven't seen him since then."

"Went back to the mountains? Where was he before that?"

"That's not important."

"Not important!" echoed Mark as they started walking again. "Do you suppose supplying him with ammo all this time isn't important either? Hiding information such as that could get you in big trouble. And now the town is in danger—"

"How dare you be angry with me! I thought you were Nate's friend."

"I am, so long as he doesn't risk getting us all killed while he insists on dodging the Indians. Tara, you should've told someone about this a long time ago."

"I did tell someone once. They almost caught him. It was a mistake and I regretted it."

Mark stepped in front of her and stopped her. "I remember when you didn't care a lick about Nate. What in the hell could he have said to make you turn around and do this?"

Tara narrowed her eyes at him and spoke harshly to hide her embarrassment. "I changed my mind about him, and I don't care who thinks I'm wrong. I know I'm doing the right thing and I expected that you would too, or I wouldn't have come to you. Nate has a right to his freedom and you must make this new committee understand that. He must get away from the Indians."

"They would never try to help Nate now with the town in danger like it is."

"But the town isn't in danger. The Indians are surrounding Mount Defiance because it's some kind of sacred mountain to them. Nate told me they did it years ago too. Now they're doing it because they're determined to capture Nate. But you and I are the only ones who know that so you must tell it to the committee."

Mark's attention was diverted to the street. She followed his eyes and saw the distinguished-looking, gray-haired and bearded cavalry officer strolling towards them. "Who's he?" she asked.

"That's Major Elliot, the head of our committee."

Tara saw something in his eyes that scared her. "You wouldn't tell on me, would you?" she said. "I did what I thought was the right thing. Please believe me, Mark. I'm begging you."

Tara's heart raced as the major moved closer. He nodded to them as he passed. "Good evening, folks."

"Evening, sir," replied Mark.

Tara was relieved when the major walked on by. She waited until he was well out of hearing distance, then said, "Nate was always your friend. Now he's in trouble and he needs your help."

"All right, I'll help," said Mark, "as long as everything stays peaceful. But I don't have a good feeling about this."

"I do. Thank you, Mark." Tara threw her arms around him and gave him a hug. "You won't regret this, I promise."

Mark smiled his appreciation for the hug, and they continued their walk until they arrived at her front door.

"Is there a certain place on Mount Defiance where I could find Nate?" asked Mark. "Would you tell me that much?" He could clearly see Tara's reluctance to share anything. "It's just in case I get a chance to talk to him. It'll be between me and you."

"On the south side by Elkhorn Creek there's a waterfall with a hollow in the rock behind it. He stays mainly around that area since it's forbidden ground to the Indians."

Mark nodded. "Well, I'll talk to the committee in the morning and see what I can do."

"Thanks again, Mark. Nate will appreciate this too."

"If it had been anybody else I would've said no. But with you it's different." He gave her a warm smile, which she returned, and they bade one another good night.

Tara watched him walk away until he disappeared into the dark and the sound of his footsteps faded away. Then once again the pounding of the Indian drums reminded her that Nate was somewhere in the midst of them. Quickly she entered the house and ascended the stairs to her room. The rest of her family was asleep.

She stepped out of her dress and petticoats, put on her nightgown, and took down her hair and brushed it out to its soft fullness. Soon she was in bed, but tormenting anxiety would not let her sleep. While she tossed and turned, trying to block the monotonous drumbeats out of her mind, she heard the grandfather clock downstairs in the parlor strike eleven, then twelve. No matter what happened at the committee meeting tomorrow, tonight Nate was still trapped on the mountain. Tomorrow might be too late to help him.

She looked over at the carving of Daredevil that Nate had made for her. Sitting on the windowsill, silhouetted by moonlight, it almost seemed lifelike. It was a symbol of something strong and wild, like the man who had fashioned it.

She finally arose from her bed, walked to the window, and gazed in the direction of Mount Defiance. In the dark all she could see was the faint glow from the many bonfires. She wanted to know what Nate was doing and if he was safe. The Grotto was too small for him to spend all of his time there. He had to go hunting. Or perhaps, having been captured, he was spending this night in one of the camps. It was frightening to contemplate, and she hastily pulled the curtains shut and stood with her bowed head pressed against them.

She couldn't go back to bed now, and she couldn't live with this curiosity. She must know if he was still safe. She left the window and groped in the dark for her riding clothes. When she couldn't find them she grabbed a blue-flowered calico work dress and slipped it on. As she pulled on her stockings and shoes, she stopped to reconsider the risk she was about to take. She was actually preparing to venture into the mountains at night, alone, near camps full of stirred-up Indians. She was scared to death, and she figured what common sense she had had gone missing. But she knew that no matter how long she thought about it, she was going to do this anyway.

Putting on her red coat, she tiptoed across the hall from her room and down the stairs. As soon as she had slipped out the back door she broke into a run towards the stable. After taking her saddle from its rack, she went into Molly's stall and got the horse ready. Then she slapped Molly's flanks, grabbed the mane, and swung up on her back as the horse trotted outside.

Keeping the light of the Indian campfires in front of her, Tara urged the horse into a run and they raced from the town into the starlit night. The sound of the powerful hooves underneath her drowned out everything else and Tara felt less nervous. But as the orange light from the camps took on the form of individual bonfires, she wondered if she could find a way to sneak through to the mountain.

She entered the woods surrounding Mount Defiance and moved Molly along at a walk. She could see a Cheyenne encampment a half mile ahead. The beating drums were louder now and she could hear Indian chants. She rode as close to the camp as she dared to go, then started traveling a wide circle around the southeastern end of the mountain, checking the number of camps and distance between them.

It took two hours of cautious searching to find a way through to the mountain that looked safe. It was where Elkhorn Creek flowed down towards the valley. In this place the banks on both sides rose up five feet to make a draw. The creek wasn't running high this time of year and there was a two-foot space between the water and the bank. Tara tied Molly in an obscure place amongst the trees and proceeded into the draw on foot. Once in the draw there was only the light of the moon to see by. While she kept watch around her she picked her way over and around rocks, almost tripping a couple of times. She felt clumsy and conspicuous and wished she had the Indian slyness that Nate had.

The Indian drums sounded all around Tara now and were so deafening they drowned out the noise of the rushing creek. Her heart thumped wildly but she pressed on, not stopping until she was at the end of the draw. The creek's banks eventually flattened out, providing no more protection. She had gone a hundred yards in a short time and was now inside the ring of Cheyenne encampments.

Rather than follow the twisting path of the creek to the Grotto, she opted for a shortcut, which proved difficult. This was a foreign place to her at night. She tried to remember what it looked like in the daytime but her fear made it hard to think. So she ran aimlessly on, following the direction she thought was right.

It seemed like forever before she picked up the sound of the waterfall. She followed the fixed, steady sound, appreciative of the guidance it afforded, until it led her to the Grotto. The long-missed sight of it stopped her short and rendered her breathless. The falls and pool displayed an infinite, eerie beauty as they shimmered in the moonlight. It gave Tara a very strange feeling as for the first time ever, this spot seemed haunting. Over thirty years ago a tragedy had taken place here. She imagined a little boy, a brave's son, drowning, and no one there to help. That was far back in the past, but even so, Tara felt she could sense his spirit hovering in this place. For a moment she forgot about the Indian drums still pounding away and walked slowly towards the water.

All of a sudden a hand grabbed her across the mouth! She tried to scream but couldn't utter a sound. Then a familiar voice spoke in her ear. "Don't scream. Don't make a sound. I mean it! You promise?"

Tara nodded and Nate took his hand away. She stood wide-eyed and shaking, looking into Nate's stern countenance.

"What are you doing here, and in the middle of the night to boot?" he demanded, gripping her shoulders. "I told you never to come here, especially now that the Cheyenne are..." His gruffness was replaced by surprise. "How did you get here?"

"I-I don't know," Tara stuttered. "I-I just, I found a way through on Elkhorn Creek, in a draw."

"Oh, yeah, the draw." But there was something more puzzling to him. "Why?"

"I was so worried about you. I was afraid the Indians had gotten you. I had to know if you were all right." She watched him anxiously, hoping to gain his approval for her impulsive action.

Nate couldn't admit he was touched by her concern. There were a lot of things he wanted to say. He wanted her to know he had missed her in the last six months. He wanted her to know that he was afraid for her risking so much to come to him. But he said none of this. "I told you that this is forbidden ground to the Indians. As long as I'm here—"

"But you don't know, Nate. They may come here anyway."

"No, they wouldn't. It means death to them. But of course, I'll be leaving now anyway. There's no way you're going back by yourself." He seemed to notice Tara's fear for the first time. "Hey, I'm sorry I scared you. It was just a surprise to find you here."

Tara swallowed hard and nodded. "I told Mark about you. He's on a new town committee. He's going to try to get them to help you. If he can do it, you would have the cavalry on your side as well."

"Good, but I won't expect a miracle. My real problem's down there," he said, gesturing towards the Indian camps.

Tara didn't want to dwell on the enormity of that problem. She needed all the courage she could muster for the return trip. "Well, do we go now or wait?"

"We go now. At sunup they'll stop drumming and be able to see and hear us easier."

So they began the descent down Mount Defiance. It went much quicker since Nate knew the easiest route, and soon they were at the edge of the draw.

"It's almost sunup," whispered Nate. "We don't have much time left. Come on. Stick close to me and do whatever I do."

They started into the draw and began working their way through the rocks as fast as they could. They were only halfway through when the drums stopped beating. Nate and Tara slowed down, conscientious of every sound they made. Even their breathing seemed loud.

As they neared the other end it seemed the hardest part was over. Then Tara's foot slipped, sending a big rock splashing into the creek. Nate grabbed her and flung her with him against the bank. He pulled his rifle in beside him, and they hugged their knees close to their bodies. Although they didn't hear footsteps, they both felt the presence of the Cheyenne warrior on the bank above their heads. While they sat like statues in the darkness, their hearts pounded furiously.

This was the closest Nate had ever come to being captured, but this time there were no tricks to pull, nothing to rely on but sheer hope, not just for himself but for the girl beside him who was risking her life for him.

Soon Nate heard the brave walk away. He waited a minute more, then quietly stood up and put his ear against the bank. Satisfied that it was safe, he motioned for Tara to follow him out of the draw.

The sky was beginning to turn pink in the east when Nate knew that all was not well. He suspected they were being followed and speeded up the pace. After hearing the definite sound of moccasin steps not far behind, he touched Tara's shoulder and they started running wrecklessly, pushing plants out of their way and ducking under low-hanging branches.

A horse's neigh sounded through the forest and Tara remembered Molly who was still tied up. Encouraged by this new means of escape, Tara turned and ran in the horse's direction. If she reached Molly in time, she would be safe and would be able to act as a decoy for Nate.

It was too late when Nate looked around and realized Tara was missing. He stood paralyzed with worry until he heard galloping hooves and whipped around in time to see her on the horse, disappearing through the trees. "Tara, no!" he shouted, afraid Indians on horseback would chase her. She was already gone so Nate headed in the opposite direction, hoping the braves would follow him instead. They did, but it would be one more of their efforts that would fail. Nate led them on until they lost his trail and returned to their camps.

Tara turned her horse towards home, but she wasn't even in the valley yet when the blood-curdling sound of Indian yells broke out behind her and she turned to see three braves on horses chasing her. Terrified, she urged Molly to go faster. The scared horse tried to respond to Tara's voice and sharp slaps of the reins, but she was already going as fast as she could. The Indians were gaining on them. Tara kicked the horse again and held on tight. Then she gasped in horror when out of nowhere two braves on foot appeared in her path. It was too late to turn so she crouched down, ready to run Molly through them.

The braves were quick. The nearest one grabbed Molly's rein and jerked it so hard that the horse slid on her hind legs and nearly sat down and Tara was thrown off. Molly's shrill whinny and Tara's scream pierced the breaking dawn. Then the other Indian was on top of her, jerking her to her feet. She fought to free herself but to no avail. The first brave came to the aid of his companion and, despite Tara's struggle, they subdued her quickly.

The frightened and bewildered horse ran away with the empty stirrups swinging at her sides and Tara was alone with her captors. One look at their dark, wild, scowling faces scared her into submission. One brave took a rope from his belt and tied her hands in back of her. Then with ironlike grips they took hold of her elbows and shoved her towards their camp. The three braves on horses followed behind them.

Tara begged to know what would be done with her, but they stared solemnly straight ahead and said nothing. She didn't know if they even spoke English.

Their camp was in a big clearing with about twenty tepees set up in rows. Several grazing ponies were tied to stakes driven into the ground and a few dogs ran loose. It was daylight now and the women, some with babies strapped to their backs, were cooking over fires in front of their tepees. They and the older children stopped to look when the braves walked by with their prisoner. There was no sound except for a dog's bark and a baby's soft cry. The dozens of cold stares sent chills up Tara's spine. She was living a nightmare she had thought could never happen to her.

They took her to a far edge of the camp where some children playing there hastily backed out of their way. They directed her to a tepee, opened the leather flap at the entrance, and forced her inside. She was thrown down on a blanket where she watched in dread as all five Indians entered and looked gravely down at her. They spoke words she couldn't understand, then one brave rushed out of the tepee. He returned with a much older brave.

"Tell us your name," the new brave said to her.

Tara felt relief, though very little, to hear English spoken, but she remembered what Nate had warned her of months ago. She was from the family of the Broken Bow and her identity must be kept a secret. "No!" she answered.

An enraged younger brave pulled a knife and started towards her. Tara ducked her head, and the older, English-speaking brave stopped him with his arm.

"My name is Tara," she said, her voice breaking. "Tara Sinclair."

Chapter 10

Later on the same morning he'd been separated from Tara and narrowly escaped the Indians, Nate was walking through the valley north of Mount Defiance. He had walked here before, but this time he decided to keep on going. He was no match for a band of Indians. He must get himself away from the camps.

There were things he wasn't eager to leave behind such as visits with Tara and her reports of how his sister was doing, and Timber Fork and the Broken Bow, the only places he had ever really considered to be home. But he put those thoughts out of his mind, for the sooner he left the Territory the better off the town would be.

A rustling noise behind a clump of bushes startled him, and he ducked behind the bushes and held his rifle at the ready. Cautiously he crept around the bushes, and there stood a riderless black horse, saddled and bridled and peacefully grazing. He went to the horse and picked up the reins.

"Oh no, she didn't make it home," he whispered. His plans to leave the Territory abruptly changed. He wouldn't go anywhere as long as Tara was in trouble.

Nate mounted the horse and gathered up the reins. After scanning the horizon and making sure Tara was not nearby, he turned the horse in the direction of Timber Fork and kicked her into a trot. Taking a roundabout trail to avoid Mount Defiance, he rode to within a mile of the town before he stopped and dismounted. "You've got an important job to do, girl," he said as he petted the horse's muzzle. "You know your way home. Now you have to go there." He slapped the horse's flanks hard. "Go on, git!" He watched Molly gallop away and began planning his next step.

*   *   *

"The meeting will now come to order!" shouted the brown-haired, blue-eyed Captain Blaine, the man who had ended the dance early the night before. The Timber Fork schoolroom became silent. "Now, gentlemen, the first thing on the agenda is to elect a secretary, treasurer—"

"We don't have time for that foolishness, Josh," bellowed Major Elliot, sitting on the platform behind him. "We're here to discuss business."

Some of the men laughed and applauded their approval.

"Yes, sir," answered the captain meekly. "Gentlemen, one of our members, Mr. Mark Curtis, has made it known to me that he has a matter of urgency to cover. I believe he may enlighten us about the situation with the Indians. Please give him your attention. Mark, the floor is yours."

"Thank you, Captain," said Mark as he rose and turned to face the others. "The purpose of this committee is supposed to be to seek peaceable relations with the Indians, who right now seem to be a threat to Timber Fork. I think first we need to determine why the Indians have come here. I got that information yesterday from a reliable source whose name I must withhold. Nathaniel Hunter is on Mount Defiance and the Indians are after him, not us."

"Nathaniel Hunter? You mean that Indian who was dodging all those trackers?" asked Captain Blaine.

"That's the one."

"I thought sure he'd be dead by now," said another man.

"Oh, he's very much alive," said Mark. "Anyhow, some of you tried to catch him and turn him over to the Indians. I'm asking you to let him be free to come back to town."

"But that could be dangerous for us," said one man. "We went through that last year."

"I know," Mark replied, "I was there. And I was never satisfied with your decision. Nate Hunter has not broken the law, and we don't have the right to deny him freedom."

Major Elliot said, "I agree with you. The Indians haven't given Timber Fork trouble on his account up to now. Consider your request granted, Mark."

"But, Major," one committee member said, "those hostiles may be gearing up right now for a massacre."

"The cavalry has dealt with their kind before and they know it," said Major Elliot.

"Oh, like you dealt with 'em after the massacre?" shouted someone in the back. "By doing nothing?"

Several men strongly voiced their agreement.

"That has been explained," said Major Elliot. "Our hands were tied."

There was an obvious contingent that expressed dissatisfaction and wanted to keep the argument going, but the major quelled the attempt with a bang of his fist on the table. When it was quiet he looked back at Mark. "Will that be all?"

"No," said Mark. "The Cheyenne almost have Nate in their hands now, and I think we should stop them from getting him."

"Now, Mark, be reasonable," said the major. "What the Indians do with one of their own people is hardly of any concern to the United States Cavalry."

"That's right. This matter is for Nate and the Indians to resolve," said one man.

Opposition to Mark's idea was strong but he was prepared to stand up to it. He had given a lot of thought to what Tara had said and decided it was a good cause. "I can't believe it," he said. "You all are the same people who once said that his family shouldn't have to go back to the Indians. Now that the Broken Bow has been wiped out by massacre, you're all backing off like cowards. You're afraid to fight for what you know is right. And you have the nerve to blame the cavalry for not doing anything."

"I ain't afraid," someone near the back called out. "I just don't think it's any of my business."

A couple of others agreed.

Edward Sinclair stood up. "I would like to remind you people that Nate Hunter has never lived with Indians. It was his ancestors. He is one of our people." He pointed a finger at the men who disagreed. "And whether you like it or not, we are responsible for him."

"Hold it right there," said Major Elliot. "You say he's never lived with Indians? I didn't know that. That could change the situation."

"Now, Major," said Captain Blaine, "surely you don't think it would be in our best interests to take sides with this Nate Hunter. That could lead to an Indian war."

"We're not talking war, Captain. Let me make it clear that there will be no violence, especially over such a trivial thing."

"Is it really so trivial, Major?" asked Mark.

"You want to have an Indian war, don't you?" said one man.

"He didn't say that," said Edward Sinclair.

"Well, that's what yer askin' fer," drawled another man. "You ain't gonna talk them Injuns into givin' up Nate."

"We don't need to fight the Indians," said Mark. "There are other ways."

"Name one!" roared a big man with a dark red mustache and beard.

"I know, Jed," Mark replied. "You'd like nothing better than a bloody war."

"Damn right! I hate those red devils, and that goes for your Injun buddy that you're tryin' to help out. He may be pullin' the wool over y'all's eyes but not mine. He's a renegader and he's up to somethin' with his Injun friends."

"That's crazy, Jed, and you don't have anything to back it up with," said Mark.

"The hell I don't. Just look at all them savages whoopin' it up every night around the mountain you say he's on. You don't think they're sharpenin' up their knives so they can lift some scalps?"

"That's enough!" declared Major Elliot. "Mr. Jed, whoever you are, I'll remind you that we're here to keep the peace with the Indians, not kill them."

"And I'm here because it's my duty to be here," Jed replied, "even if I don't agree with your cockeyed ideas."

"Gentlemen, please," said Edward. "Mark, I'm with you all the way. I was always friends with the Hunter family and I won't go against Nate now."

Mark smiled gratefully. "Of all people, Mr. Sinclair, it's good to have you on our side."

The back door opened and everyone turned to see who the latecomer was. In walked Hiram Curtis who took off his hat and looked sullenly at the committee. "I'm sorry I'm late. I have bad news." He looked at Edward Sinclair and felt sad for what he must say. "Tara Sinclair is being held for ransom by the Cheyenne."

The room fell silent and Mark stared unbelieving at his father.

"That's impossible!" said Edward, clearly shaken.

"That can't be," added Mark. "I just saw her last night, at the dance."

"I'm sorry, Edward," said Hiram. "Apparently she left during the night and went up to Mount Defiance. The Indians got her early this morning. Her saddled horse just came back to your barn."

"How did you find out and what do they want from us?" asked Captain Blaine.

"I talked to an Indian on the road outside of town. Says his name is Beartooth. They want Nate Hunter found and returned to them in three days or else..."

"Or else what?" asked Edward.

Hiram turned his hat over and over in his hand while he looked uneasily at the floor.

"They'll kill 'er, that's what," said Jed.

Edward closed his eyes and his hands shook.

"I told you them skunks were up to no good," Jed went on as he leaned back and rested his hands on his suspenders. "Lord knows what they'll do to her. It's a cryin' shame. Maybe next time you'll listen to me."

In an instant Mark was after him, grabbing his collar. "For heaven's sake, shut up! How dare you talk like that with her father here, you bastard!"

"Break it up!" shouted Major Elliot. "Mark, sit down now! Jed, we don't need that kind of talk." He waited until his orders were obeyed and everyone was watching him. "Now I assure you, Mr. Sinclair, that we'll do all we can to get your daughter back. You have the United States Cavalry on your side."

Edward nervously sat down and waited for the major to give his orders.

"This shouldn't be a problem," continued Major Elliot. "We know where Nate is now. All we have to do is go get him."

"But that's just what the Indians want," said Captain Blaine. "You're not going to give in to them, are you?"

"Ordinarily I wouldn't, but a young woman's life is involved here. Getting her back is the first priority. Then we can talk about further actions."

"Beartooth said some of his people were packing up and moving out today," said Hiram. "His party will stay until the demands are met."

"Good," said the major, "then we'll spread out and close in on the mountain from different directions to make sure Nate doesn't get away. Litton, Collins, Markham, take a bunch of men and follow the trail along the creek from the east. Both Curtises, you and the rest of the men go with Captain Blaine straight in

79

from the south. Let's get going." He turned to Captain Blaine and lowered his voice. "And Captain, keep an eye on that Jed. We do want Hunter alive, you know."

"Yes, sir."

Captain Blaine left with the committee members, leaving the major alone with Edward and Mark, who were still shocked by the news of Tara's capture.

"Mark, I'm sorry about having to go after Nate," Major Elliot said. "I wanted your case to win, but I didn't expect this to happen."

"I understand," replied Mark.

After the major was gone, Edward turned to Mark. "How did you know where Nate was? Who did you talk to?"

Mark shook his head. It wasn't the right time. "I'll tell you sometime, Mr. Sinclair." With this he left to join the search.

*   *   *

Edward spent the day with his family, waiting for word of Nate's capture and Tara's release. Not until early evening did Mark appear at their door, tired and frustrated. He was ushered into the parlor where in shame he faced the hopeful expectancy on the faces of the family.

"Well!?" prompted Edward.

"We couldn't find him," said Mark.

"What? What do you mean you couldn't find him? You said he was there!"

"He was there. We saw his tracks. He was there, maybe just yesterday." He shook his head. "I don't know what happened."

"Edward, what are we going to do?" said his wife Margaret. "We can't leave Tara with those Indians all night. I'm afraid they'll hurt her and I know she's scared." She began to cry.

Edward put his arms around her. "Now, darling, don't worry. Tara's going to be fine. We must have faith."

"Why did it happen?" Margaret sobbed. "She had no reason to go to Mount Defiance. Why would she go there?"

"I don't know," replied Edward. All of a sudden a look of revelation appeared on his face. "Mark, did my daughter give you the information you told the committee?"

"Yes, sir," said Mark, barely above a whisper.

"But how on earth did she know about Nate or—"

"I don't know any more." Though Mark did know more, he decided he didn't know as much as he'd like to and planned to investigate on his own.

*   *   *

Nate returned to the mountain that night after the searchers had gone. He was despondent, knowing that he alone could do nothing to help Tara. He sought refuge from this mental torment in the Grotto. In this den of escape he always found it easier to be alone with himself and think. Just as the haunting beauty of the falls and surroundings captivated Tara, he, too, sensed that certain unknown feeling, and when he was there, time stood still.

But even as he basked in the security of his hideout, he could feel Tara's fear and loneliness in the midst of a strange people. Knowing she was there because of him made him feel worse.

It was a sleepless night for Nate, but early the next morning he had a visitor. He first heard the slow thud of a horse's hooves in the woods nearby. He knew the person was alone so he hid behind a tree and waited to see who it was. When Mark emerged from the brush, Nate stepped into his sight. "Why, Mark Curtis!" exclaimed a smiling Nate. "I can hardly believe my eyes."

Mark returned a smile as he dismounted and looked Nate up and down. "I can't believe it myself."

They laughed as they firmly shook hands and slapped each other's shoulders.

"How did you know I was here?" asked Nate.

"Tara told me you were on Mount Defiance. When we were up here yesterday I noticed your tracks around here. I figured you'd come back to this place. Gosh, it sure has been a long time. You look good."

Nate's smile faded. "I don't feel so good."

"You know about Tara?"

Nate nodded and walked to the big, flat rock beside the waterfall where he sat down and folded his legs. "It's all my fault, Mark," he said.

Mark sat down next to him. "What do you mean?"

"I found her standing here the other night," Nate recalled. "She came to see if I was all right. I couldn't believe she got here without being seen. We went back the way she'd come. When we were on the other side of the camps some Indians heard us and started after us." His eyes were fixed on the water's gently rippled surface as he pictured the incident again. "We were running, then all of a sudden I turned around and she wasn't there. Last I saw her she was riding off on her horse. I thought she'd make it home." He shook his head in disbelief. "I shouldn't have let her out of my sight."

"Don't blame yourself," said Mark. "You know, the Indians want you, Nate."

"You think I don't know that?"

"I mean, in exchange for Tara." Nate looked up in surprise and Mark continued, "They gave us three days. Everybody was up here yesterday looking for you."

This news threw a scare into Nate. Until now his quarrel had just been between him and the Indians, but now they were involving Tara, a tactic which preyed on his heart. "And I guess it'll be bad for Tara if they don't find me."

"Maybe they'll extend the time."

"No, they wouldn't. Why would you want more time? You're supposed to find me and here I am."

"I can't turn you over to them, Nate. I admit, when I came up here today I had that idea in the back of my mind. But after meeting up with you again, well, I'm your friend and I won't betray you." He gave Nate a pat on the back and stood. "There'll be another way to get Tara out of the camp. The town committee is having another meeting this morning and we're going to talk about it then. That's where I'm heading now."

"So soon?" asked Nate, not wanting to be left alone again.

"I only wanted to see how you were doing?' replied Mark. "There'll be other times for catching up on everything."

Nate stood also and shook hands with his friend.

Before mounting his horse, Mark said, "You know, they say in town that you're impossible to get a hold of, even to talk to. But all they've ever used on you is force. They've never given you a fair chance to say what you want.'

Nate smiled. He knew Mark was one to be trusted and he began to feel better.

*   *   *

Promptly at eight o'clock the second committee meeting came to order.

"Now gentlemen, we must make a decision quickly," said Major Elliot. "Here's how the situation stands. The Cheyenne have demanded that we deliver the Indian fugitive, Nathaniel Hunter, into their hands in order to retrieve Miss Sinclair. The deadline is tomorrow night, and we can well figure that we won't be able to meet their demands by then. I need suggestions."

"I say let's stop fiddle-footin' around and teach them Injuns a thing or two," shouted one man. "They can't just steal one of our people and expect us to bow down to their wishes."

"He's right!" yelled another. "There's just one sure-fire way of straightening 'em out and that's by attacking 'em!"

This set off a rash of excitement with some men jumping up and yelling for war. Mark Curtis and Edward Sinclair listened to the reaction with dread but held their peace.

"Aren't you going to do something about this outburst, Major?" asked Captain Blaine above the commotion.

"I was afraid it would come to this, Captain," replied Major Elliot. "I thought it over last night. An attack is inevitable. I just needed the townsfolk to reassure me of it."

"But, sir, we have orders—"

"To hell with the orders! We'll not let that girl die in that camp while we waste our time on futile strategies. An attack is the only way to save her now." He turned to the rowdy men and slammed his fist on the desk. "Let's have it quiet! Right now!" He had to repeat his command before the men finally silenced themselves and were seated. "The Cheyenne have forced us to this decision," the major explained. "We will plan an attack."

"Will we continue to search for Nate?" asked Hiram Curtis.

"I'll send out a small search party but we'll concentrate mainly on battle preparations. Even if we find Nate, the Indians must be taught a lesson. Tomorrow night at dusk we'll take them by surprise."

"But tomorrow night is the deadline they gave us," said Captain Blaine. "They'll be expecting us to do something then."

"I know, but it's our only chance," Major Elliot replied. "We need the time to get ready. And we'll need to make careful plans on how to retrieve Miss Sinclair."

Edward stood. "You can't rescue my daughter in the middle of a battle, Major. The Indians may do something to her before we get to her. It's too risky."

"Mr. Sinclair, whatever happens from here on, there will be some danger. But the lives of my fellow cavalrymen and me are dedicated to her safety."

Edward reluctantly sat down, realizing that trusting the major was the only hope he had for Tara's safe rescue.

"Now listen closely, everyone. Jennings, both Curtises, and Smith, you go and look for Nate. Split up and take different areas. Tell me where you'll be so we can find you if necessary."

"I'll take the south side of Mount Defiance along Elkhorn Creek," said Mark, hoping no one noticed his urgency to speak up for that area.

"Very well," said Major Elliot. "Captain, send a wire to Fort Mason and tell them to send a company of soldiers and enough supplies and ammunition for two weeks immediately. They must be here by noon tomorrow. If they give you any problems, tell them it's an emergency and they'll have to trust my judgment until I can give them an explanation. Have them make camp by the lake ten miles south. We don't want the Indians to suspect anything."

"Yes, sir." Captain Blaine saluted the major and left to carry out the orders.

"The rest of you sit tight and wait for further word. And remember, what you've heard here is strictly confidential. Meeting adjourned."

Chapter 11

In the Grotto Nate was thinking on his own idea that Mark had unknowingly inspired. He no longer felt helpless, but what he was about to do would test the depths of his fortitude, perhaps at a high cost. He mulled over his feelings for the girl he might never see again if he became her ransom. She had been the one to help him pull his life together when it was a hopeless cause. Now his own life seemed less important, and it was his turn to do something for her.

He picked up his rifle and began the trek down the mountainside. In an hour he stood on the outskirts of the Cheyenne encampment, filled with apprehension. Strong feelings that he had buried away a year before were moving to the forefront again. These people were his family's murderers, yet he shared their blood, and he had never been able to reconcile that. He refocused his thoughts on Tara and what he had to do. His own mental conflicts would have to wait for another day.

As he walked boldly into the center of the camp, the women and children didn't give him a glance but continued their work and play. The few who did notice stared curiously. He looked like one of them yet he was different.

Nate disregarded the stares and looked for Tara but she was nowhere in sight. Suddenly he found himself standing face-to-face with a Cheyenne brave who gave him a hard, expressionless gaze. Nate studied the rigid face of this one of a people whom he resembled in so many ways.

The brave eyed Nate's clothes and hair inquisitively, but it was his neck beads that drew the most attention. He fingered this telling specimen of Nate's heritage and a knowing look crossed his face. He knew who was standing before him.

"Take me to the chief. I believe his name is Red Feather," said Nate. Met by the warrior's blank stare, Nate searched his memory to awaken the language he had not recently practiced. *"Taaxa'e vehoo'o."*

The brave motioned for Nate to follow, and he led him to the largest tepee in the camp. The tent flap was opened and the brave entered after Nate.

Inside, the light was dim and it took a moment for Nate's eyes to adjust. When they did he saw a scene he had imagined a thousand times as his father had described it, the chief's council sitting in a half circle around a small fire. In the midst of them and across from Nate sat Red Feather, a noble chief of the Cheyenne. He was middle-aged and very muscular. His long black hair hung down in two braids but was hardly visible under an array of eagle feathers. There was an unsightly battle scar on the left side of his chin.

The confrontation between the chief and Nate seemed predestined, for though each had never seen the other before, neither needed an introduction.

"The Wise One Above has blessed us with the return of our Cheyenne brother," said Red Feather.

One of the council spoke. *"Hamêstoo'êstse kâhamaxe."*

Nate laid his rifle in the center of the circle, then unstrapped his gunbelt and dropped that next to it. He looked to see if the brave was satisfied.

"Motšêške," the brave added.

Nate impatiently took his knife from its sheath and added it to the pile. He was then motioned to sit down.

"This is a great day," said Red Feather. "You are wise like the fox, swift like the deer. Like the shadow of the eagle you make new trails and go where we cannot follow. We call you *Netse Mâhta'sooma*, Eagle Shadow."

Eagle Shadow, Nate repeated to himself. He was pleasantly surprised to learn that he had attained a measure of respect among the Cheyenne. He hoped he could use it to his advantage. "You've captured a white girl," he said. "Is she all right?"

Red Feather nodded. "She is well. She has not made trouble for us."

"You said you would let her go if you found me. Will you do it?"

There was a long silence as the chief looked at all of his council then back at Nate. "I cannot let the white girl go."

"What? Why not?"

"That is not in the terms we gave to the white man. We said if you were returned to us in three days we would not kill the white girl. Now you are here. She will live. But the white man must give our land back to us or we keep her."

Nate was confused. Mark hadn't said anything about additional terms for Tara's release. Something here didn't fit. "What are you talking about?"

"Many moons the white man has taken our lands and killed our meat. The Wise One Above has said the time has come for us to fight back."

"But you come from the plains in Nebraska Territory," Nate said. "The white men here have not taken anything from you."

"They come here from our land on the plains, like you do. If we keep the white girl they will do what we say."

"The white men who did you wrong are few. Those few are bad. But you want to punish many good white men."

"All white men are the same." Red Feather began to describe the sorrows of his people, using vivid hand gestures to emphasize his words. "Red man had land for many moons. The white man came and took our land. They have no mercy for us. They kill the buffalo that provides our meat, clothes, and shelter. In the winter our little children die because we have no food. It is not right that we suffer and be forced to leave the land of our fathers. It belonged to us from the first."

Nate became leery of the stand the Indians were taking. He had figured by turning himself over to them he would solve the dispute, but now the Cheyenne were demanding things far beyond his control. He could see a storm coming, a hostile encounter between two peoples with which he felt close. It would be a fight in which he wouldn't want to choose sides. "I agree with you," he said to the chief, "it's not right. But using an innocent girl to make threats isn't the way to settle the problem. The white men would be willing to make peace if you gave them a chance."

"They make peace their way, not ours. They make treaties and break them. Our time has come. We will take revenge."

Nate stared hard at the unrelenting chief and struggled to rein in his temper. "You cannot use that girl to barter with." His guard came down. "*I* will not allow you to use that girl to barter with."

In that instant Nate was grabbed by the brave on his right, and he felt the cold, sharp blade of a knife pressed against his throat. He looked out of the corner of his eye at the arm that held the knife and didn't move a muscle.

The chief wasn't so eager to punish Nate. He gestured for the brave to release him.

Nate turned to see who had held the knife and recognized the brave by the long scar down the side of his cheek, the scar Buck Hunter had given him. In the moment that Beartooth and Nate's eyes met, a look of malice passed between them. It was interrupted by the chief's harsh voice.

"He is wise but quick to speak. Now you will remember this. I will not spare you the second time." He pointed to Beartooth. "Beartooth is a great tracker and a great fighter, more than any brave here. He does not like your words to us."

"I don't want to make trouble for you," said Nate. "All I want is for you to let the white girl go and give her people a chance to be your friends."

"No more chances," Red Feather protested. "The white man must pay us back before the moon rises tomorrow."

"But that's not enough time for what you're asking."

"Then the white girl will belong to Beartooth."

"What?" Nate looked at Beartooth, who gave no indication of what he was thinking.

"Beartooth thinks the white girl is beautiful," said Red Feather. "He wants her. If the white men do not meet the terms, Beartooth will have her. He will be good to her."

Nate felt rage boiling up inside of him but held it in check. "She belongs with her own people. Please let her go."

"No!" said Red Feather.

"I will take her place," Nate pleaded with him. "I will be your hostage. Do what you want with me." The chief's silence unnerved Nate, and he glared at Red Feather with dark, fiery eyes. "You're making innocent lives suffer just like you did on the Broken Bow." He pointed an accusing finger at the chief. "You murdered my parents and I can never forgive you for that! But even that didn't satisfy you. You've stayed on my back like a hound for over a year. Well, now you have me. It is enough! What more do you want?"

Red Feather signaled Beartooth, and he and another brave grabbed Nate by the arms and yanked him to his feet. Nate tried to throw their arms off but they only held him tighter.

"Eagle Shadow has no respect," said Beartooth.

"Don't tell me about respect," Nate snapped. "And you listen to me, Beartooth. If you lay one finger on that girl I'll kill you!" He looked at Red Feather. "And you too!"

Red Feather's dark eyes glared at the brazen Nate. "I can have you punished for this."

"Go right ahead," replied Nate through gritted teeth. "But I'm only the least of your problems. If you keep that white girl, her people will be after you and they'll kill you. I promise you that, Red Feather!"

The chief uttered another command and two more braves stood and assisted Beartooth and the other Indian in taking Nate from the tepee.

"Neve'nêheševe!" Nate hissed as he put up a violent struggle. It took all four braves to wrestle him to the ground, then while three of them held his legs and shoulders, Beartooth lashed his wrists together behind his back with a rope. With his hands rendered useless Nate yielded to the fight.

He was taken to the north end of the camp where he heard a young woman's anguished cries. He looked up and saw Tara being forced from a tepee by two braves. Nate's captors let him stop to watch as she was led towards a thick wooden post that had been planted in the hard ground.

She looked tired after two days in captivity. Still in her blue calico dress, her face had lost its color and her hair hung loose and uncombed.

"Please don't tie me here," she begged. "I won't do it again, I won't!"

Her earnest pleas were too much for Nate, who lunged and strained his wrists against the bonds. But the braves powerfully subdued him and he could do nothing except helplessly watch.

Tara was positioned against the post and a rope was looped several times around her waist and tied. Nate found it difficult to muster enough calmness to say her name. "Tara," he called softly.

She turned at the sound of the familiar voice. "Oh, Nate," she whispered in disbelief.

Nate managed a hopeful smile. "Don't be afraid, Tara. Everything's going to be okay, I promise."

Tara winced as the braves yanked Nate away, and she followed them with her eyes until they were out of sight among the tepees.

Beartooth and his companions took Nate to a tepee on the northwest end of the camp. They left him alone inside, still tied, with one brave outside the door to guard it.

As Nate sat staring at his mostly barren surroundings consisting of a center pole hung with tools and utensils, and blankets and skins scattered about the tepee, minutes stretched into endless hours. He couldn't understand what had gone wrong in the chief's tepee, how Mark had gotten wrong information, yet he somehow felt that it was his own fault, that he had ruined Tara's chances for release. *First time in a Cheyenne camp,* he thought to himself, *and I threaten to kill the chief. Good work, Nate.* He had allowed his vengeful feelings from the massacre to get in the way, even though he had told himself he wouldn't. He cursed himself for letting his temper get the best of him. He knew now that diplomacy wouldn't work, and he had no faith in the cavalry either. He alone was powerless in the face of Red Feather's band, so he was left devoid of answers.

By afternoon Nate was tired of thinking. He felt hunger pangs, and his arms were aching from not being able to move. Then he heard voices outside the tepee and he straightened up expectantly. The tent flap opened and in walked a pretty, young Cheyenne girl, clutching something behind her back. The girl knelt down and studied his face a brief moment as if trying to decide if it was safe to go near him.

The sight of her brought back a memory for Nate. "You look a lot like my sister," he said. He knew she hadn't understood him but it didn't matter. It was nothing more than a thought spoken out loud.

He smiled at the girl, a gesture that was eagerly returned. Perhaps she had heard of him in stories around the campfire and her curiosity brought her to the tepee. Immediately she relaxed in his presence. She brought her hands from behind her back and set down the bowl of stew she had been holding. Nate leaned forward to get a better look. His mouth watered as he smelled the meaty aroma but his hands remained bound. The girl looked at him and hesitated. Finally she reached into her moccasin, pulled out a tiny knife, and held it up for him to see.

She didn't have to convince him. He eagerly turned around and held out his wrists. As soon as she began to cut the rope, Beartooth entered the tepee. She cowered in fear and the brave grabbed her by the elbow and stood her up. He reprimanded her and sent her back outside with the stew. Then he helped Nate up and, with a firm hold on his elbow, shoved him outside where two other braves waited.

Nate quickly forgot his hunger and fatigue; all of his senses were alert. The Indians would not get him without a fight, but he would hold his contention until he knew what they intended to do.

One brave took out his knife and cut the rope from Nate's wrists. Nate was greatly relieved to have his hands free, but he looked at Beartooth questioningly.

"The chief has decided," said Beartooth. "Your heart is bad. You will visit the forbidden ground where the water flows over the rock. There you will die by the hands of the evil spirits."

Nate almost laughed at Beartooth's earnestness. They were sending him home. He rubbed his sore wrists. "The chief's coward to tell me himself?"

Instantly Beartooth slapped Nate's face hard with the back of his hand. Nate stood quietly for a moment, feeling the sting of the blow. But his pride could not tolerate such an indignity for long, and without warning he balled up his fist, reached back, and swung towards Beartooth's jaw. His aim was true and the Indian was knocked off his feet. Then Nate threw himself on top of his victim and dealt a couple more blows before the other braves pulled him off.

Beartooth picked himself up and glared at his assailant. "I did not agree with the chief's decision," he growled. "I would have killed you myself." He shoved Nate in front of him, and they began hiking up the mountainside.

In an hour the Indians stopped with Nate in the woods within hearing distance of the waterfall. Beartooth took Nate's weapons from another brave and handed them back to Nate. "Now you will be punished for your bad heart, Eagle Shadow," he said.

Nate walked away from the Indians, glad to be free but more worried than ever about Tara.

He was met at the waterfall by Mark Curtis who eyed him with contempt. Nate was immediately filled with dread.

"I've spent all day looking for you, Nate," said Mark.

"Oh, I've been busy," Nate replied as he set down his weapons and knelt on the rock beside the creek to get a drink of water.

Mark's hand clamped down on his collar and yanked him to his feet. "I just saw you with three Indians. Now tell me the truth. Are you a traitor?"

"Take your hands off me!" demanded Nate as he jerked himself free. "It's not what you think. I'm not in alliance with the Indians. I turned myself over to them this morning. I wanted to get Tara out."

Mark remained skeptical. "Then what are you doing here?"

"You should have heard what I heard in that camp today, Mark. The Indians are going too far. They're causing big trouble now."

"What do you mean?"

"I mean it's not just me they want. They want the land down in Nebraska Territory that was theirs before the white settlers came."

"Good grief!" exclaimed Mark. "What are we supposed to do about that?"

"That's what I wondered. So I said things to the chief that I shouldn't have and they threw me out."

"But they said you would be Tara's ransom. They didn't mention anything about land."

"Exactly what did they tell you?"

"An Indian named Beartooth told my pa they wanted you returned to them in three days or they'd kill her. That's it."

Nate's eyes blazed. "Beartooth, I should've known! He held back on you. He didn't give you all of the chief's terms."

"Why would he do that?"

"Because if they don't get their land back they'll keep Tara and she'll be given to Beartooth. And he wants her. What am I going to do, Mark? I thought I could take care of this by myself but I can't. I need your help." His voice shook with rage. "If we don't get her out of there, that damn Indian'll rape her."

Mark's face went pale at the thought of it. He struggled to maintain a level head. "Listen, there's a lot of people working on this. I came here to tell you what was decided in the meeting this morning. The cavalry and settlers are going to spring a surprise attack on the Indians tomorrow night."

"Attack!" exclaimed Nate.

"It was the only thing left to do. I was thinking, since you know all about the Cheyenne, you can help us plan the attack."

Nate paced back and forth in frustration. "You forget that it's Cheyenne blood that flows through my veins. And you expect me to help you plan an attack against them?"

"Let's face it, Nate. The Indians brought this on themselves. Now I know how you feel about turning on them—"

"No, you don't. Whatever they may have done to me in the past, I can never forget that I'm one of them." He tried to shut the idea of an attack out of his mind, but Mark's voice came through to him steady and firm.

"An attack is the only way to get Tara out of there. It's going to happen whether you throw in with us or not. It'll be for Tara's good, though, if we can get help from someone who knows about Indians firsthand. You're the only one who can give us that help, Nate. And you've been in the camp now. You know the layout."

"Oh, why did it have to come to this?" whispered Nate. Though his first visit in a Cheyenne camp hadn't left him with a good impression, he kept in mind that it was only a couple of Indians who made him mad and their actions didn't speak for a whole people. He remembered the girl who had wanted to help him while he was captive in the tepee. On the other hand, Tara was the main girl who occupied his mind. "Okay, I'll help," he said at last.

"Wonderful!" said Mark. "I knew you'd join us."

Nate thought for a moment then sat down on the edge of a rock and picked up a stone. "Now pay close attention so you can remember this. Here's Red Feather's camp." With the stone he drew a circle on the ground. "From what I saw, Tara's being held towards the north end, right about here." He marked the place with an X. "At the time of the attack tomorrow night she may be in a tepee or be tied to a post there. Now you don't want her to be in the middle of the battle so your best bet is to attack from the south. The men could be divided into three groups with the main force going straight in and meeting the Indians head-on. The other two groups would advance secretly on the east and west sides, then sit and wait. But they have to keep quiet. The success of this thing depends on the second and third groups' positions not being given away." He drew lines to show the directions the soldiers were to take. "Then the east and west flanks will move in at an angle from the north and form a barrier between Tara and the fighting. The Indians will be surrounded."

"That's good," Mark agreed. "I think we can handle that."

"Don't underestimate the Indians," said Nate. "They might have scouts in the woods around the camp. You have to be careful that they don't ambush you."

"We'll be on the lookout."

"Who's going to rescue Tara?"

"I will. I have to get her to where Elkhorn Creek turns into the valley. They'll have soldiers to meet her there and take her home."

Nate nodded. "I'll back you up."

"Thanks, I'll need it. I'll tell these plans to Major Elliot as soon as I get back and see what he thinks."

"I'm sure you know not to mention my name," said Nate. "A half-Cheyenne making up plans to attack the Cheyenne probably wouldn't look good to him. You can take the credit."

They stood, but Mark seemed reluctant to leave.

"What?" prompted Nate.

"Well, I'm a little concerned. There's division among the men. Some are mad because the cavalry didn't do anything after the massacre. The cavalry defends themselves, saying they didn't have enough information to go on. Then they say that there are a number of white captives and they just don't have the manpower to—"

"Look, I have more reason than anybody to want revenge, but that's over and done with. I don't care about any of that, Mark, and neither do you." He walked up close to Mark and jabbed a finger in Mark's chest, emphasizing his intense frustration. "This is *not* just another white captive. This is Tara. You *make* them understand that."

Mark was taken aback. He realized for the first time that his friend's feelings for the captive girl were stronger than he thought. "You love her, don't you?"

Head bowed, Nate nodded and whispered, "Yes."

His answer disheartened Mark whose deep feelings for Tara had never gone away, but at this moment somehow he knew that the rift between him and Tara would never be mended. "Does she know?"

"No." He looked up at Mark. "I'm sorry. I know how you feel about her."

"Don't apologize. You're not taking anything of mine. She'd be quick to tell you that."

"It doesn't matter anyway. It's a dangerous life I live, too dangerous to ever bring Tara into it."

"You already have."

Jealousy had manifested itself. Nate felt Mark's eyes boring down on him, waiting for him to meet his gaze, but Nate would not.

Finally Mark broke the coldness of the moment. "There's something you should know about Tara. She commands respect and she deserves to have it. She has a big heart. It may be hard to reach, but if you do she'll give it all to you. If you have that you're very lucky."

Nate marveled that Mark, the offended one, would give him advice so freely. "Why would you tell me this?"

Mark's lighthearted self took over. "Oh, I suppose we could have one of those duels like they used to have in the old days. I'd whup you too," he said, drawing a smile from Nate. "But what good would that do either of us? Hell, she'd be on your side anyway."

"No, she wouldn't."

Mark looked out across the pool by the waterfall. "No, there's no division between us, Nate. We have the same objective." He offered his hand for a handshake.

Truly appreciative of Mark's loyalty in the face of what had transpired, Nate grasped him firmly by the wrist. "Thank you."

Mark walked to his horse and picked up the reins, but again he hesitated.

Nate knew the reason why and voiced his thoughts for him. "One of us could fall tomorrow night."

"Yes," replied Mark. "If I do, will you see that Tara gets out all right?"

"I promise. And if anything happens to me you'll do the same?"

"I will."

Chapter 12

Major Elliot was satisfied with Mark's plans, and he set to work with Captain Blaine filling in the details and how to implement them. When Monday arrived, the soldiers and settlers began to prepare for the attack that night. Before noon two hundred and fifty cavalry soldiers arrived from Fort Mason with Colonel Jackson O'Brien in command. Major Elliot and the town committee met them at the lake ten miles south of Timber Fork where they unloaded supplies and ammunition and set up camp.

The major met with Colonel O'Brien and explained the situation with Tara and the Indians and his reasons for summoning assistance from Fort Mason. The colonel approved of the plans, then asked to meet the person who was to rescue the girl. When Mark was brought before him he was surprised by his young look.

"How old are you, boy?" asked the partially bald, war-toughened Colonel O'Brien.

"Nineteen, sir."

"I see. Rescuing that girl will be no easy task, you know. She's at the mercy of the Indians and you never can tell what they'll do next. Are you aware of what you'll be up against?"

"Yes, sir. I've fought Indians before."

"Where?"

"At Fork Brooks, in Oregon. Also, Tara Sinclair is a friend of mine, and I will not leave that camp without her."

"You have grit. I like that," said Colonel O'Brien. "Ever thought of joining the cavalry?"

"Yes, sir, I have."

"Well, you'd be an asset to the military, I'm sure. You can go now."

Men were sent to scout the area around the Indian camp and guard against ambush attempts. In the cavalry camp the soldiers and volunteers were separated into three divisions, the main force under Colonel O'Brien and the east and west flanks each commanded by a captain. Edward Sinclair and Mark Curtis' positions were both on the west flank.

Late in the afternoon the company departed on its mission. At dusk they rode through the woods a mile south of the Indian camp, a silent movement of men and horses. The main force staked its position and prepared to wait the allotted ten minutes while the east and west flanks moved up and took their places. The two divisions left their horses behind and walked single file around the sides of the camp. They closed in to within fifty yards of the camp and spread apart until there was a man behind every tree.

As soon as ten minutes were up, a bugle call sounded the charge and the attack was under way. The earth seemed to shake as the horses' hooves thundered boldly into the quiet camp. Two of the surprised Indians fell beneath the hooves, but their fellow warriors grabbed rifles and bows and arrows and mounted a tough defense such as was characteristic of them. In a few short moments the dusk came alive in a blaze of gunfire.

Indian women scrambled about in confusion and screamed for their children. The little ones were terrified and didn't know which way to go. Some stood where they were and cried. Before long most had found relative safety with their mothers in the tepees.

The Indians started out at a disadvantage, being on the ground and shooting at men on horseback, but by firing a rapid succession of arrows and bullets and hitting their targets several times, they forced the enemy to seek cover.

* * *

No one on either side knew that Nate Hunter watched from the woods north of the camp as his own plans were being flawlessly executed. Within five minutes of the initial assault he noticed soldiers and volunteers entering from the east and west and forming a battle line across the north side of the camp in front of his position. He checked the magazine of his Henry rifle and made sure it held its full complement of fifteen rounds, then silently moved closer to the fighting and watched for Mark to appear.

He soon spied Mark behind a tree about twenty feet away. When he caught Mark's eye he pointed and held up two fingers, indicating that Tara was in the second tepee from where they stood. Mark nodded and cocked his revolver, ready to make a run for it. Nate made a quick check of their immediate environs to see if it was safe, then he worked the lever of his rifle to chamber a round and signaled for Mark to go.

Mark darted into the open and headed straight for the tent flap of the second tepee with Nate following closely behind. Nate crouched beside the tepee while Mark went inside. It was only a moment before Mark emerged with an ashen-faced Tara clutching her red coat. Nate was relieved to see that they had located her all right but he didn't allow himself to bask in it. They still had a long way to go to get to safety.

Apparently she'd been left alone in the tepee, but as the trio began to make their way back to the woods, nearby gunshots rang out. The Indians had spotted them.

While Mark forged ahead, shoving Tara in front of him and shielding her with his body, Nate found where one shooter was hiding, took aim, and fired. Shot in the neck, the Indian fell dead, and Nate continued following Mark's path. They soon found that they were going to run into more opposition than they expected. Several Indians had already managed to break through the ring of cavalry and volunteer troops, and Mark, Tara, and Nate were being fired on with bullets and arrows from two directions. With no words spoken, Nate and Mark worked in sync, Mark firing on the attackers on their right and Nate taking on those on their left, each employing implicit trust in the other for his life.

They had to alter their original escape route and head in an easterly direction, but they moved when they could, racing from the cover of one tree to the next. At one point, as he ran in the open, Nate heard the lever of a gun behind him. He turned around, dropping to one knee as he did so to throw off anyone who was trying to target him, raised his rifle and pulled the trigger in time to kill the Indian who had trained his sights on Tara.

Soon the three of them crouched near a cluster of granite rocks, boxed in on three sides by Indian shooters. Mark pushed Tara down behind him and got off a couple of rounds, killing two attackers. Nate propped himself up on one knee and started chambering rounds and firing in rapid succession. He made every bullet count, taking down an Indian on every shot. Mark covered for him while he reloaded the magazine; in no time he was ready to fire again.

As soon as Nate saw a break in the attack on them he gave Mark a shove. "It's clear! Go!"

Mark and Tara ran from their hiding place while Nate kept his eyes trained on his sights and his finger on the trigger. They had gone about fifty feet when new shots and arrows began whizzing by them. From their protected spot behind a tree Mark gestured to Nate that he was going to take Tara into a different direction to avoid confrontation with Indians. A moment later they both ran off to the right, disappearing from Nate's view.

"Damn," Nate muttered to himself. He'd been separated from Mark, and because of the location of these new shooters, he wouldn't be able to follow the direction Mark had taken. He quickly considered his options. If he could make it to the cover of the woods he could circle around and take out the shooters from behind, but he must work fast to be able to meet up with Mark again on the other side.

There was one shooter he knew was blocking his nearest escape route to the woods. He counted the rounds fired, and when he knew the Indian had to stop to reload, he made a mad dash for the woods.

Once in the woods where he felt only a little safer, he ran full speed, ducking under branches and jumping over logs and low bushes. When he neared a position in back of the Indians who had forced Mark into the other direction, he slowed down and crept stealthily along until he found them, two braves taking cover behind a fallen log, one with a bow and arrow, one with a rifle. Nate was breathing hard from running, but he struggled to quiet his breathing so as not to give away his presence to them.

He decided to go for the one with the rifle first; a bow and arrow would react slower than a gun, but as he took aim, out of the corner of his eye he saw the other Indian pull back his bowstring. Only too late did he see the danger posed by this. He heard the thud, then saw Mark, still out in the clearing, slouch over, the arrow stuck deep in his chest. Tara's scream drowned out Nate's gasp of disbelief. He stood frozen for a moment, his mind exploding in confusion. Then he whipped the rifle up to his shoulder and glared down the barrel at the brave who shot the arrow. He pulled the trigger, hitting him square in the back. He switched his aim to the other one, but that brave was already running away and quickly slipped from his view.

He knew he needed to get to Tara fast and he wouldn't be able to carry the rifle. He stashed it under a huge fallen log near his feet, unholstered his gun, and raced out to the troubled pair in the clearing. The Indian yells and gunfire were deafening now, but he could hear Tara sobbing and crying out Mark's name, and he could see Mark fighting the sharp, dizzying pangs and forcing himself to rise to finish his task. The next instant Nate was there, grabbing Mark and easing him down on his back.

"Thank heaven," Mark gasped as he let himself fall.

When Nate saw that Tara was panic-stricken and unable to take her eyes off Mark, he threw his arm around her shoulder and half pushed and half pulled her to a nearby thick clump of trees. "Are you okay?" he asked.

Her nod was accompanied by a blank gaze and Nate wasn't convinced. His eyes did a quick once-over of her body. "Are you sure? You're not hit?"

"No," she replied.

"Don't move then. I'll be right back." Again he darted into the open and arrived at Mark's side.

"No, Nate," Mark said breathlessly, clutching his bleeding chest. "Don't get yourself killed for me."

"I won't leave you out here in the open," said Nate. He lifted Mark by the shoulders, and while his right hand kept his gun poised, with his left arm he dragged Mark out of the range of gunfire. In the woods beside the clearing, he holstered his gun and knelt beside him, and immediately a weeping Tara was there too, holding Mark's hand.

Mark opened his eyes halfway and whispered something to Nate, who bent down and put his ear close to Mark's mouth. "Take it out.... Please, take it out."

"No, Mark, you'll bleed to death."

"I'm dying anyway. Take it out." It was a grave demand.

Nate understood Mark's desire. He didn't want to die with something of the enemy buried inside him. "Hang on to me," he said, placing Mark's hand on his knee. With nervous hands he grasped the stem of the arrow and gave it a hard yank. Mark cried out, and Nate grabbed the wound, trying his best to hold it shut, but the blood flowed out freely between his fingers.

A coughing spell overcame Mark and blood began trickling down his chin. He threw his head back and fixed his eyes straight ahead while waiting for the sweet release of death. He struggled for a breath. "Remember what we agreed on... if I was killed."

"I know." Nate nodded, tears stinging his eyes. Mark went into convulsions and Nate felt the urgency of their parting. "Mark, I'm sorry I couldn't do better giving you cover," he said, his voice breaking.

Soon after, Mark's eyes closed, his breathing silenced, and his hand fell from Nate's knee.

"Mark, no!" Tara sobbed. "Please don't go."

Nate stood and turned his back on the scene. He held up the arrow and stared at the sharp, bloody tip, then in a flurry of anger he broke it over his knee and cast it aside. Leaned against the trunk of a tree with his head in the crook of his arm, his fists clenched, he let the tears come while he wondered what had gone wrong that Mark had been made to pay such a price.

The sound of Indian whoops was coming closer. Nate wiped his eyes and turned to look. The Indians were advancing on the soldiers and forcing them to retreat to the woods. The spot where Nate and Tara were would soon be a battleground. "Come on," he urged Tara. "We've got to get out of here!"

With her eyes fixed on Mark, she seemed not to hear him, but he took hold of her arm and compelled her to come with him. He led her further away from the clearing, to the log where he'd stashed his rifle earlier. "Get down, stay down low." He pushed her down behind the log and ducked behind it himself.

For Nate the battle was only beginning. He reached for his holster, pulled his gun, and took aim at a Cheyenne brave at random. "This one's for Mark," he whispered just before pulling the trigger. The Indian went down. He aimed and shot again, taking down another warrior. The more braves he shot at, the more his anger built up. There was no end to the revenge he wanted for Mark's death.

He emptied the chamber and crouched behind the log to reload. As fast as his hands could move, he slid bullets from his cartridge belt and inserted them in the gun. Just as the last one went in, a hard blow to his right forearm jerked him back. With a grunt of pain he dropped the gun and grabbed his wounded arm. Tara uttered a weak scream and fainted.

Nate lifted his hand and looked at his arm. Blood was oozing through the hole in his jacket. It appeared the bullet had only grazed his arm but it had taken a hunk of flesh with it, and the resulting stinging pain spread throughout his entire arm. But his fight wasn't over, so with dogged determination he picked up the gun and pulled himself up to the log. He had to use his left hand to hold up his gun arm, but he could still shoot, and soon he had fired through another round of shells.

By now the volunteers and cavalry had retreated to the woods where Nate and Tara were. There they held their ground but not without a struggle. The battle was long and both sides were becoming weary of it. Many and much-needed soldiers and some volunteers had been killed or wounded while fighting in the clearing, and the Cheyennes' numbers had dwindled as well.

The night was dark now, lit only by the moon and Indian bonfires. That light was dimmed with gunpowder smoke and the smell of it was in the air. Arrows were stuck in tree trunks and logs. The moaning of a suffering victim could be heard amid the tumult.

Nate looked at Tara and was glad she wasn't awake to witness more of this scene. He himself wanted it to end, but as long as Indians kept coming into his line of vision, he kept firing on them. His hurting arm taxed his strength, and frequent dizzy spells forced him to put his head down. Soldiers, Indians, fires, guns—he saw and heard everything in a daze. He didn't know why he was fighting. He had exhausted his hate and revenge, and now there was only remorse. Shooting at Indians had become nothing to him.

To his right he saw Tara's father behind a tree several yards away. He kept glancing at Edward Sinclair, then one time he discovered Edward looking back at him.

Edward's expression wasn't friendly. He didn't seem to recognize Nate as one for whom he'd once taken a stand. On this night Nate was another Cheyenne, and Edward pointed his gun at him.

Nate stared in disbelief at the barrel. "Mr. Sinclair, I'm on your side." He held his breath until Edward turned it away, and they got back to fighting with no more words spoken. Little did Edward know that Tara was on the other side of Nate, just out of his view.

A rifle blast sounded next to Nate and he whipped around, afraid for Tara. She had come to and was holding his rifle. He looked at where the rifle pointed and saw a dead Indian, his chest blown open, a spear still clutched in his hand. He swallowed hard and looked back at Tara. "You saved both of our lives."

She had dropped the rifle, and her face had gone white. He holstered his gun, grabbed the rifle, and took her by the hand. "Come on, we're getting out of here." He stayed on the lookout, and when it was safe they left their place behind the log, ducked down, and scooted into the forest. They never looked back at the battle.

Chapter 13

As Nate and Tara hiked up the mountainside, the sound of the gunfire grew faint. Still, the bitter memory of the violence lingered in their minds, and with the moon hidden from view by thick foliage overhead, it seemed to be the darkest night these woods had ever seen.

Nate let them stop in a small clearing near the top of a ridge. He set down the rifle and dropped to his knees to catch his breath. "Thank heaven you're all right," he said with unsuppressed relief.

Tara wasn't responding. She had not said a word during their run up Mount Defiance, and now she stood breathing heavily and staring trancelike into the dark.

Nate went to her and laid a hand on her shoulder. She jumped and shied away from his reach, shaking beyond control. "It's all right," Nate reassured her. "There's nothing to be afraid of. I'm not going to hurt you. I want to help you." Slowly he reached out his hand to her again. "It's okay, Tara. Let me touch you."

Tara raised her head and watched him out of the corner of her eye. His hand came to rest lightly on her shoulder and she did not move away.

Nate saw her eyes becoming moist and her lip quivering, and he offered his other hand to her. "Come on," he urged. "It's okay."

Tara looked at him and suddenly realized he was not to be feared. He had rescued her from the Indian camp. She burst into tears and rushed into his arms.

Nate hugged her tightly. "It's all right, Tara. You're safe now."

"Why did you and Mark take such chances for me?"

"Mark loved you," he softly replied.

"And I watched him die," she sobbed.

"I know. I'm sad too."

Tara pressed her head against the soft leather of Nate's jacket, and little by little the haunting recollections melted away into the warmth and security of Nate's arms. At first she had been afraid that she was a burden to him, but in a few short moments she knew it was different. She sensed a caring and sincere attitude in him that she hadn't sensed before. When he said that she would be safe now she knew she could believe him and she was not afraid.

She remained in his patient and comforting clasp until she stopped crying and was calm. Then she saw the tear in Nate's jacket on the upper right arm and the spot of blood. "Nate, your arm!"

"It's nothing to worry about. I'm fine."

"Does it hurt?"

"A little. It'll go away."

"You're just saying that. It needs to be wrapped. We need to find some fresh water."

"First put your coat on. You're freezing." He picked it up from where she'd dropped it and helped her put it on.

A short ways from where they stood was a small stream that trickled over smooth boulders. Beside it Nate removed his holster, knife belt, and jacket and bent down to wash his hands on which Mark's blood had mingled with his own and dried. Then he sat down and leaned against a log. Carefully Tara peeled his shirt away from the wound while he flinched and tried not to show how much pain he was in.

The sight of the bloody wound troubled Tara. "You ought to see a doctor, Nate."

He shook his head. "It's not as bad as it looks."

"Well, I hope you're right." She turned up the bottom of her dress and ripped a lengthy piece from the hem. After dipping it in the stream, she knelt beside Nate and blotted it on his arm, carefully wiping away the blood. Then while he held it in place, she tore another piece from her dress to use as a bandage. Nate discarded the bloodstained piece he was holding, and Tara wrapped his arm with the second piece and tied it.

As Nate watched her work he felt guilty. She had done so much for him ever since he'd lived in the mountains, and now, when she had just been through so much and needed the comfort of her home and family, she insisted on doing still more for him. He felt indebted to her but had nothing to give. There was something he would tell her though, something she must know, and this night would be his only chance to say it, for as they had run from the battle a little while before, he had made a decision which would never allow his involvement with Timber Fork or the Cheyenne people again.

He slid his shirt back over his shoulder and smiled at her. "Thank you, Tara. It doesn't hurt so bad now."

"It's I who should thank you," she replied. "You risked your life for me tonight."

Nate meekly looked away. "There are soldiers at the bottom of the mountain where Elkhorn Creek enters the valley. I'll take you to them."

Tara hesitated, then asked, "When will I see you again?"

Nate didn't answer, but he stood up, picked up his jacket and other belongings, and held out his hand to her. "I want to talk to you."

Tara took his hand and let him help her up. He led her through the trees to the top of the ridge to view the land west of the mountain.

It was a magnificent, memorable sight that Tara saw before her. The timber on the west slope stopped three-fourths of the way up, giving her an open panorama of the Lewis and Clark range. Miles upon miles of beautiful, wild country stretched out under a myriad of stars and a full moon that was peeking from behind a cluster of illuminated clouds. Towering peaks and wide plateaus emerged from an ocean of darkness, their eerie outlines silhouetted against the glowing night sky. Long ridges spread out across the vast, sleeping land before either gradually descending or breaking off sharply into the depths of the blackened valleys.

"It's so beautiful, so peaceful," said Tara in awe, "not like down there." She glanced over her shoulder in the direction of the Indian camp.

"For the past year this has been my home," Nate said as he swept his arm across the scene. He turned to face her. "You're the one who sustained me all that time by bringing me what I needed. I've never known anyone with such patience and kindness. It was rough between us at first, but you just don't know how much your visits meant. I could never repay you if I tried the rest of my life. All I can do is thank you. I know that's not much."

"I did it because I wanted to," said Tara. "I didn't want to be repaid."

Nate smiled only a moment then gazed out at the mountains, mulling over how to put the next thing he wanted to say. When he looked back at Tara's fair, girlish face and innocent blue eyes barely visible in the moonlight, the task was made easier. "That wasn't all I wanted to tell you. I know we only agreed to be friends, and I know that's all I am to you. But you've become more than a friend to me, Tara. I don't know how it happened..." He stopped abruptly and bowed his head. He soon raised it again. "I want you to know that I love you." He turned away again. Facing her was becoming very difficult. A hand touched his shoulder.

"Nate, what's wrong?"

"I just... I wish I'd told you before now."

"But at least you told me."

"There's more to it." He turned back and looked squarely at her. "I'm going away tonight. I'll probably never see you again."

Tara's heart skipped a beat and she found it difficult to speak. "Why?" she asked in a forced whisper.

"I don't belong here, Tara. I'm to blame for all of the Indian trouble. I should've done this a long time ago."

"But it's not your fault. You couldn't help what happened."

"If I hadn't been here it wouldn't have happened, and you wouldn't have had to spend three days in an Indian camp. Yes, I could've helped it, you know I could've."

"But I'm not blaming you for what happened to me. Everything's okay now—"

"No, everything's not okay!" He pointed towards the bottom of the mountain. "People are dying down there and you call that okay? Tara, my life is not worth the many others that were killed tonight." He shook his head. "No one else will die because of me. Please understand."

Tara was crushed to realize how final his decision was. "You were wrong about what I feel for you. I love you too, Nate."

He closed his eyes. She couldn't have dealt him a harder blow if she had a hammer. He remained aloof to hide the pain. "You could anger a lot of people if they knew you said that to me."

"I don't care." Her voice shook with emotion. "I've wanted you to love me for so long, but I didn't think you would. I've been so horrible to you in the past."

Nate was not prepared for this turn of events. Her confession would make his leaving into a heartbreaking task. He halfway chuckled when he realized the irony of the whole thing. "Isn't it something? We've known each other all these years and only now we fall in love."

Tara stepped closer and reached out to him, and they embraced. When a moment later he found himself looking deep into her eyes, his face so close to hers, he couldn't resist the powerful pull her gaze exerted on him. He pressed his lips to hers in a tender kiss. A second kiss was longer, then he slid his arms further around her and held her close.

Tara couldn't move. She knew that this was what she had secretly wanted, to display her affection for him. But her sense of fulfillment was instantly overcome by loss because he would leave her. She buried her face in his neck, determined that she would not be the first to let go.

"Believe me, I don't want to do this," he said as he pulled away from her. "I'd better take you to the soldiers now."

Tara backed away from him. "There's no need. I can make it myself. If you're going to go, go now."

"You're absolutely not walking there by yourself."

"I know the way from here. I cannot say goodbye to you in front of anyone."

He picked up his gunbelt, pulled out the gun, and held it out to her. "Take this with you." She reluctantly took it.

"Where are you going to go?" she asked.

"I'm heading north, to work for Canadian fur traders. I can hunt for them."

He bent to pick up his jacket, but the sound of Tara's sniffles tugged at his heart, and he turned and looked at her. "Don't cry, Tara, you'll soon forget. There's somebody else out there for you who can give you everything you want. Nobody ever knew about us. There'll be no harm done."

He took his time putting on his jacket, knife, and gunbelt, and then stood ready to say goodbye.

Through tear-filled eyes Tara beheld the rugged yet serene look in his eyes, the prominent chin, the black hair whipping in the night breeze. She felt the warm touch of his hands when he placed them on her cheeks.

Again he took her in his arms and they kissed, then a final hug. "I'll never forget you, Tara Sinclair."

"Nor I you," she whispered.

Foregoing one more chance to look into her face, he firmly pulled her arms from his shoulders and turned away. Tara clutched him until the tips of his fingers slipped from her reach. Then he picked up his rifle, rested it on his shoulder, and strode off into the darkness, never looking back.

As soon as he had disappeared, the loneliness closed in on Tara and she felt like he was already miles away. She looked out at the Lewis and Clark range whose beauty only minutes before had taken her breath away. It didn't affect her now, and quickly she turned and started walking. She must return home now and not let anyone see the emptiness in her heart. She would try to forget as Nate had said, but that would mean erasing the past year of her life.

A cloud covered the moon and the woods became darker. Tara knew the direction to go, but she began to fear what lay in the unseen forest ahead. Scenes from the battle came to mind and she couldn't block them out. She remembered so vividly the arrows that narrowly missed her as she ran from the tepee, the look on Mark's face just before he died, and the Indian she had shot in the chest with the rifle. She thought she heard cracks of gunfire far away, but was it real or had she imagined it? The call of a hoot owl above her head made her jump and she started running as fast as she could. Suddenly a root tripped her and she fell. Thinking for an instant that someone had grabbed her, she lay on the ground, screaming in terror.

It seemed but only a second later that she was being picked up and held in Nate's arms.

"It's okay, I'm here," he said. "I was following you. I wasn't going to let you go back by yourself." He picked up his gun from where she had dropped it on the ground and holstered it.

He heard the sound of footsteps and whipped his head in the direction from which it came. A cavalry soldier on foot appeared. Nate let Tara go and backed away, but it was too late. He had already been seen holding her.

The soldier walked towards Nate, pointing a threatening finger. "What in the hell do you think you're doing with her?"

Nate stood his ground, alert and ready to ward off accusations. The soldier stopped advancing. "I wasn't doing anything to her," said Nate. "She was scared, and I—"

"Don't you lie to me! I saw you lay your hands on this girl. Look what you've done to her."

Tara was crying hysterically and unable to speak in Nate's defense.

"I was not doing anything," Nate insisted. "I swear it!"

A look of revelation spread on the soldier's face. "I know who you are. You're the half-Cheyenne who's been on the run, aren't you?"

Nate did not reply.

"That does it. You're coming back with me if I have to drag your dead body."

"I haven't done anything wrong," said Nate. "If Tara wants to go back with you she can, but don't come near me."

"I'm warning you. You won't get away with this."

Nate saw the soldier put his hand near his gun and held up a hand to stop him. "Don't try anything. Please don't. I don't want to have to defend myself." He knew he was a fast draw, probably no match for the soldier, but he prayed he wouldn't have to prove it.

The soldier moved his hand away from the gun. Then Tara looked up and saw the way the two were eyeing each other. "No, please stop!" she sobbed.

"I'll give you one more chance to turn yourself over to me before I kill you," the soldier was saying.

"I swear I did her no harm."

"It's the truth!" Tara shouted.

The soldier had already gone for his gun. It never left the holster, for Nate readily responded. His gun was drawn; a shot pierced the night, and the soldier lay still. Tara screamed and began shaking. Nate stared for a moment, his right hand still holding the smoking gun, his left hand still resting over the hammer. His wounded arm hurt something fierce, but he paid little attention to it as he held onto it with his hand and walked to where the body lay crumpled on the ground, with the head twisted to one side, eyes open and vacant.

"Oh, no, I've killed him," he whispered. Seeing the insignia on the man's shoulder, he added, "And he's a lieutenant." In frustration he kicked at the ground and shouted at the dead man. "Why did you do that?"

"What was he doing here?" said Tara's anguished voice.

"I bet he was one of the soldiers who was going to escort you home. He was looking for you." He put away his gun and knelt in front of Tara, who sat with her face in her hands. "You saw it, Tara. I did it in self-defense." She did not answer or look up. "I had to do it, didn't I?" He gripped her shoulders, demanding some form of reassurance. But all she could do was nod. He helped her up and ushered her away from the scene.

When they had gone some distance they stopped to collect themselves and figure out what to do.

"Take me with you, Nate," said Tara. "Take me wherever you're going."

"What?" asked a shocked Nate.

"I want to leave this awful place. I don't want to be here anymore."

"You're just upset. You mustn't even think of such a thing."

"I won't be a burden to you, I promise."

He squeezed her shoulders. "You could never be a burden to me." He was truly taken by surprise. After what had just happened, he didn't think she'd want to be around him. But now he had the needed assurance that she still trusted him.

"It would be a rough trip, Tara. We have no horses, no shelter. I can protect you most of the time, but I might not be able to protect you from some things, like an early winter blizzard, illness, dangerous animals..." He shuddered at the thought.

"I understand. But don't worry about me. I'm strong."

For a moment he stood transfixed by her beauty, which had not been diminished a bit by her recent experiences. But then he turned away, rubbing both hands through his hair in frustration as reality struck him. "What are we doing? This is crazy. My life is no kind of life for you. You belong at home with your family."

"Do you really think that I could go home now, back to a normal life, pretend like all this never happened?" Her voice began to break. "Pretend like I never knew you?"

"You have to," he whispered. She opened her mouth to object, but he stopped her. "Don't you know that you have a family that's worried sick about you? That's been on edge for days waiting for you to be released unharmed? Do you want to forget that?"

"No, of course not! I will find a way to get a message to them. The first place we come to where I can do that. I will let them know."

He gripped her shoulders and spoke firmly. "Tara, they may think you're dead." He paused to let that sink in. "Nobody will miss me."

"I'll miss you."

He walked a few feet away, folded his arms, and stood looking at the ground. "Why are you doing this? You have such a power over me. You're offering me what I want. It would be so easy for me to listen to you."

"Then listen to me!"

"No!"

"Don't you think you deserve a measure of happiness the same as anybody else?"

"Not at the expense of those who care about you. Tara, for months when I knew I was falling for you, I dared not even *think* about the possibility of us being together. You belong with your family, with all the things they can do for you."

"This is no different than other people who leave their families forever to come to the frontier."

"Other people don't run away with someone who's thought of like an outlaw."

"I don't think of you as an outlaw. Don't conform to other people's labels of you." She searched her heart for the words that would explain herself to him. "It's been six years since my family left Chicago and came here to the frontier, but I don't know the frontier. I want you to show it to me. Show me your world. Teach me your ways. I want to learn them."

105

She had put a different slant on it, redirected Nate's thinking. She didn't want to run from anything; she wanted knowledge, knowledge that he could give her. But were her feelings genuine, or did she just want to be with him? One look into her eyes and he would know. She wouldn't be able to fool him. But he avoided her eyes, afraid of what he would find there. He hoped she was telling the truth; he also hoped she wasn't telling the truth. His heart pounded as his gaze met hers. In that instant he knew. She meant every word she said. She desperately wanted to cross over into his world, to know what he knew, to discover the secrets of the wilderness passed down for generations of his father's family.

It seemed that time stood still while Nate weighed this decision. The silence of the dark woods enveloped them and heightened her anticipation while slowing his thoughts to a meandering, reflective pace.

"All right, I will," he said at last, eliciting a grateful smile from her.

He took her by the hand and led her to the Grotto, a fair hike from where they were, to retrieve supplies he had stored. They sidestepped behind the waterfall into the pitch-black cave. Nate felt his way to the rock beneath which was the hole containing the wooden box of supplies. There were two woolen blankets rolled up and tied with strips of rabbit skin. He handed these to Tara, then he picked up boxes of ammunition which he carried outside into the moonlight. He took the small box of shells for the Colt .45 and filled his cartridge belt. He dumped the rest into his leather pouch along with bullets for the rifle. Now all was ready.

With blanket rolls in hand they walked back up to the ridge, and Nate waited while Tara looked back in the direction of her home. There was nothing to see but woods, but in her mind's eye she saw the neat white two-story home and store that she was leaving behind. Her stomach was tied in knots. She was rife with fear and excitement all mixed together. "Okay, I'm ready," she said.

Nate understood her fear of venturing across a threshold from the known into the unknown. He had experienced something akin to it himself when he first came to the mountains following the massacre. "Do you trust me?" he asked.

"Yes."

"Good. We must keep moving most of the night. They will come looking for you, and our trail may be picked up as early as tomorrow, unless by some miracle it rains." He hesitated. "They may figure out that you're with me."

She understood the unspoken thought that he was sending her, to consider the resulting scandal and her reputation. "Then they should know that I'm safe," she answered with a smile.

His concerns dismissed, he smiled back. "Come on, let's go."

Chapter 14

All through the night Nate and Tara plodded through the forest, rarely stopping to rest. This wilderness was completely foreign to Tara, but she was confident in Nate's direction. When the ridge they were following veered off to the west, he turned the course northward and they started down to the valley. Their fast pace made them hungry in the early hours of morning, and Nate pointed out edible berries which they picked to eat.

The sun was beginning to rise when they had crossed the valley and ascended a hill covered with quaking aspens. They stopped and Nate shed his jacket and cumbersome belongings. The sunrise was a welcome sight to both of them, from its first promising glow in the pink eastern sky to its full burst of brightness.

"You're not hungry still, are you?" Nate asked.

"No."

"Good, because we don't have anything to eat."

Tara laughed at his carefree attitude. If he wasn't worried about where their next meal was coming from, neither would she be.

"What happened when you were in the Indian camp, Tara?"

"I was kept in a tepee with a brave and his wife. She was about my age. I tried to talk with her but she spoke no English. She wasn't very talkative anyway. On the second day in the afternoon I was left alone in the tepee and I tried to escape by digging out. The woman came back and saw me. She hollered and some Indians came and got me and tied me to that post. That's when I saw that you were captured. A couple of hours later they took me back to the tepee. I tried to get someone to tell me what they had done with you, but it was no use. Even up to the battle I thought you were still in the camp, and I was surprised to see that you were free. How did you get away?"

"Oh, the chief didn't like some things I said and they threw me out. The evil spirits in the Grotto were supposed to kill me."

"And after all the time they spent looking for you," Tara said, smiling. "Well, I'm glad they let you go. What did you do when you weren't in the Indian camp?"

"I talked to Mark a couple of times."

"Did you?" Tara was eager to hear about Mark when he was still alive.

"Yeah. I'm glad I got the chance. He asked me to come up with an attack plan, so I did."

Tara was astonished to learn of the major part he had played in the battle.

"If only I'd done what I knew I should've last summer," Nate continued. "The Indians weren't here then but I knew they'd be back. I *knew* they would. I was going to leave and go somewhere far away. Only one thing stopped me. I didn't want to leave the place where you were. But I was selfish. Now Mark is dead and a lot of others on account of me."

"Please don't do this to yourself, Nate."

He seemed not to hear her. "My father always said it was so important that Lena and I be proud of our Cheyenne blood. He made us hold our heads high and said that our heritage is what makes us stand out in a land that was fast being lost to the white men. Now I feel like I've betrayed him. I've killed some of my own people. The ones I shot while rescuing you, I had to do that. Afterwards, though, I could've left, but I chose not to. I was so full of hate for them. I could think only of what they did to Mark, and you. But the blame doesn't fall on the Indians. It falls on me. Their blood is on my hands."

Tara saw his hand quickly brush against his cheek. She put a hand under his chin and turned his head towards her. His eyes were moist, and she reached out to hold him.

"Mark was my friend," whispered Nate as he hugged her tightly. "I'm so ashamed of myself."

"You have absolutely nothing to be ashamed of," replied Tara. She ached to solace him the way he had done for her the night before. He had upheld her with his quiet strength and, as always, kept his own weaknesses concealed. Tara knew she was seeing a side of him that no one had ever seen, and she felt grateful that he had let her into this corner of his heart.

*   *   *

There were still two hours of daylight left when they stopped beside a stream and made camp. As soon as a fire was built, Nate left Tara with his gun while he took the rifle and went hunting. He later returned with a pheasant which they plucked and cooked for their supper.

While Tara rested, Nate spent the evening deep in thought. The coming years suddenly loomed before him. He would look back no more for now there was a future to plan for, and Tara would share it, as his wife. But she was a Sinclair and that made a difference. While his family had always been content with the simple things of life, her family had built their name on wealth and distinction. Nate knew he was no match for that.

He watched Tara asleep by the fire and instantly made a decision. He would simply provide for her in the way to which she was accustomed. But how was he to do that? He remembered his mother's words to him, *You can be whatever you want to be.* Then that old dream came to mind. He had wanted to be a ranch foreman. Perhaps now he would renew his pursuit of that goal. But his excitement soon waned as he imagined Tara Sinclair as the wife of a ranch foreman. He must do better than that. Sinclairs were used to owning things whereas Hunters had never had any land to their name. Hunters were always hired hands; Sinclairs were bosses.

With an open mind he delved deep inside himself. What did he really want to do? He must not say no to anything. Just a few seconds on this line of thinking and he had made up his mind. He was born for ranching. He would someday have a ranch of his own and he would work for no one. Hired hands *and* a foreman would work under him. It would take years to fulfill such massive plans, he knew, but he would make her proud. Perhaps he would carve out his own empire as Jerome Sinclair had.

He saw movement out of the corner of his eye and turned. Tara was coming to sit beside him. He was eager to tell her of his plans. "Tara, I've got an idea. I'm not going to be a hired hand forever. I haven't figured out the particulars yet, but how would you like us to head up something like your father's Split Timber or even the Broken Bow, to stand on top of a hill and look out as far as you can see at our land and our cattle grazing on it?"

Tara's eyes grew wide.

"That's right," he continued. "We're going to have our own ranch someday."

She didn't respond in the way in which he expected, and his soaring mood was deflated in a hurry. He picked up a stone and tossed it into the stream. "You don't believe me. You're so used to the way I've always lived you don't think I can ever do better." He arose, walked back to the campfire, and added another log to combat the growing night chill.

She followed him and sat down on the blanket next to him. "You know what? If I can leave my warm, comfortable house and nice things and come out here with you and learn to fight grizzly bears, I guess you can own a ranch."

He laughed. "I know I'm a far cry from a rancher right now, and I know I'll have to prove myself to you. But all dreaming aside, as soon as we come across a place where people can do such things, will you marry me?"

"Yes, I will," she replied with a warm smile.

"You will right away? You won't wait?"

"No," she replied with certainty.

"Good. Now that you've run away with me, I need to make an honest woman out of you." He took from around his neck the rabbit's foot that Lena had given to him. "This is supposed to fight off evil spirits and bring good luck." He flashed a smile. "The truth is, it's worthless. But it means something to me, and I want you to have it." He reached over and, slipping her hair out of the way, put it around her neck. "It's all I have for you now."

"This is enough," said Tara. "I will treasure this." As she searched his eyes, she knew there was more he wanted to say but he wasn't sure if he would. "What is it?" she prompted.

"It's just... well, ever since the massacre there's been a scar on my heart. But I can't feel it anymore. You've made me forget something I never thought I could."

"Oh, Nate." She put her hand aside of his face.

He found himself irresistibly drawn to her and burned with desire to express his love. "I never knew it could be like this," he whispered before pressing his lips to hers.

Tara was responsive to his fond aggression and slid her arm around his neck.

A moment later when she backed away from him, Nate bowed his head, sorry that he had offended her. He looked up to see her unbuttoning the front of her dress, and he caught her hands and held them. Shaking his head, he whispered, "You're still the boss's niece to me."

Tara lowered her eyes. He was placing her on a pedestal which, a few months before, was what she had wanted. But that girl no longer existed. She was leaving that life behind and entering a new one, and she needed to feel his strength. Gently she guided his hands around her waist and moved closer to him. "It's all right, Nate," she whispered into his ear.

She was offering to fulfill his wildest dreams and he suddenly felt grateful to her. He laid her down on the blanket and took over the task of her dress buttons while caressing her neck with kisses.

He made love to her, a slow, quiet entwining of souls by firelight. Afterwards, propped up on one elbow and looking down at her hair fanned out on the blanket above her head, he sighed happily. "I must be as dumb as a post not to have noticed your beauty a long time ago."

"My father would take a switch to you if he heard you say that."

"Your father could hold a knife at my throat and it wouldn't scare me. But now if you were to threaten me, that's different."

"You rascal!" Tara laughed. "The people in town never said this about you."

Nate took on a thoughtful expression. "What do the people in town say about me?"

"They say you're smart and clever. To some, you're an elusive mystery; they're not sure what to think of you. And some even..." She stopped short, ashamed to report what some people said about him.

"I want to know everything," he urged.

"Some, but only a few, call you a half-breed."

He traced his finger down her bare white shoulder. "And you?"

She smiled mischievously. "I used to call you a half-breed."

He feigned being insulted. "You know, you could've told me that thirty minutes ago."

Tara burst into laughter, an uncontrolled, contagious laugh, and he joined in with her.

"If you ever do invite me to dinner," he said, "I'm not sure I'd want to come."

"Why is dinner at my house so important to you?" she queried when she had regained her composure.

"I've just always wondered what your kind of people eat."

"If you think my kind of people are that different, how come I could never get you to show any respect to me back on the Broken Bow?"

"Because aggravatin' you was more fun, and I could do it all I wanted to. I knew you wanted to get me fired, but I also knew the boss wouldn't do that because he was too nice."

"Yes, he was," she agreed. She turned more serious. "And also because you were a top hand. I heard him say so many times."

Nate looked at her in surprise. "I never knew he thought that."

"He did. He really liked that about you."

His teasing grin returned. "Well, then I'm sure he wouldn't fire me for this either," he said as he pulled her blanket-wrapped, feathery frame close to him and began lavishing her face and neck with kisses.

Chapter 15

In Timber Fork Tara's disappearance had caused bewilderment among the men who had been in the battle, none of whom could recall seeing her once the attack was in full swing. Having confirmed that the Indians did not still have her, they searched from dawn to dusk, never finding more than a few tracks here and there.

The endless waiting and wondering was hard on Edward and Margaret Sinclair, but in spite of their worries they remained loyal to their longtime friends, the Curtises, in the face of their loss. On Thursday following Mark's funeral, the Sinclairs accompanied the Curtises to their home to visit for a while.

Julie had taken her brother's death especially hard. He had been the oldest, and for as long as she could remember she had looked up to him for protection and with respect. Now as she sat by herself in the parlor, staring mournfully at his gunbelt, which lay on a table by the window, she felt lonely and scared, feelings not at all new to her. She was reminded of the young lieutenant she knew in Oregon whom she had not told anyone about. He had promised to marry her. She had loved him and she had watched him die at the point of an Indian spear. Her youth had died with him.

Now she pondered Mark's incomplete life, reflecting on his one sadness, a girl whom he had not often spoken of but deep down inside whose love he did not want to let go. Even the gun that now lay before her had been carried into battle to defend the life of that girl.

It was not like Mark to let such things get him down, so there had been dreams for the future to take the place of the one he'd lost. He was an adventurer at heart. He always wanted to see what was outside Timber Fork and Montana Territory and was intrigued by faraway California. Though he talked of it often, Julie always knew that part of him belonged to Montana, and he may never have left the little town where they lived. Maybe he knew it too, for he never actually made plans to go away. But he was young and he may have changed his mind if he'd lived longer. Now the thought that his dreams would never be fulfilled hung over Julie's head like a black cloud.

She heard Edward's voice speak softly behind her. "Julie, you shouldn't stay in here by yourself."

"I know. I don't want to be alone. But I don't want to be around anybody else either. I just can't stop thinking about that night, how afraid I was when he and Pa left to attack the Indians."

"How did you know about the attack? We weren't supposed to tell anyone."

"Mark told me after I begged to know what the men were doing for Tara. Then when he told me I wished he hadn't." With a distant look in her eyes she remembered the horror of that night. "I sat up with Ma and we waited and prayed. We heard Pa ride up outside and we stood to watch the door, thinking all was well by then. He came in and we looked for Mark to follow him. The look on Pa's face was different than I'd ever seen, and Ma kept asking where Mark was." Julie's voice began to quiver. "Then Pa hugged her and started crying, and even before he said anything we knew." Her shoulders started shaking and she covered her face with her handkerchief.

Edward sat down beside her and put a hand on her shoulder. "You can be very proud of him. He was always thinking of others. His main concern was getting Tara home safely. And when the committee was discussing Nate Hunter, Mark put up an impressive argument in his behalf. I had to agree with him."

"I hope Nate's all right," Julie said as she wiped away tears.

"I saw Nate in the battle," said Edward. "He looked different from the way I remember him. He seemed... much older. And he'd been shot."

Julie looked up in alarm. "Was he hurt badly?"

"He didn't look it to me. But I don't know what got into me. I pointed my gun at him. He was like a stranger and enemy at first, and I was surprised when he didn't try to defend himself. I know he saw me first."

"Nate would never hold up a gun to you, Mr. Sinclair."

"Oh, I don't know. A year and three months is a long time for a person to live alone in the mountains. It could have changed him. Who knows what goes through that man's mind?"

All of a sudden Julie remembered her talk with Tara the Friday night before she was captured, when Tara had reluctantly revealed something. "I think I understand now about Tara and Nate."

"What do you mean?"

"Tara never told you this because she was afraid of getting herself or Nate in trouble. She has always known where Nate was, Mr. Sinclair. Since last year she had a place where she would meet him. She took him bullets to hunt with that she bought with her own money from your store. She feels differently about him now than she used to."

Edward stared at her in disbelief.

"Friday night when they sent us home from the dance she was worried because Nate was on Mount Defiance, surrounded by Indian camps. She didn't want to admit how she felt about him but I could tell. And that's why she rode up to the mountain that night."

"You're not saying that..." Edward's voice trailed off.

"She's in love with him."

Quietly Edward stood up and walked to the front window. He stared blankly at the street outside with his hands in his pockets. He was remembering Mark saying how Tara had persuaded him to plead Nate's case before the town committee. "And all this time I knew nothing of it. How could I have been so blind?"

"You weren't blind. It was just well-hidden."

"So why do you tell me this now, Julie?"

"Because now neither of them can be found. I believe they've run away together."

Edward whirled on her. "No, she wouldn't do that! Tara would not run away and leave us to wonder like that."

"Wouldn't she, if she was afraid of the Cheyenne capturing her again? And if she believed that she would be okay with Nate? I think she would."

Edward realized that it was indeed likely. After all, why shouldn't Tara's best friend know something like that?

"I don't know where they would've gone," Julie was saying, "but it was their choice, and I don't think any good will come of searching for them."

"Stopping the search would be like giving up on Tara. I won't do that."

There was a knock at the door and Edward answered it. He invited Captain Blaine in and shook his hand.

"You're one of the Curtis family, are you not?" Captain Blaine asked the young woman.

"I'm Julie, Mark's sister."

"I'm very sorry about your loss, Miss Curtis."

"Thank you."

The captain turned to Edward. "I've been looking all over town for you, sir. One of our search party found this by a stream on Mount Defiance. I thought you should take a look at it." He held out a piece of brown-stained cloth. One could see the blue-flowered print around the frayed edges.

Edward took the specimen in his hands and beheld it in horror. It was a piece from Tara's dress and there was no mistaking the stain to be dried blood.

"Don't be discouraged, sir," said Captain Blaine. "We've combed the mountain and haven't found any other evidence to suggest that she's hurt. We'll keep you posted."

Edward nodded and Captain Blaine left.

Julie was not distraught as Edward was. As soon as she saw the piece of cloth her mind started to work. "Wait a minute, you say Nate Hunter was shot?"

"Yes, in the arm."

"Then if Tara was with him later on, she would've used a piece of her dress to stop the bleeding. Mr. Sinclair, this is Nate's blood. I know it is."

What seemed improbable at first now seemed very logical to Edward, but then a new worry surfaced. "Oh, I hope he's all right. He must bring my daughter home to me."

* * *

Julie sat in the officers' tent across a table from Captain Blaine.

"It certainly is a surprise to see you here this afternoon, Miss Curtis," said the captain.

"I'm here to ask a favor of you. It's a rather large favor, maybe even outrageous." When she saw that he was prepared she began, "First you should know that the missing woman, Tara Sinclair, and I have known each other for years. We are best friends and I wouldn't want anything dreadful to happen to her, of course. I come here now because I would like you to call off the search for her. Perhaps when you hear what I have to say you'll consider it."

Captain Blaine raised his eyebrows. "Yes, I would be very interested in what you have to say."

"Tara's not in any trouble. She simply ran away. She would come home if she wanted to."

"And where do you think she would've gone? Where could she have gone? There's no other settlement for miles."

"I don't know where they would've gone. But I'm sure they're capable of—"

"Just a minute. What do you mean by they?"

Julie was at a loss for words. She had meant to skirt around Nate's name.

Captain Blaine leaned forward in his chair. "What do you know, Miss Curtis? You need to tell me."

Julie looked down at her hands folded in her lap. "I'm supposing that she's with Nate Hunter. He's the half-Indian who—"

"Yeah, I know who he is. Does Tara Sinclair know him?"

"Very well. She's known him for years as I have."

"Why do you think she's with him?"

Again Julie was silent and avoided the captain's eyes.

Her reluctance to talk revealed much to Captain Blaine. "I see. Still, there has to be more to it. He was holed up in the mountains for over a year, I understand, and no one came in contact with him."

"Tara saw him. She regularly took him ammunition to hunt with."

"And no one knew this but you?"

"Yes, until this morning. I told her father."

"And he believes this?"

"You mean you don't?"

"Well, to be frank with you, I do find it difficult to believe that all this would've gone on with only a young woman like yourself to know about it."

"Look, Captain, I had no obligation to tell you anything about Tara's personal life. Now that I have you think I'm a liar."

"I'm not calling you a liar, Miss Curtis. I'm merely saying—"

"That I don't know what I'm talking about. Yes, I know what you're saying. And stop calling me Miss Curtis. My name is Julie."

"Very well, Julie, I don't mean to be insulting, but I hope you don't think I can call off a whole search operation because of the testimony of one woman who's playing a hunch."

"This is no hunch, Captain Blaine. I know it was their decision to go away and you won't find them around here. Please leave them be."

"I would like nothing better than that so I could wrap up this mess and go home. But Miss Curtis, I mean Julie, I just can't do that. It's too ridiculous."

"You are wasting your time. Your search range only reaches to Mount Defiance and shortly beyond. Nate Hunter's senses are as sharp as the best Indian hunters. You don't think he's just sitting there in the woods with Tara waiting for you to come and rescue them, do you? If you really want to find them, put men out in the mountains further away from Timber Fork."

"I'm sorry, Julie, but I'm very busy. Maybe we could chat some other time?"

His attitude infuriated her. She stood up and gathered her shawl around her. "Forgive me, Captain. I won't bother you again."

A private entered the tent and saluted the captain who rose to return the salute. "Sir, we've found some tracks. We think it's those of the girl."

Captain Blaine asked, "Where at?"

"In the valley north of Mount Defiance, sir. There are other tracks along with it, a man's tracks. They lead north."

"And how old are these tracks?"

"Must be around two days or so."

"Thanks for the information. You're dismissed."

The soldier left and Captain Blaine sat down again, visibly embarrassed. "I am so sorry, Julie."

"It's all right, Captain," replied Julie, sitting down again. "I don't hold grudges."

"I'm relieved to hear that," he said, smiling. "But north. Why would they go north?"

"It's as good a direction as any. Now will you consider my request?" She saw that the captain was still reluctant. "Do you think I would ask you to stop looking for my best friend if I didn't believe she was safe?"

"I will think on it. In the meantime perhaps you will allow me to make up for my unpleasantness to you by serving you dinner here this evening?"

Julie stared at him, speechless.

Captain Blaine smiled. "I see I've taken you by surprise. I know this may not seem like the proper time and I will understand if you decline. But I feel I owe it to you, and I'd like to find out more about you and about this couple that you seem to know so well. And it's not often that I'm privileged to have a lady join me for dinner."

"Well, I'm not surprised, given your approach." He appeared disheartened and she quickly tried to fix it. "I'm sorry. That was uncalled for. I would be happy to come."

"Good. My cooking isn't half bad."

*   *   *

Julie found Captain Blaine to be a pleasant dinner companion, more easygoing than when he was doing his job as a cavalry officer.

"So you're from Richmond, Virginia," he said, laying down his napkin after dinner.

"How did you like it there?"

"Oh, I really don't remember much about it," replied Julie. "We moved away when I was four and went to Chicago. My father worked with a wainwright there." She smiled when she recalled those days. "I remember Pa coming home all the time saying how he was tired of fixing broken wheels that were going to take people west without him."

Captain Blaine laughed. "Itchy feet, huh?"

"Very much so. It's aggravating sometimes. Me, I would like to settle down, maybe be a schoolteacher." She picked up her cup of tea and caressed it with her fingers. "Chicago is where we met the Sinclair family, all nineteen of them."

"Good heavens! They must've ruled the city."

"Almost. Tara's father owned the largest dry goods store in the city. His brother, Jerome Sinclair, was a banker and was on the town council, and his sister, Mary Sinclair McBrae, ran a very elegant hotel and restaurant. Tara and I were eleven years old when our families decided to move. Jerome Sinclair heard about land here in the Territory ideal for grazing cattle so he went into ranching and established the Broken Bow while Tara's father remained a merchant plus took on the Split Timber. Their sister stayed in Chicago."

"That's unusual that they would've left a place where they had deep roots planted," said Captain Blaine.

"Well, when Edward Sinclair's brother was alive they would do just about anything together no matter how foolish. It wasn't as if they were taking chances though. Anything they got into was bound to be a success. I think it's impossible for the Sinclairs to fail at anything involving money."

"Then too, the call of the open West is something many people can't resist."

"I know what you mean. My brother always wanted to answer that call."

There was a moment of uneasy silence, then Captain Blaine cleared his throat. "So what about this Nate Hunter? Tell me about him."

"Nate's parents came here in '61 from the Platte River in Nebraska. They went to work for Jerome Sinclair on the Broken Bow. I remember the first time I saw Nate. He's a very interesting person, a little mysterious and intriguing. I liked him instantly but Tara couldn't stand him."

"Seriously? Why?"

"He wasn't in her social class. But that was fine with me because sometimes I was jealous of Tara's being so pretty. But I didn't have to worry about her trying to steal Nate's attentions." She laughed as another memory came to mind. "I remember when we were around thirteen Tara said to him one time, 'Don't you know how to treat a lady?' And Nate looked at her very calmly and said, 'Of course I do, whenever I see one.' I laughed so hard and Tara got mad at me."

Captain Blaine chuckled, then asked, "So now are you envious of Tara?"

"No, of course not. On the surface they seem very different from each other, but I think they're more alike than either one ever cared to admit. Both are not afraid to speak their minds or stand up for something. Each of them is loyal to have as a friend; they'll bend over backwards for you. And both of them are pretty determined people. No, it's not hard for me to imagine them being drawn together if they spent much time around each other." She brushed the subject away with her hand and took a sip of tea. "So where are you from?"

"I hail from Lexington, Kentucky."

Julie leaned back in her chair and smiled. "I don't detect an accent."

"Well, like you I've moved around a bit."

"Why did you become a soldier?"

"Family tradition. My father was a soldier and his father before him. It never once occurred to me to be anything else. So I started out in the Ohio State Militia and joined the Union Army during the war." He laughed and shook his head. "I was just a young private, never been in a battle before. I was scared half to death."

"Apparently you got through it unscarred," said Julie.

"There are invisible scars. I lost an older brother at Bull Run and another brother in the Wilderness Campaign."

"Oh, I'm sorry."

"Thank you."

"So why do you like being a soldier?"

Captain Blaine contemplated his answer for a while. "Because I like order. We bring law where there is no law. It's a very disciplined life and I like that." His blue eyes studied hers for a moment. "Did you know that there was a cavalry soldier killed on Mount Defiance the night of the battle?"

Julie braced herself. She sensed that Captain Blaine had asked her here just to tell her whatever he was going to say next. "Really? I hadn't heard."

The captain nodded. "Lieutenant Sam Wyatt. He was with the group waiting to pick up Tara after she was rescued. When she didn't arrive, he left the others to look for her. He was found later, shot in the chest."

"How awful!"

"We, that is, the cavalry officers, think that Nate Hunter did it."

"Captain Blaine, you must be mistaken!"

"I wish I was but I doubt it."

"How dare you accuse a friend of mine that way. Nate Hunter is not a murderer!"

"All I know is, we have a dead soldier. Tara Sinclair and Nate Hunter were on the mountain that night. Nate has a gun. Tara wouldn't try to get away from a soldier. Nate probably would, and if physically detained he might retaliate."

"I don't have to sit here and listen to this." As Julie stood up and stormed towards the door she knew in her heart she couldn't dispute the captain's theory. She stopped before the door and bowed her head, tears stinging her eyes. "I tell you, Nate wouldn't do that. Is this all you wanted me to come here for, just to get me to tell you everything about him?"

Captain Blaine came and stood behind her. "No. I'm sorry I brought this on you at such a time. Please don't leave."

"If Nate did do such a thing, he would've had a very good reason."

"I'm sure I can believe you. Listen, do you feel certain that they'll be coming back here?"

"Oh yes. Tara would at least get word to her family."

"We will need to talk with Nate eventually. But I'll see what I can do about calling off the search. I'll have to have permission from the Sinclairs first. You do understand that?"

"Yes, thank you."

In the days that followed both Julie and the captain would have many discussions with Edward and Margaret Sinclair. Within two days the search would be disbanded and the town would turn its attention toward a small band of revenge-seeking Indians who had survived the battle.

Chapter 16

Far to the north, Nate and Tara were still trudging across miles of mountainous wilderness, a majestic but lonely landscape fraught with unseen dangers. The autumn air grew colder as they moved deeper into the Lewis and Clark range, and the highest mountains were already capped with snow. The mountainsides were covered with rich evergreen forests dotted with deciduous patches clothed in brilliant oranges and golds. Squirrels and chipmunks scurried about, finding and storing their winter's food supply, and white-tailed deer and elk were growing thick coats of fur.

Tara's thoughts only occasionally wandered to home for she had found forgetfulness in Nate's companionship and in this untamed, unpredictable country. It was profoundly inspiring to her to see the frontier just as it looked when Lewis and Clark passed through over a half century before, so much so that she was almost offended at the occasional discovery of a steel trap, intrusive evidence of man.

She learned much from Nate about survival in the wilderness and reading the signs of nature. She found out how to identify the tracks of nearly a dozen animals, how recently they had passed by, and where they were going. She learned how to find game and sneak up on it without it being aware of human presence. He taught her not to fear the wilderness but to make it her ally.

At night he taught her how to read the sky like a map, how to tell the time of night and even the time of year by the positions of the constellations, and how to use them to establish direction like a compass.

It was with amusement and awe that Nate sat watching her one evening as she gingerly skinned a jack rabbit, seemingly unaffected by the bloody sight before her.

She saw him out of the corner of her eye and paused, more uncomfortable with being watched than with performing her task. "What?" she inquired.

"Nothing," he answered. He continued to study her hands as she resumed skinning the animal. "Did your father or brother ever go hunting?"

"No," she replied, shaking her head. "Cattle ranchers, you know. We're a beef-eating family."

For all the fortitude Tara displayed during the day, reminders of her vulnerability overtook her in the night when she would jerk to sudden wakefulness in a cold sweat, crying inconsolably, unable to shake off the effects of being a captive and of the ensuing battle. Instantly Nate was there holding her, his soothing voice whispering in her ear.

"It was just another bad dream. They will go away. Time always does that." Although she would never admit it, he knew exactly what was the source of her torment. "Nothing was your fault," he assured. "You don't have anything to feel guilty about, nothing at all."

Wide-awake now, he sat leaning against a log, enclosing her in his blanket in front of him. With his face next to hers he pointed to the luminous patch that divided the night sky. "Look at that Milky Way. It looks like a cloud, but it's really thousands of stars further away than either of us can imagine. And do you hear that wolf howling at the sky? It's coming from that peak over there."

Used to their intense lessons in the daytime, she asked, "And what does that tell me?"

He looked very seriously at her, as if about to explain some secret of nature. "Nothin'."

That elicited a smile from her and the night lost some of its fear.

On their third day on the trail they stopped to rest on a huge rock perched high on the eastern slope of a mountain. Tara opened the bandage on Nate's arm to look at the wound. She was worried because he never used his arm for anything unless absolutely necessary. He kept it by his side and never said a word about it.

"Nate, we really need to get you to a doctor."

"I don't need a doctor. I'm all right."

"But your arm isn't getting any better. Promise me we'll find a doctor, or at least somebody who knows something about it, as soon as we can."

"Okay, I will."

Tara rewrapped the bandage after which she sat back and pondered for a moment. "Do you believe in God?" she asked. "Or the Great Spirit or whatever else the Indians worship?"

Nate smiled at her blunt wording of the question. "*Heammawihio*, the Wise One Above," he corrected her. "I never figured there to be any difference between them." Prompted by her bewildered look he attempted to clarify himself. "The Indians really aren't so different from the white man. They all believe in a supreme being who watches over us. They just call him by different names, that's all."

"I guess I never thought of it that way."

"Neither did my ma. Lena and I learned a lot from Pa, but one thing Ma made sure we learned from her is Christianity. When she taught us to read, it was from the Bible. I've read the whole thing, cover to cover. Have you?"

Tara grinned sheepishly. "No, I'm afraid you've got me there."

When they were rested, they crossed over the ridge and descended the west slope where they followed the Teton River for a ways.

Tara noticed that the wilderness seemed different and it took a while for her to figure out why. Then it hit her. All the usual sounds were gone. The mountains were haunted by a strange silence. "Listen to the silence, Nate. The

121

wind is still. No birds are singing. No leaves are rustling. Only the river moves. What's it mean?"

"There's a storm coming."

"How do you know that? There's not a cloud in the sky."

Nate nodded towards the mountains to the northwest. "They're behind the mountains. Besides, the animals tell us everything we need to know. They've already found cover so we should do the same before long. It'll come, you'll see."

There were a few clouds visible as, an hour later, having left the riverside, they came to a shallow ravine in a meadow.

"What's this?" Tara asked as she followed the long, winding gully with her eyes.

"Probably was a tributary of the river at one time."

"Let's go into it."

Nate consented although he didn't feel like it. He was tiring easily and the periods of lightheadedness that had begun in early afternoon were becoming more frequent. He did not want to say anything. He had never been seriously ill and he wasn't going to start now. But his condition worsened as they walked. He felt weak and shaky, his whole body ached, and his dizzy spells made it seem as if the ground was rolling like an ocean under his feet. He realized that his arm had become infected, but he was certain that if he could just rest for a few hours he would be fine. Suddenly his blanket roll and rifle slipped from his grasp and his knees buckled.

Tara turned in time to see him collapse, and she gasped as he rolled to the bottom of the ravine. She rushed to his side as he attempted to rise, but he was clearly disoriented. In spite of his weak protests she helped him to a nearby rocky bank where he could sit and lean back somewhat comfortably. She tried not to let him see her trembling hands as she settled down next to him and struggled with a frightened mind to determine what she could do.

"Nate, I'm going to look for help," she said at last. "You need to be in some kind of shelter."

He beheld her in utter astonishment. "What are you talking about? There's nobody—"

"We're on somebody's trap line. Somewhere there's got to be a trapper. And he has to have a place to live."

"Yeah, and a haystack has to have a needle," he whispered between breaths. "Tara, don't go."

"Don't worry about me. If there is such a person, he'd live by the river. I'm just going to go back there and follow it north. I'll take your gun. You keep the rifle." She reached around his waist, carefully pulled the gun from his holster, then placed the rifle in his hands. "I'll be back very soon," she said, squeezing his hand.

She made her way to the other side of the ravine, climbed out, and started at a run westward toward the river. She made a mental note of memorable trees and rocks along the way so she could find her way back. When she reached the riverbank she followed its twisting course as it cut its way through heavily wooded landscape. Thick brush often drove her away from the banks, where she followed old animal trails through pine trees and berry thickets which scratched her face, neck, and hands and hindered her pace.

She went on until she was worn out and breathless, then she went further still. She looked up at the sky where clouds with dark undersides were building. Nate had been right; there would soon be a storm. She prayed she would find someone or something that would be of help to them before the rain came and made it difficult to get back.

* * *

As Nate lay in the ravine he worried about Tara and was sorry he'd let her go. He knew her search for someone would probably be futile, and with a storm on the way their situation would only grow worse.

He was startled by the sound of vicious growling and raised his head to find three timber wolves trotting back and forth at the top of the ravine opposite him, panting hungrily. They knew Nate was in no condition to put up a fight, so with barred teeth and gray fur standing on end, they prepared to descend on their victim.

As Nate stared into their menacing yellow eyes he remained calm but cautious. He picked up the rifle, pointed it at the sky and fired once. The loud bang spooked the wolves and they shied away, out of Nate's sight. They soon reappeared above the ravine, and he fired a second shot, driving them back again. He was sure they were still there so he fired a third shot after which he heard them run away. He waited to see if they would come back, but apparently they had decided to look for peaceful hunting elsewhere. He laid his head back down and was fast asleep within moments.

* * *

Tara figured she had gone at least of couple of miles and she was beginning to lose hope of finding anyone. She wanted to go back to Nate before the storm hit, yet she couldn't turn back having been unsuccessful.

She rounded a bend in the river, the brush gave way to a pretty clearing, and there before her eyes, not far from the water, stood a small log cabin. Her mouth dropped open and she was sure she was seeing the most beautiful sight ever. Although she was already breathing heavily, she broke into a run across the clearing strewn with stumps, obviously cut with an axe, and arrived at the door shouting for someone to come to her aid.

Continued shouting and knocking brought no response. She walked around the cabin and called out, "Hello, is anyone here?" She was answered only by silence.

She went back to the door and pushed against it. The unlatched door eased open and she entered, cautiously at first. Seeing it unoccupied, she took a quick look about at her new find.

The interior was simple and sparsely furnished. It wasn't in a shambles as Tara expected but rather tidy. In the wall across from her was the fireplace. In between the fireplace and the door was a little table made of rough-hewn boards and a chair. In the corner was a log-frame bed bearing a pitiful-looking straw-filled mattress. It would suffice for their needs, and Tara wasted no time setting out for the return trip.

She remembered the way well, and before long she stood peering into the ravine where Nate lay still. The wind had started blowing furiously. She scrambled into the ravine, knelt beside Nate, and shook him awake. He didn't seem to know where he was, but she jostled him until his eyes focused on her. "Nate, I found a cabin. There's nobody there right now."

"How far is it?" he whispered.

"It's a little ways. But I need to get you there so I can take care of you better. I know you don't feel like it, but do you think you could walk? I'll help you." He nodded and she began gathering up their belongings. She tied the two blanket rolls together; holding the leather tie of one of them, she could drag the load in one hand. He insisted he could carry the rifle, so she put her other arm around his waist to support him as they hiked out of the ravine and headed towards the river.

A drizzling rain set in before they arrived at the river's edge, and shortly thereafter it became a downpour.

"We're losing daylight," Tara warned.

"Don't worry. I can keep going," replied Nate.

But as they trudged over the same ground that Tara had traveled the whole afternoon, now wet and slippery in places, his weight grew heavier against her and taxed her strength. Their pace was slowed by the cold, driving rain and the swirling wind as it howled across the valleys and ridges. She felt him shivering and heard his feet dragging and prayed that he'd be able to make it as far as the cabin where she could get a warm fire going.

It was almost completely dark when the shape of the little cabin loomed in front of Tara and she breathlessly announced, "Here we are." She leaned into the door, and once inside, dropped the blanket rolls and helped Nate to the bed. He collapsed onto the bed, shivering violently.

On the wall next to the door was a wooden shelf on which sat a kerosene lamp and some matches. Tara lit the lamp and its light flooded the cabin. After helping Nate out of his wet clothes, she found a dry shirt inside his blanket roll and helped him put it on. At the foot of the bed was a box containing several woolen blankets and animal skins. She covered Nate with blankets and dried his hair with a small towel.

Next to the fireplace was a neat pile of logs and dried kindling. Tara used some to start a fire, and once a few logs had been added, the cabin became warm and comfortable, and Nate was able to sleep. Tara peeled off her rain-soaked clothes and bundled up in a dry blanket. She laid their clothes out by the fire to dry and proceeded to search the cabin to see what kind of supplies were on hand. To her great relief, the crudely made cabinets were filled with food—jerky, beans, cornmeal, flour, coffee, sugar, and bottles of whiskey. Unless the cabin's owner was lying dead in the woods somewhere, he was definitely planning to return. She didn't expect him to arrive during the night so she settled herself in front of the fire with a steaming cup of coffee.

She felt only a little uncomfortable taking over a stranger's home and helping herself to his things. Her brief sojourn in the mountains was already roughing her up and she was developing the survival instinct that true frontier people all possessed.

For a couple of hours she sat by the fire, wide-awake and deep in thought, before she heard Nate stirring and arose to check on him. What she saw made her heart sink. There he lay, his face and neck glistening with sweat, his breathing short-winded and laborious, and his chin quivering from chills.

She laid her hand on his forehead, although she already knew the diagnosis. "Nate, you're burning up with fever."

He did not hear her; he was dazed. There were blurred images and a voice coming from a distance. He was cold and wanted more cover, but then a wave of heat rushed through his body and he pushed the blanket down from his chest. There was a moment of relief, but then the blanket was over his chest again. Maybe he only thought he pushed it down. There was blackness. He was snapped out of it by the comfort of a cold, damp cloth on his burning forehead.

He found it increasingly difficult to hold onto consciousness for the painless peace of sleep was ever luring him away. It was an overpowering force and he would easily succumb to it, drifting off and coming back, again and again.

When he did sleep, it brought him little comfort, for frightening images invaded his dreams. There was someone standing above him who looked like his father. Nate reached out to him but his figure faded into the dark. Suddenly Nate was at the bottom of a hill looking toward the summit, waiting for something. For what he didn't know. Then dozens of flaming torches appeared at the top of the hill and Nate felt terror, a very familiar kind of terror. He had been here before. Those torches had terrified him before. From far away he heard Indian yells. They grew ever louder and Nate knew what was about to happen.

Desperately he fought to turn the Indians away but they kept on coming. They closed in all around him, shooting arrows and raising spears. Their whoops and yells became deafening as arrows pierced his body. In pain and anger he yelled at the top of his lungs.

His yell unnerved Tara and she placed a hand on his to solace him. He broke free and slapped her hard with the back of his hand, almost knocking her to the floor. She returned to his side and grasped his arms with her own shaking hands.

"Nate, it's just me. It's Tara," she kept repeating. "I won't hurt you." She sat on the bed, placed his head in her lap, and clasped his wrists, yearning to break through his delirium and reassure him of her presence.

Hot tears coursed down her cheeks. She didn't try to hold them back for now she was truly scared. They had talked about the possibility of her becoming sick, but the idea of anything happening to him, her guide through the wilderness, her protector—her lover, had never even been considered. "I've known you to be tired, Nate Hunter," she cried, "but never beaten. You're strong. You can pull through this."

In a few minutes when he seemed more calm, she went to the cabinet that contained the whiskey and brought a bottle back to the bed. Holding him up by the shoulders, she prompted him to drink. When he'd had enough she put it on the little table next to the bed, then she brought a chair over to the bed and sat by him till he slept again.

* * *

Sometime in the night Nate's hand took Tara's, and she bolted upright in her chair and looked around. She realized she had fallen asleep sitting beside him. His eyes were open and she leaned forward. "Can I get you something?"

"Some water," whispered Nate.

Tara went to the water bucket by the door and dipped some of the fresh river water into a tin cup. She brought it back and held up his shoulders while he drank it in big gulps. Then before she could stop him he took the cup from her hand, turned it upside down and let the remaining water splash down his sweaty neck and chest.

Tara set the cup aside, picked up a cloth and wiped his brow. Then she rearranged the rabbit furs that served as a pillow under his head.

"How long have I been here?" he asked.

"Just overnight. It's probably a couple of hours till daybreak."

He weakly reached up and fingered the rabbit's-foot charm that hung about her neck. "What's to become of you?"

"What are you talking about?"

"I never should've brought you out here. I'm sorry."

She caught his hand and held it. "I'm not leaving here without you." She forced a smile. "And if you'll remember correctly, it was my decision to come, not yours."

The corners of his lips turned up in a smile. "Oh, yeah, I forgot." He was asleep again before he took the next breath.

Chapter 17

Morning came and Tara unwrapped Nate's bandage and examined the wound again. But this time she noticed something she hadn't before. She moved the kerosene lamp to the table by the bed to get a better look. "Oh, no." She gently pushed his perspiration-soaked hair away from his pallid face and nudged him awake. "Nate, you're still carrying a piece of the bullet in your arm."

"Damn," he hissed, clearly frustrated. He hesitated for a moment, not wanting to tell her what he knew he had to. "You're going to have to cut the bullet out, Tara."

Tara's eyes widened and she vigorously shook her head. "No, I can't do that. Please don't ask me to do that."

"Listen to me, Tara." She started to object again, but his voice stopped her. "There's no choice, do you understand what I'm saying? You *have* to do this for me."

She swallowed hard. "I know. But I don't know what I'm doing. I could maim you for good."

"Then I'll learn to shoot with my left hand," he whispered between breaths.

She struggled to calm her nervousness and think. "I need to tie you down."

"No, I won't move."

She couldn't keep the tremors out of her voice. "I have to, Nate. This is going to hurt."

"I won't move," he sternly repeated. "Just please don't tie me."

"All right." She took a deep breath. "What do I do?"

Nate remembered seeing his father do this one time. Although his knowledge was primitive, he was the closest thing to a doctor on the Broken Bow and he was occasionally called on in that capacity. "Is there a small knife here somewhere?"

Tara rummaged through the cabinets, reaching behind and under the contents, until she found a paring knife, which she tested for sharpness.

"Now hold it over a flame till it's hot," he instructed her, "very hot."

She lit a candle and repeatedly passed the blade through the flame, turning it over several times, till it was too hot to touch. "Okay, I'm ready."

"Give me some whiskey." He downed as much whiskey as he could, then gave her the bottle. "Pour some over the wound." He grimaced when she did. "If I pass out," he warned, "keep going till you get it out."

She nodded, then placed a small piece of kindling wood in his mouth for him to bite. He reached above his head with his left arm and grasped the corner post of the bed.

When the burning knife touched his arm he drew in a breath and bit down hard on the wood. Searing pain shot through his arm and he struggled with a tired mind to think of something else. His eyes were fixed on the ceiling and tears rolled down his temples and dissolved into his hairline. Beads of sweat clung to his forehead and upper lip and trickled down his neck and heaving chest. He heard Tara's anguished voice.

"I can't get it, Nate."

He spit out the piece of wood. "Don't stop! Keep going!"

With renewed resolve she tried again. He gritted his teeth against the agony, but he never uttered a sound except for his breathing. His arms defied all temptation to move, and Tara was astonished at the control his mind exercised over his body.

"Okay, I've got it!"

He didn't hear her for everything started spinning around him, his hand slipped from the post, and he lost consciousness.

Tara was momentarily alarmed, but she calmed herself as she knew she had to do. "Don't worry, Nate. I'll take care of you." She set aside the sharp, bloody piece of lead and, holding the sides of the wound together as tightly as she could, hurriedly wrapped his forearm with a clean strip of cloth.

She looked down at her hands, which were covered with his blood, and the emotions she'd held in check for the last few minutes surfaced. Stifling her tears, she grabbed a towel to wipe her hands. Her eyes fell on the bullet again and she became curious. She filled a bowl with water and rinsed off the bullet, then held it close to the lamp to inspect it. She knew enough about ammunition from working in the store to know that it was from a .45-caliber revolver. An uneasy feeling was developing in the pit of her stomach and she quickly put the bullet down and out of her mind.

*   *   *

Tara waited and watched Nate for hours while he slept. At times he lay so still that she could hardly see him breathing and she would lay her hand on his chest to feel his heartbeat. And it was always there, steady and constant. Finally, no longer able to keep her eyes open, she laid her head on the edge of the bed to rest.

Chapter 18

Nate opened his eyes. Things were blurry but he blinked a couple of times and began to focus. He licked the inside of his dry mouth and wondered how long he'd slept. He turned his head and looked around at the cabin. From the two windows in the north and west walls he could see that dusk was settling in and all was still and quiet. Tara was asleep in the chair beside him, her head resting on the bed. He reached over and touched her tousled hair. She stirred only a little then settled back into slumber. He continued to finger her hair until she awoke.

Tara rubbed her sleepy eyes and thought for a moment. Then she remembered the events of that morning and turned to look at Nate. He looked pale and very drained but his eyes were open, watching her. She put forth a hand to feel his forehead. "The fever broke." She took hold of his hand and squeezed it. "Thank goodness," she whispered. When she felt Nate's hand clasp hers in return, a great burden was lifted; she knew he would be fine.

"You did good," he said to her.

"So did you."

"This is the second time you've saved my life. I guess I better stick close to you."

"How'd you ever survive before you were with me?" she said with a smile.

"Barely. Did you save the bullet?"

"Yes." She handed him the bullet and waited to see what he'd say.

Using his good arm he scooted himself up in the bed to a sitting position and studied the piece of lead in his palm. "This is from a revolver. The Indians only have rifles." He looked up at her. "I was shot by a white man."

His statement confirmed what she had suspected but didn't want to think about.

Just then the bray of a mule outside startled them both.

"It must be the trapper coming back," said Tara.

"Get me my gun."

When she had done so, she suggested, "Maybe I should go meet him out there first."

"No, you stay here with me. He's likely not to be happy about this." He pointed his gun towards the door. "Listen, if we get through this without any shots fired, you do the talking. You can get anybody to do anything."

Tara braced herself and watched the door. It opened and in walked a man probably in his sixties, with gray hair and a face full of short, stubby whiskers.

Upon seeing his uninvited guests, he dropped the bundles he was holding and leveled his rifle at them. Nate cocked his gun while Tara held up a hand to stop both of them.

"Wait a minute, don't anybody shoot."

"We don't mean any harm," said Nate. "We had to borrow your cabin for a little while."

"My name is Tara Sinclair. I'm from Chicago," Tara offered, trying to diffuse the situation with charm.

The man looked up and down at this young woman in a ragged blue dress, her hair tied back with a strip of leather. "Chicago!" he echoed in a gruff voice.

"Well, Timber Fork, we're both from Timber Fork."

"There's a fella in Timber Fork by the name of Sinclair, got a store."

"That's my father's store. If you've been there I may have waited on you."

"Oh, no, I would've remembered that."

She saw him eyeing Nate questioningly. "This is Nate Hunter. He used to work on my family's ranch. He got sick and we needed a place to stay. I'll be happy to replace anything we've used, when I'm able."

The trapper looked from one to the other. "Somehow I think I'm missing part of the story."

"You can have the whole story when I know that no one is going to shoot anyone," said Tara.

Nate and the trapper cautiously lowered their weapons, then the trapper pulled up a chair and sat down opposite them. He was dressed in buckskin pants, a faded and patched red flannel shirt, a dark blue neck bandana, and a coat that had seen better days.

Nate and Tara both saw his gaze fix on Nate's Cheyenne neck beads.

"Are you with him?" he asked Tara, "I mean *with* him?"

She nodded. "Yes."

The trapper narrowed his eyes at her in disapproval, almost disgust.

In her customary manner, Tara turned the conversation around and put him on the defensive. "So what is your name, and where have you been for two days, and don't you know that leaving your cabin unlocked invites bears to ransack it for food?"

Humbled a bit, he replied, "I'm Thaddeus Montgomery. I've been up at Milestone at the trading post, stocking up on supplies for the winter, and as for bears, I've not met any as bold as you." He chuckled and looked at Nate. "That was smart to get her to do the talking for you."

Nate smiled. "That's what I figured."

"Well, I s'pose I don't mind if y'all bunk here a little longer."

"Thank you, Mr. Montgomery," said Tara. "We are very appreciative."

"Thaddeus to you, pretty lady. How 'bout I rustle up some dinner while you tell me the whole story?"

131

*   *   *

The next two days saw Nate getting progressively stronger. It appeared that his arm would make a full recovery and his ability to shoot wouldn't be hindered. It was impossible for Tara to keep him down; he had to keep busy and make himself useful.

Thaddeus approached him one afternoon as he sat outside on the woodpile, whittling a piece of wood. "The girl says you're planning to pull out of here in the morning."

"That's right."

Thaddeus scratched his cheek and looked up at the sky. "The weather's not gonna hold much longer, and you've still got a lot of hard country to cross before you reach one of those Canadian fur settlements. You're likely to run into snow."

"The thought's crossed my mind."

"Well, I think you'd be wise to winter here."

"You've already been more than kind to us, Thaddeus. I know it's for her sake, not mine. And you like being by yourself. That's why you live way out here."

"What you're sayin' is true." He glanced in the direction of the cabin. "But I'm worried about her. She's young, Nate. And whatever mistakes she may have made in choosing her companions, she doesn't deserve to die out here."

Nate gave him a half smile. "You understand if she stays I stay."

"Yeah, I know. I can abide you if you can abide me."

"All right then, we'll stay. Thanks for the offer. I'll go tell her."

Later in the cabin as they each poured a cup of coffee, Thaddeus raised his for a toast. "To a mighty short winter."

Nate raised one eyebrow. "Never in Montana."

Chapter 19

As autumn was swept off of its feet by the icy white monster of winter, the trees dropped the last of their leaves and shivered against the forceful north winds. The animals of the high country readied themselves for the months ahead. Bears went into hibernation, and wolves, deer, and elk seemed to be hungrier than usual as they anticipated the coming months.

One morning Tara, Nate, and Thaddeus awoke to find the season's first snow on the ground outside. Thaddeus' mule Maxwell romped and frolicked like a colt in the powdery white stuff.

Tara had never felt so small and insignificant as she did in this vast wilderness. Here the snow was more deep, the cold more penetrating, and the wintry silence more foreboding than anything she'd experienced. On stormy days, the sky seemed to close in on them and the wind howled like an animal. The cabin was buried up to its windows in snow, and the pathway from the door tunneled through six-foot drifts. On clear days the glittering landscape and blue sky belied a harsh enemy to those not prepared to meet its grip. The names she heard Nate use for these time periods, the Moon of Popping Trees followed by the Moon of Strong Cold, added another dimension to her understanding of the seasons and made more sense to her than the conventional knowledge she was used to. She was keenly aware that mere log walls and a roof were all that came between them and certain death. She was wary yet not afraid. She felt connected to these mountains; they became a part of her soul and she could not fear what had become her ally.

Nate and Thaddeus fashioned snowshoes out of willow branches soaked in water and laced with leather. With these they spent the days checking traps, hunting, and chopping and hauling wood, while Tara tended the cabin and cooked. They were never hungry or cold inside the cabin, just tired from the work, and so they took to retiring early and arising late. Tara was given the bed, and the men slept on the floor, made plenty comfortable by an abundance of furs. On days when poor visibility prevented outside excursions, they repaired snowshoes, sewed together animal skins, dried jerky, and talked in front of the fire.

Their forced closeness allowed them to learn nearly everything about each other's lives. Nate and Tara were surprised to learn that their host had been married twice and outlived both wives and a daughter before he secluded himself to this distant corner of the earth. This wild country indeed seemed a friend to those who were running from something, and in that fact the little cabin's occupants found their common ground.

*   *   *

It was December and winter was still young in the Lewis and Clark range when Nate spent a morning chopping wood in the forest behind the cabin. Tara, with fur coverings over her wrists, palms, and leather shoes, had made several trips carrying the wood back to the woodpile. It was near noon when he quit chopping and helped Tara carry back the last of the logs and stack them.

As they neared the door of the cabin Nate pointed to boot prints in the snow leading to and from the door. "Someone's been here."

"He sure didn't stay long," said Tara as she opened the door. "I was in here just a little while ago and there was no one—Thaddeus!"

Thaddeus lay on the floor, beaten and bleeding, his left eye black and swollen almost shut. All about him the room had been ransacked. Nate and Tara rushed to his side and helped him as he struggled to rise.

"What happened? Who did this?" asked Nate.

"A low-down, dirty thief, and I'm gonna kill that son of a bitch!" He started to sway and they grabbed his arms to steady him.

"You're not going after anybody," said Nate. "I'll do that. Tell us what happened."

"You just missed 'im, Tara, when you were here last. Good thing too. He just busted in here like he owned the place. He had a gun on me and made me hand over all my tradin'-quality furs, every last hairy one." He put a hand over his ribs and took a deep breath, which appeared to be painful. "And he took your rifle."

Nate turned to see where his rifle should've been leaning against the wall, but the spot was barren.

"I seen 'im around Timber Fork before," added Thaddeus. "His name's Jed. He could see that somebody else was stayin' here. He demanded to know who it was. He seemed like he knew of you, Nate."

Nate repeated the name to himself. "I don't know him."

"I do," said Tara. She looked at Nate. "He thinks you're a renegade, and that you're in alliance with the Cheyenne." She turned to Thaddeus. "But how could he have traveled this far in this weather?"

"Aw, he's only half human," replied Thaddeus, irritated. "The other half's grizzly."

Nate was already headed for the door. Thaddeus' voice stopped him.

"He's a dangerous man, Nate. You watch yourself."

Nate's eyes registered a hint of surprise. It was the first time Thaddeus had shown any real concern for his welfare. "I will."

Nate hiked southeast, far up the mountainside, following the tracks of Jed and his mule. He could tell that Jed was heavy-set, and he was in no hurry as the tracks became more recent as Nate went on. Why he would leave a trail so carelessly was a mystery to his pursuer. Certainly anyone who could loot a cabin as quickly as this man had could travel faster than he now was. Nate concluded he must be expecting to be followed and eager for a confrontation.

Just when Nate knew he wasn't more than a half mile behind Jed, the trail became confusing. It wound in circles and made sharp turns for no reason, even backtracking in one spot. Jed knew he was being followed and Nate guessed that this was meant to be a delay being used to Jed's advantage. He hurried faster. He must not give Jed time to set a trap.

Soon Nate got his answer to the unusual behavior when the trail led to a mass of huge boulders. Jed was going to try to ambush him in the rocks. Now he must rely on his wits to keep himself out of trouble.

While he listened for the slightest sound and his eyes scanned the rocks for hiding places, he followed the tracks southward beside a rock wall until he came to a crevice wide enough to walk through. The tracks went on beside the wall, but Nate ventured into the passageway. It became thinner, then wider, and went uphill until it opened onto a flat ledge. Here the snow had been partially dusted off by wind, but he could see a footprint leading back northward. Jed had taken the long way around the rock.

Nate turned north and, after searching the rocks with his eyes for signs of Jed, climbed higher, his feet not making a sound. The trail was lost as the wind had left the rocks completely bare of snow. He ventured away from the ledge and further into the forest of boulders. Suddenly he picked up a muffled sound, like a heavy footstep, coming from the rocks above him. A second sound like the first told him where it came from and he pivoted his head to that position. In a flash he glimpsed a figure on the rocks above and caught the unmistakable shape of a gun. Nate threw himself under the nearest rock as a gunshot echoed through the boulders. He saw the puff of smoke where the bullet ricocheted off of the rock across from him. He breathed a sigh of relief.

Now Jed began shouting at Nate. "All right, renegade, come on out! I seen ya, I know where y' are."

Nate wisely kept his mouth shut. He knew better than to carry on conversation with the enemy.

"I said come on out, Nate Hunter. You're in one hell of a predicament and you know it. I got ya covered and there ain't nothin' else you can do. Now are ya chicken to come out and face me?"

But Nate knew that there was something else he could do. He simply wouldn't do anything. If he stayed under the rock, sooner or later Jed would have to come and get him. He'd have to take his eye off of Nate's rock, giving Nate a chance to make a move.

"I'm waitin' for ya!" Jed was saying. "Anytime you're ready!"

Nate was determined to beat this strange man at his own game. After all, Jed was the crook and he should be the one cowering under a rock, not Nate.

He studied his surroundings. There was a passageway around the side of the rock going back between two large boulders. The one on Nate's side of the path was the one on which the enemy stood. Quietly he eased himself out from under the rock, into the path, and stood up. He proceeded into the narrow crevice. There must not be one audible footstep, not one sliding of a stone. Jed need only walk to the edge of his boulder, peer down ten feet into the crevice, and Nate would be at his mercy. The width of the crevice even prevented any effective use of a gun.

But Nate was sure of himself. Many a time he'd been in similar situations in his familiar country where he'd had plenty of practice evading trackers.

With full confidence and agility Nate hiked through the passageway with noiseless ease. Jed kept hollering threats, which Nate didn't mind. The voice told him precisely where the thief was and assured him that Jed didn't suspect anything.

Coming out of the passageway, Nate turned to the left and began ascending the back of the boulder. On smaller rocks he found footing and handholds, which he tested first to make sure they were steadfast and could hold his weight. Upon reaching eye level with the top of the rock, he peered across at Jed, who was still watching the rock under which Nate had hidden.

Nate pulled himself up to the summit and stood on this highest rock under the wintry blue sky. With the footsteps of a cat he walked to within five yards of the stranger. Then he broke into a run, and before Jed could protect himself, Nate jumped him, grabbing his neck in a headlock. The force of the impact sent both sailing over the edge of the boulder and they crashed in the snowy clearing ten feet below. There was a mad scramble as each tried to get to his feet before the other. They both stood at once and for the first time got a good look at each other.

Nate saw before him a big, heavy man with a dark red mustache and beard. His skin was tan and weathered from the sun, and deep lines crossed his forehead under the brim of an old hat. He was a homely person, dressed in layers of leathers and furs.

"You think yer smart, don't ya?" said Jed. He took a swing with his right fist but Nate ducked, then returned the gesture effectively. "So you scored another point. Looks like I'll have to do you in proper-like." He threw a punch that landed Nate on the ground.

As a full-fledged fight broke out, they each moved as fast as angry wildcats. Jed was decisively bigger than Nate and had great strength. But whereas Jed had the bulk, Nate had the cunning, quickness, and surefootedness, and he easily held his own. He had gained experience from little crowd-pleasing skirmishes with fellow hands on the Broken Bow.

136

As the punches flew, the fight moved from the clearing to the edge of the rocks near the woods. Nate endured a kick in the stomach, then got in three good swings at Jed. The big man powerfully returned the punches.

Nate breathlessly leaned against a tree while tasting the blood from a broken lip. Determined not to give his opponent any rest, he launched another fist attack. After a minute more of rolling on top of each other in the snow and throwing punches, Nate executed a wallop that landed Jed against a boulder groaning in pain.

"You won't win, Nate Hunter!" gasped Jed between breaths. "Yer kind are nothin' but trouble."

Nate glared at him with fiery eyes. "How do you know me? Who are you?"

Jed taunted him with a snicker but said nothing.

Nate's patience had almost run out. "Listen, I want to know right now what you want with me!"

"It's very simple. You're a dirty, rotten renegade, Hunter. You may've been foolin' some o' the soft hearts in Timber Fork but you never fooled me for a minute. You belong with them scalpin' redskin friends o' yours. It was you who started that bloody battle, and I seen you tryin' to kidnap that perty little Sinclair girl too. Now nobody can find her. I'll wager she's dead and all 'cause o' you."

There was a pause as Nate took in the man's accusations. "I don't know where you get your information. But I've never seen you before and—"

"Oh, yes you have. Think! Or maybe I was too far off and you didn't git a good look at me. I was a little off aim that time, but it don't matter much now. I got me a second chance to finish the job."

"What are you talking about?"

Jed pointed to the bullet hole in the arm of Nate's jacket. "I did that to ya."

Nate was taken aback. In a few seconds he relived the moment in time when the bullet struck him, then the deadly fever. So this was the man of mystery, the white man with the .45-caliber revolver. The distaste that Nate had always harbored for all those who drove him to live the life of a fugitive was about to manifest itself in the face of this one man. He forgot about Thaddeus' furs; he was fighting solely for himself now. He unstrapped his gunbelt and tossed it aside, reached for his knife, and held up the glinting blade. "Defend yourself," he challenged.

Jed unbuckled his holster, cast it aside, and pulled his own knife. "All right, Hunter, since you're so eager to git finished off, I'll fight ya till only one of us stands. Agreed?"

"I wouldn't have it any other way."

Nate hunched over and moved in closer and so did Jed. They eyed each other cautiously, sidestepping in tight circles, looking for an opening. Finally Jed broke the pattern with swift swipes with his knife. Nate parried the blows and slashed out with his own knife.

Before long they had felt out each other's combat ploys and were moving faster. They drove for each other's throats, but neither could draw blood. Then Nate made one slow move, just one, but a dangerous mistake. He found himself caught in a headlock with a knife touching his throat. His desperate hold on Jed's wrist was all that kept the blade from his flesh. He dropped his own knife and struggled to save himself. It was two persistent forces against each other and the stronger would win. The knife pressed harder against Nate's neck, and his wrists ached trying to hold it back.

Suddenly a deafening rifle blast from nearby startled them both out of their wits, and they each heard the bullet whiz past Jed's ear. Jed's headlock on Nate loosened, and Nate took advantage of Jed's diverted attention. He thrust Jed's arm away, dropped to his knee to pick up his knife, and scrambled out from under him.

When he looked at where the shot came from, Nate was flabbergasted to see Tara atop the boulder with his rifle that she'd retrieved from Jed's mule. She held it pressed against her shoulder, level and unshaking, and worked the lever, ready to fire again. With one eye closed, she trained the sights on Jed. Nate was astounded by her action, but his mouth dropped open at what she said next.

"The next one will be between your eyes," she threatened.

Jed looked at the barrel of the gun, and when he had overcome his disbelief, he switched glances between Tara and Nate, finally narrowing his eyes at the girl. "I see," he said knowingly. "What's the matter with you, Tara? White men aren't savage enough for you?"

Nate bristled, but he wasn't about to go near Jed who still had a rifle pointed at his head.

"What would your daddy say about this?" asked Jed.

"You leave my daddy out of this," replied Tara evenly. "He's put you in your place more than once."

Jed glared at Nate. "Well, this ain't 'xactly fair, is it? If I kill you, she'll kill me."

"Tara, put the gun down," instructed Nate.

She immediately lowered the rifle.

"All the way down. I will finish this fight myself."

She reluctantly laid the rifle on the ground. Instantly Nate lunged at Jed before he knew what was coming. He yanked the man backwards over his outstretched leg and tripped him, then pounced on top of him and raised his knife. But Jed's full attention was back on the fight and he ably shoved Nate off of him.

Nate stood and backed up, slowly, while Jed advanced, making false starts to try to confuse him. Suddenly he was swooping over Nate and wrestling him to the ground. With his hand he hacked on Nate's wrist, weakening his hold on his knife. Then he grabbed it and wrenched it out of his hand.

Nate found himself lying with both wrists pinned down and staring into Jed's face. Each of Jed's big hands held a knife, either of which he could raise from Nate's wrist and bring down into his chest in a flash. Anticipating this move, Nate clawed the snow with his fingers and grabbed handfuls. Jed raised his own knife for the final stab, and with lightning speed Nate's freed left hand hurled a clump of snow at his eyes. His aim was true and Jed was momentarily blinded. Nate put a foot in his stomach and shoved as hard as he could.

Now Nate was on his feet, realizing with dread that he was without a weapon in the face of an enemy bent on killing him. Jed drew near, deftly brandishing a knife in each hand, but instead of moving away, Nate moved towards him and grabbed the hand that held his knife. Jed attempted to gore him from the other side but Nate caught hold of his wrist and held it back.

As he tried futilely to wrench his knife free, Nate discovered he would need both hands to do it. He must let go of Jed's right wrist, a risky move. But he needed his weapon more, so he dedicated both hands to the effort, retrieved the knife, and jumped aside to evade the impending blow. Out of the corner of his eye he saw Jed's arm sweep down and could hear the knife slice through the leather of his jacket. Nate felt the sting of the blade as it struck him on his left side under the ribs.

Jed backed off, the mean smile showing beneath his beard. His eyes were met by Nate's unwavering gaze, which swore vengeance. With the fury of an injured wildcat, Nate threw himself at Jed, dealing blows with his knife. But Jed held him off and Nate retreated back to the rock.

He leaned against the rock, dizzy and his head throbbing. He knew this was no way to fight a fight. He would have to get hold of himself and come up with a strategy. He needed to appear weaker than his opponent, so he breathed heavily, made no rush to get back into the fight. He staggered a couple of steps and his half-closed eyes appeared distracted, yet they followed Jed's every move. So when Jed drove for the kill, Nate came alive in a flurry of action. Jed tried to retreat but he was clumsy and slow. Nate dropped down, grabbed Jed's right leg and put a deep gash across his knee. Jed fell backward into the snow with yells of torment and cursing. Nate pounced on top of him. Jed found enough energy to throw his attacker off and struggle to his feet. He had difficulty balancing himself while the blood ran profusely down his leg.

There were signs that one or the other would go down soon. Both were weakening their defenses. Jed was more seriously injured but Nate was exhausted. He knew he must finish this fight soon before it finished him.

Taking advantage of Jed's slowed reflexes, Nate darted behind him. Before his foe could spin about to face him, Nate had thrown himself on Jed's back and locked his arms around his chest. He closed his hand on Jed's right hand and forced him to turn his own knife on himself. Nate dropped his own weapon and threw himself wholeheartedly into what he was determined would be Jed's final stand.

While Jed struggled with all his might to keep the knife from entering his chest, Nate used every last ounce of strength left to push on the knife. The cut in his side was burning worse, and every muscle in his body ached with exhaustion. He knew that if he missed this chance there would never be another for he wouldn't hold out any longer.

The shining blade quivered under the pressure while Jed's knee weakened him until finally, his hand slipped from the handle and his own knife was driven deep into his chest. He uttered a deathly gasp as Nate turned the knife. Jed staggered a step, then his entire weight fell back on Nate, who jumped out of the way.

Nate stood in the midst of the churned-up snow and looked down at his victim. The knife was sunk to the hilt in Jed's chest, but his eyes still flared as with short, painful breaths he forced out a few words.

"You stirred up a hornet's nest in Timber Fork, Hunter.... . They been goin' at it with Indians ever since you left."

Tara had arrived at Nate's side. "What are you talking about?" she questioned Jed.

"Indians got everybody scared.... . It's been real bloody.... . Lot of people are dead."

Tara's eyes widened. "Who? Who's dead?" Jed saw her but made no attempt to answer. She frantically knelt down, took a firm hold of his collar, and shook him. "Who is dead? Tell me their names."

His last breath escaped him and he lay silent. Tara stood, frustrated and upset. Nate, panting heavily, watched her, but neither said a word.

Nate painfully bent over, picked up his knife, and washed the blood off with snow. He sheathed it and staggered back to the rocks. His body felt hot but the cold winter air burned in his lungs and made him nauseated. He slid his hand into his jacket and felt his bleeding cut. It was about two inches long and not deep but the freezing chill heightened its sting. He collapsed to rest at the base of a rock.

Holding up her dress, Tara waded through the snow to his side and knelt in front of him. "Are you all right?"

He nodded. "How'd you get up on that rock without me hearing you?"

"Everything I know I learned from you."

He raised his eyebrows and smiled meekly. "I guess that's the third time you've saved my life now."

"You are a lot of work," she teased.

Chapter 20

Back at the cabin the mood was quiet and somber as Tara helped Nate wash off his knife wound and hold a wet rag against his bloody bottom lip. Jed was dead but his last words still echoed after him.

"You're thinking about what he said about the situation in Timber Fork, aren't you?" Nate finally asked.

"Yes," replied Tara as she poured him a steaming cup of coffee.

"You needn't worry. I know your family's fine."

"How do you know?" She sat across from him at the table, eager to talk about it, earnestly seeking any form of reassurance.

"Because they live in the town, and the cavalry's there."

"But there's a great number of Cheyennes in the Territory. The town was already afraid of a massacre before I was captured. I knew that they were there for you, not us. But now after the attack..." She shook her head. "I never even thought about the consequences until now. But you would've known that the Indians would want revenge. I know you've thought about it, haven't you?"

He didn't like the sudden accusing tone in her voice. "I have, but I don't believe a word of what Jed said."

"Why would he lie about that?"

"Because that's how he was. My kind offended him, and he wanted to turn you against me."

Thaddeus discreetly donned his coat, picked up his rifle and slipped outside.

"Maybe, but that doesn't make me less afraid. I don't want to abandon the plans we've made, but I need to know, Nate. Papa may have been involved in the fighting, Mr. Curtis too."

Nate looked away from her and uneasily rubbed his forefinger over a crack in the table. "You don't know what you're asking."

"Yes, I do. You can come into town with me. It's time for you to face the people and explain yourself. I will stand by you, I promise."

"I know you would, but it's not enough."

She reached across the table to grasp his hand. "Please, Nate."

There was a long pause. She could see that he was deeply troubled.

"I would never deny taking you home," he said at last, "and I'll do that when the snow breaks. If there's any pain and suffering you can take care of it, if there's any loss you can grieve it, but I won't stay with you."

"What are you saying?"

"There's no place for me there."

"But there could be—"

"No, Tara, you have to choose between me and your family."

141

"Don't ask me to make such a choice," she replied, her voice quivering.

"You made it once before, when you came with me."

She walked to the fireplace and stood watching the glowing embers. "Did I ever tell you that I saw my aunt and uncle's bodies when they were brought back from the Broken Bow?" she asked, fighting back tears.

He shook his head.

"They didn't want me to, but I did." She gritted her teeth in anger at the memory of it. "They had both been stabbed more than once, and they were burned so that the only way we could recognize them was by pieces of their clothing."

Nate bowed his head, sickened by the horror of what she'd seen.

"You understand what I'm afraid of?" she continued.

"I'm truly sorry you have those memories."

"But you still won't come with me into town." He wouldn't answer and she covered her eyes with her hands. Then, while tears coursed down her cheeks, she removed the rabbit's-foot charm from around her neck and placed it on the table in front of him.

Crestfallen, Nate beheld the charm for a moment, then picked it up and started for the door. He looked back at her. "Jed only wanted to divide us. It looks like it worked." He picked up his rifle and opened the door. "I'll be back before dark."

*　*　*

Tara spent the next hour tortured by her thoughts. She contemplated the unsavory man who had crashed into their winter solace, bringing disturbing news of home, which now seemed ever so far away from this serene place. Now she had hurt Nate, and for what? A phantom fear originated by a man she knew couldn't be trusted. Thaddeus' return didn't help matters. He spoke not a word, but she knew he was aware of the situation and she knew he had an opinion. She finally asked him for it.

"Well, if you were my daughter, I'd want you home," he said. "But I have to say, I think Nate's right about your family being all right. The cavalry would've known what they were getting into when they attacked the Indians. That place would've been heavily fortified. Ain't no doubt in my mind that your people are fine."

Her eyes reflected her gratitude for the comfort his words brought to her. Now she knew what she had to do, and she wasn't going to wait for Nate to come back to do it. She bundled up in her coat and, in the face of Thaddeus' disapproval, ventured out into the snow and began following Nate's tracks. They led her to the river, then turned north and followed beside it.

The sound of the rushing water was absent as the river was frozen except for a thin stream out in the middle. She followed the top of the bank as it rose steadily higher above the river.

She had hiked at a brisk pace for nearly half an hour when the trail opened onto a large, round meadow. Crossing this white field, Tara felt small against the great umbrella of cloudless blue sky. The snow was flat, marred only by the solitary pair of tracks that seemed to go on infinitely. The fir trees and leafless aspens loomed across the meadow, their topmost branches reaching to touch the heavens. The more Tara walked, the more she seemed to stay in one place. She was weary and her feet were cold, but she plodded on as fast as she could.

She didn't realize the land had ascended so much until she walked to the edge of the plateau and peered over a two-hundred-foot drop. A cold wind blew up from the river below and, having no obstacle to break it, it played against the cliff freely. The rocks near the edge had been dusted bare of snow. She followed the Teton River with her eyes until its winding, threadlike course disappeared in the distance. To the northwest lay the endless expanse of the Lewis and Clark range, a whitened mass of rugged terrain stretching to the horizon. She hurried faster to catch up to Nate.

She found him sitting on a rock across the meadow in a stand of trees, a freshly killed pheasant lying on the ground at his feet. His back was turned to Tara and he didn't look at her when he spoke. "You shouldn't be walking out here without a gun."

"I know. I was impulsive, like I always am." She sat beside him, but his icy silence matched that of the atmosphere. She tried to think of a way to break it. "Thaddeus doesn't say a lot, but I know he's grateful to you for bringing back his furs. They amounted to probably half a year's worth of supplies."

Nate acknowledged her with a nod but remained somber.

"I'm so very sorry, Nate, sorry that I let the word of someone like Jed come between us."

Nate studied her face such that Tara wondered what he was thinking. Then he took the rabbit's-foot charm from inside his jacket and held it out to her. "You want this back?"

She reached for it only to have him snatch it away. She looked on, dejected, as he walked to the edge of the cliff and threw the small object out into the wind where it quickly vanished.

"You presume a lot, don't you?" he said, walking back to her. "Sure, it was just a silly old rabbit's foot. But when I gave it to you I counted it next to sacred. And when you gave it back, it was like you were throwing away everything we had. You tore my heart to pieces, Tara. It wasn't just because you wanted to go back. It was that you didn't trust me. You made me equal to that lying thief who shot me once and then tried to kill me today. And I know you wished I left him alive so he could tell you more of his lies and tear you away from me."

Tara was at a loss for words after this scolding, and she took a moment to gather her thoughts to respond. "Is that what you think?" Tears stung her eyes and she fought to quell the lump in her throat. "I followed you to that fight this afternoon because I knew how much Jed hated you, and I knew how dangerous he was. And I was not for anything going to sit in the cabin all afternoon waiting to see if you were going to come home or not." She couldn't control her emotions any longer. "When I saw you fighting I was more scared than I've ever been before. Of course, I didn't let it show. I had to keep a steady hand on the rifle, and I was prepared to pull the trigger on him if I had to. I know it wouldn't have been a fair fight, but I didn't care. All I cared about was that you were safe." Not wanting him to see her face, she turned away and quickly began retracing her path back to the cabin.

"Tara," he called after her. She stopped and he went to her and took her in his arms. "Forgive me," he whispered as he hugged her tightly.

"There's nothing to forgive." She moved back to look at him. "I came here to tell you that you don't need to take me back to Timber Fork in the spring. When I decided to come with you I knew that I could be putting myself at risk for many dangers. That's part of life out here. And you've risked so much for me. I know you turned yourself over to the Indians for me."

He beheld her in surprise. He had never mentioned it to her.

"Yes, I know." She smiled. "There's no way that the Indians could've ever captured you. Anyway, part of the sacrifice means leaving my home behind, not knowing what goes on there, not fretting about things I can do nothing about. My place is with you, no matter what."

He turned away and stood silently for a while. "No, Tara, that shouldn't be part of the sacrifice. I was angry when you mentioned going back because it's not what I wanted. But it's what we need to do. If we're ever to live like normal people, if we're ever to run a respectable ranch..." He looked deep into her eyes. "If we're ever to have a family, I can't be on the run, living like a fugitive. Like you said, it's time for me to go back, and that's what we're going to do."

"I know this is hard for you," she replied. "I don't pretend to know how much, but it will be all right."

He collected his rifle and pheasant and they started on the trail back to the cabin.

"So tell me," Tara began, "when you were going to take me back home and then leave me there, just how far away were you going to go?"

"Probably not very," he laughed. "I never seem to get too far away from where you are."

Chapter 21

Winter held its tight grip on the wilderness until mid-April before subsiding to make way for spring. It was the Moon of Greening Grass, and a fresh, new land began to emerge from the silent, snowy landscape. The ice in the Teton River gradually thawed and the river ran fast and overflowing with melted snow, a natural irrigation system that quenched the thirst of an awakening land. Tender green leaves sprouted where only barren, skeletal branches had been. The air was penetrated with the scent of green, growing things and with the chattering of squirrels and the chirping of birds.

The arrival of spring signaled the time for Tara and Nate to leave Thaddeus' plain and simple hospitality, a moment that proved more sentimental to Tara than she had anticipated. With this ramshackle cabin as a home, she had seen the wilderness at its threatening worst and at its majestic best, and she felt a measure of pride at having endured it for so many months. She sensed that she had experienced the winter and the mountains in a way that she never would again but in memory, and she was somewhat reluctant to put time and distance between her and this place.

Nate and Tara packed food, blankets, and ammunition into deerskin packs that Tara had sewn from a winter kill, then they tied them onto the mule which used to belong to Jed.

"We are obliged to you for putting up with us all this time, Thaddeus," said Nate as they stood on the banks of the Teton River.

"Aw, it was nothin'. It almost makes me wanna pick up stakes and go somewhere more populated. Almost, not quite."

"Well, if you do," Tara said, "you're welcome to visit us in Timber Fork. We still owe you for things we used and you can collect when you come into the store."

"I may just do that next time I'm in town. You take care of yourselves."

So it was back across the high country again, only this time it looked very changed from the first time they had seen it in the fall. Warmer weather softened the atmosphere and graced it with a different kind of beauty. Here and there a patch of snow lingered, livening up the greens and browns with a flash of brightness.

Late in the afternoon of the first day, Nate and Tara discovered that they were not alone in this vast country. They happened upon Indian moccasin tracks and, leaving the mule tied up, felt compelled to follow them until they were led to the outskirts of a camp. As they spied five tepees through the trees, Tara became leery of being so close.

"Cheyenne! Nate, let's get out of here," she said in a voice just loud enough to make Nate uneasy.

"Shhh, not so loud," he whispered. He studied the camp a little longer. "They're not Cheyenne. I think they're Arapaho, allies of the Cheyenne. It must be a hunting party."

"We have no business here, Nate. Let's move on."

"Not just yet. I'm curious. Let's get a closer look."

Despite Tara's objections she found herself being pulled very near to the camp. Kneeling behind the bushes they got a better view of the site. To the left of the tepees was tied a string of colorful and spirited ponies. Tara immediately noticed them and, after looking at Nate, found that they had captured his interest also. In fact, he seemed to be paying more attention to them than they were worth as he looked at each one and sized them all up.

"I got an idea," he whispered, cautiously standing up and motioning for her to follow. "Come on and I'll tell it to you."

Whatever the idea was, Tara knew she didn't like it, but she followed him through the forest to the small clearing where they'd left the mule.

"How would you like some horses to ride home?" he asked.

"I would love a horse. Do you think they would take the mule in trade?"

He chuckled. "A mule for two horses? I don't think so."

"Well, I won't let you steal them."

"They have plenty. They won't miss two. It's only fair to us."

"If it's so fair then why don't you ask for the horses?"

Nate idly scratched his neck. "Because we don't have enough to trade for them."

Tara folded her arms and rolled her eyes.

"Oh, Tara, it's like a game to them. Among Indians, taking horses is an act of bravery and worthy of honor."

"You'll have no honor if you get caught."

Nate grasped her shoulders. "Honey, if I thought I was going to get caught I wouldn't do it. And just think how much faster we can get home on horseback."

The thought of it pleased Tara, but she didn't realize she was smiling.

Nate's face lit up and he slapped her arm jovially. "It's settled then. We'll stay here till nightfall, then I'll leave the rifle with you while I get the horses. You might want to rest up 'cause we'll be riding for a while after sunset to put some distance between us and the Indians."

That evening as the sun was setting, Nate was lurking at the edge of the Arapaho camp, waiting until there was enough darkness to cover him. All became quiet as the Indians settled into their tepees, save for two guards who patrolled the camp. After determining the whereabouts of each guard, Nate skirted the edge of the clearing in total silence, making his way to where the horses were standing. There were about fifteen ponies tied to trees in groups of two and three, contentedly munching on clumps of grass, unaware of the intruder. There was a brave keeping watch on the other side of the horses, and Nate concluded that he would be the only guard to worry about.

Using the trees for cover, Nate sneaked as close as he could on foot, then he dropped to his stomach and used his elbows to pull himself into the clearing. He slowed down as he neared the first group of horses so as not to spook them. The first one, a little roan mare, was a nervous creature and began to stomp impatiently as she eyed the person coming near her. Her behavior drew the attention of the guard, who began to walk in Nate's direction. Nate quickly shuffled past the fidgety mare and moved daringly close to the front hooves of the next horse. From underneath the horses' bellies he saw the feet of the brave approaching and he flattened out on the ground with arms outstretched.

The roan quieted down and soon the brave was satisfied that all was well. When the guard moved away and Nate could breathe again, he nimbly stood and began to stroke the muzzle of the horse under which he had lain. It was a sleek, bay-colored appaloosa and would make Nate a suitable mount. As he continued petting and whispered soothingly in the horse's ear, he slithered his other hand up to the branch and untied the rope. He led the animal to the next tree further back where more horses were tied, taking time to scoot stones out of the way with his heel to prevent his new charge from kicking them.

The first horse at the next tree was a little brown and white pinto. Using the same procedure, Nate slipped the pinto's rope from the branch into his hand.

Now Nate's only aim was to make a fast, clean getaway. He remembered a simple trick he had used several times before to throw off trackers. He picked up a good-sized stone and hurled it across the clearing where it landed in the brush and caused a sound loud enough to warrant the guard's checking into it. With the guard's attention diverted, Nate headed for the woods with both horses in tow.

Tara impatiently sat waiting in front of a small bonfire, the rifle laid across her knees. The sound of a soft breeze hissing through the trees and the noisy chirping of crickets filled the night as she listened for unusual sounds and kept her eyes fixed in the direction Nate had taken a while before. Suddenly she heard brush crackling and swung the rifle into position. While she kept a nervous finger on the trigger and strained her eyes to see through the dark, the noise drew nearer and soon Nate's face appeared in the firelight's glow.

Nate abruptly stopped with the horses. "I'm not too keen on being at this end of a gun." His eyes sparkled mischievously.

Tara laughed as she put the gun down and walked to the horses. "Oh, Nate, they're beautiful!" She petted the pinto and asked, "Is this one for me?"

"Yep. Of course, if the colors aren't right I can go back and trade it for another."

Tara gave him a sidewise glance. "Don't get too cocky. Let's ride."

She put out the fire while Nate attached the loose end of the pinto's lead rope to the halter to make a rein. They retrieved their belongings from the mule and turned the animal loose to fend for itself.

The full moon acted as their guide as they rode southward to the top of a ridge. After two hours of riding they watered and tied the horses and set up camp for the rest of the night in a hidden thicket.

By midmorning the next day they had turned southeastward and were riding back down the ridge. Steadily they traveled until they reached an overlook from which to view the valley below.

It was a hilly valley with few trees. The streams crisscrossing it were overflowing with the spring thaw and only a few clouds dotted the sky.

As they studied the valley Tara saw a serious look break on Nate's face and followed his gaze to the northeastern section of the valley. "What is it?" she prompted.

"I see the Arapaho. They're traveling south, single file."

Tara saw the tiny dots of the horses moving slowly in a procession. "They'll be going right across our path."

"Yep. And that could be a problem."

"Why? Can't we just wait for them to go by?"

"We could, except that something's not right about this. I expected us to be followed. Unless those Indians are meant to be a distraction so we wouldn't see something a little closer like..." He pivoted his eyes towards the foot of the mountain on their left as if he knew what to look for. "... like a bunch of braves hot on our trail."

Tara looked at where he pointed. "I don't see anything."

"A couple miles away down there." He looked back at the main party to the northeast. "It's a trap. They probably suspect which way we're going."

"Oh, no, Nate. What are we going to do?"

"We'll have to make a run for it and reach those mountains across the valley before the main group goes by. Are you ready?"

"I guess so."

"Come on then. We'll make it home by tomorrow night yet." He helped Tara mount the pinto then he mounted the appaloosa. "And they won't get our horses either."

"You mean their horses," Tara reminded him.

"I didn't see any Indians doing without. No reason we should."

They began to make their way down the mountain, but the going was slow for steep trails and loose rocks hindered the horses, and many times they had to detour to avoid thick brush. But once in the valley they galloped much of the way, stopping only to rest the horses occasionally. They kept their course headed southeast to better their chances of crossing the main group's path before the

148

trackers caught up. But the valley was wide and the Arapaho had covered a lot of ground while Nate and Tara were still on the mountain.

Still a mile away from the crossover point it was obvious to Nate that they would not make it in time. "Damn it!" he said as he pulled up his horse. "Of all the fool predicaments to get into."

"Why don't we just give them back the horses, Nate?"

"And say what? That we found them and were bringing them back to them? We'd be in trouble for sure."

"I have an idea," offered Tara, hoping her suggestion would reach to Nate's caliber for crafty thinking. "We could turn south and ride in a wide circle around the valley. That will keep the trackers behind us, and by the time we get back here, the main group will have gone by and we can cross over behind them."

Nate laughed and Tara was embarrassed. Then he said, "It's lucky I have you along. Let's do it."

Tara smiled and kicked her horse into a full gallop beside his. After riding south for almost half an hour, they turned west and began to circle the valley, keeping an eye out for the trackers. To remain unseen they stayed far enough ahead and hidden in the hills so that the braves following would have to rely solely on their trail.

When they returned to the northeast edge of the valley two hours later, the Arapaho had long since gone past. Nate and Tara were grateful to enter the cover of the forested mountains on the other side. High up in the mountain they looked back the way they had come, but there was not an Arapaho in sight. Relieved that the trackers had given up and rejoined the main party, they made camp for the night.

*   *   *

Sometime in the night Nate was awakened by something yet he didn't know what. He looked over at Tara sleeping undisturbed beside him. He put an ear close to the ground and listened. He could feel the vibration of approaching horses. Then the subtle call of a hoot owl drifted through the trees. It sounded out of place in the otherwise still night. Suddenly Nate was wide-awake. He knew an owl when he heard one and this was no genuine owl. It was the disguised signal of a brave who had picked up a trail.

He reached for Tara and shook her awake. "Tara, come on, we gotta get outta here fast," he urged.

"Why? What is it?" her sleepy voice asked.

"There's no time to explain. Just get on the pinto and ride." He helped her roll up her blanket and mount the horse. "Don't stop for anything," he instructed as he slapped the pony's flanks. "I'll catch up as soon as I put out the fire."

149

While Tara and the pinto disappeared into the woods, Nate doused the smoldering embers with dirt. Knowing it would be impossible to hide all evidence of the camp, he picked up his rifle and untied the appaloosa. His horse had already started cantering in the direction Tara had taken when he leaped and slid onto its back. Within minutes he caught up to Tara.

"I bet those Arapahos have been on our trail all night," said Nate when they stopped to get their bearings. "They're trying to wear us down."

"Well, they're doing a good job. We can't keep this up much longer, Nate. We'll get lost."

Nate pointed through the dark. "I see some rocks in there. Let's look around and see if there's a place to hide."

They rode for a few minutes around the rocky area, but it was soon obvious that the ground was too steep and rigorous for the horses to travel hastily.

"We'll have to leave the horses here and go up on foot," declared Nate.

"But the Indians will get them."

"I know and I'm sorry. But we've got to think of ourselves now."

They tied the horses in an obscure spot, and with belongings in hand they ventured further up the slope.

They hadn't gone far when they happened upon a broad crevice in the rocks. It was surrounded by foliage and seemed to Nate to be an ideal place to hold out until daybreak. With some coaxing, Tara followed Nate into the ominous darkness, gripping his arm tightly.

The crevice turned out to be a small cave, the height of it just a few inches above their heads, and pitch black inside. After listening intently and sniffing the cold air, Nate pronounced, "There're no dangerous animals in here." He felt his way warily along the uneven rock wall and helped Tara along behind him until they reached a far corner. Here they stopped, shed the packs and rifle, and sat down.

They heard the Indians ride up outside. Nate and Tara were surrounded by the drumming of horses' hooves and felt their vibration as the braves rode back and forth on the ground above their heads. Then came the familiar hoot owl signal again.

"They found the horses," whispered Nate. He lifted the rifle and pointed it toward the entrance. But soon silence settled throughout the cave.

"Are they gone?" asked Tara.

"Shhh." Nate heard the soft pat of a brave's feet as he dismounted from his horse. "They'll probably stick around till morning and try to pick up our trail again. We'll just stay put for now."

They sat in the dark and waited. An hour went by and then another. It became uncomfortable sitting pressed against the cold and clammy rock wall, but just the same they became drowsy and Tara busied herself dreaming of other places she'd rather be.

It was close to dawn when they were jerked to sudden alertness by the pawing of horses' hooves on the ground above. Nate straightened up and pointed the rifle at the entrance. Suddenly a large rock tumbled over the edge of the cave's roof outside and fell before the entrance. This started a thundering avalanche of smaller rocks, which shook the earth. Nate dropped the rifle and grabbed Tara. He shielded her as best he could with his own body as stones and dirt were jarred loose from the ceiling of the cave and fell upon them.

The avalanche was over as quickly as it began, but Nate and Tara held still for a moment to be sure.

"Are you all right?" Nate inquired.

"Yes," Tara's small, shaky voice answered.

Nate rose and went to the entrance to investigate. A moment later his voice echoed through the darkness to Tara. "The entrance has fallen in. We're lucky the whole cave didn't collapse."

"You mean we're trapped?"

"For a little while, I guess."

"Nate, what are we going to do?" She fought to keep the anxiety out of her voice. "It's like being sealed in a tomb. And it's so dark." She heard Nate's footsteps coming back, then felt his arms enfold her as he sat down next to her.

"It's okay, Tara. We will get out of this, I promise. We'll just sit tight and wait for the sun to rise. When the light comes through we'll be able to see where there's an opening."

His confidence bolstered Tara immensely, but Nate wasn't anywhere near as self-assured as he pretended to be. He kept his doubts to himself as he sat back and caressed her shoulder, cursing himself for getting them into this lousy situation.

Before long light began to squeeze in through tiny holes between the rocks in the entrance. Nate and Tara could see the sky through the holes but there would definitely be no crawling out. They would have to remove the rocks one at a time, thus risking another avalanche inside the cave.

They anxiously started the grueling task, throwing aside heavy stones until they sweated. They had not progressed far when Tara noticed it was lighter inside the cave. She looked down at her hands and dress and knew that the light which made her see them was coming from somewhere other than the small holes in the entrance. She turned around, and a beam of dim light streaming in from the upper southeastern corner caught her eye.

"Nate, look!"

He went over to inspect her discovery and found an opening wide enough for a person to fit through. "You're wonderful, Tara. We can make it through here."

"It's funny we didn't see it before."

"Just didn't think to look for it I guess. I'll go up first and see about the Indians." Spurred on by Tara's impatient excitement he climbed the rocks along the cave wall and poked his head through the upper entrance.

He couldn't hear anything to tell him Indians were present but he wouldn't trust that presumption without having a look with his own eyes. Such a look produced the sight of the flaxen hooves of an Indian pony through the bushes atop the cave. He lowered his head back underground. "They're still here," he told Tara. "Listen, I'm going out there and giving 'em a chase to see if I can't shake 'em. I'll come back for you as soon as I can. Keep the rifle handy."

He pulled himself back up and noiselessly eased his whole body out of the opening onto the grass. He hurried into hiding behind the nearest rocks and circled around to the north, taking cover between open spaces where he could.

The day had dawned fully and the braves had begun searching for signs of their horse thieves when Nate stood ready for a chase near the woods fifty yards north of the cave. "Hey, over here!" he shouted, waving his arms above his head.

All four braves whirled around and saw him, then mounted their horses and started after him.

Nate turned and ran like wildfire through the forest. As the thunder of hooves drew nearer he swerved to the left and dove headlong into the deep brush, hoping there were no snakes resting where he landed. Then he rolled under the nearest bush and waited.

The Indians hesitated near him but went on past. Careful to time his next move to where the braves were far enough away but hadn't discovered their mistake yet, Nate jumped up and continued running through the brush in another direction. His pursuers became wise to his trick and turned back.

Nate managed to stay far enough ahead of the horses, which were conveniently hampered by the underbrush. When he reached a cove a half mile away, he was breathless but there was no time to rest. He found a cluster of cottonwood trees, an excellent place to bewilder his followers. He stopped at the first one, leaped up, and caught hold of the first branch. With agile movements he climbed up and out onto a far-reaching limb. From there he sprang across to a branch of another tree. He went on in this manner, suspending his trail above the ground, until he climbed down from the fourth tree. He hoped that would hold the Indians for a while and give him a chance to catch his breath.

He trotted back into the woods where he found a temporary hiding place in a shaded thicket. As he rested he could hear the braves poking around the cottonwoods. He knew they would unravel the trail in less time than it took him to lay it down, so he must move on.

He sneaked as quietly as possible from the crackling bushes and started northeast down the side of a ridge. He picked up the rushing sound of a river and the smell of fresh water and followed it until he reached the banks where he viewed the beautiful blue-green waters of a tributary of the Teton River. He thought fast for he was leaving an obvious trail in country unfamiliar to him and he must come up with a final trick, one that would throw the trackers off for good.

A little ways upstream Nate saw what he needed, a colossal cottonwood tree with an uppermost limb hanging out over the water. He walked across the rocks by the river's edge, taking big bounds over bare, muddy spots and picking up stones and leaving his footprints under them where he could. He made it to the tree in this way, then shinnied up to the first branch. As nimble as a slender cougar he glided from limb to limb until he reached the topmost one. He eased out onto the branch and looked down at the river below. From this vantage point it seemed much higher than it had from the ground.

He scanned back up the ridge and saw brush moving close to the top where the Indians rode. He looked again at the water and decided he must get it over with before his hesitation got him caught. He took a deep breath, let go of the twigs and leaf clusters that supported him, and dove into the river. When he hit the frigid water the force of impact drove him deep below the surface. When he finally fought back to the top, the river had already carried him thirty feet. He struggled to stay afloat in the swift currents while swimming for the other side.

A few minutes later, water-logged and breathless, his ammunition wet, he drug himself out on the opposite shore and plodded back upstream to watch what the Indians' reaction would be.

The Indians trotted their horses to the riverbanks and paced back and forth. Nate saw one brave dismount, pick up a stone and point to the footprint underneath it. He then led the others to the big cottonwood. After looking up into it and out at the river, they mounted up and started back the way they had come.

Upon seeing that the braves had given up, Nate wasted no time getting on his own way. His next miraculous feat must be to make it back to the cave before the Indians did. He remembered from his and Tara's trip in the fall that this river thinned out less than a mile southwest of the place he had just crossed. He would cross down there and make a mad dash for the cave.

When he arrived at the cave he was too thrilled to see that he had beaten the Indians to notice anything else. So as he knelt by the opening in the rocks to summon Tara and heard his name called from a different direction, he was surprised. He looked up on the mound above the cave to see Tara astride the pinto with the rifle and deerskin packs and holding the reins of the appaloosa.

"You're losing your cleverness," she said with a smile. "If I was an Indian I could've shot you."

Nate laughed. "And if you were an Indian I wouldn't be coming back for you. What are you doing with those horses? Haven't we invited enough trouble?"

"The Indians left them behind to chase you. I figured we should use them as long as we could."

He gave her a sidewise glance. "You know what that means. You share the guilt with me now."

They took an indirect route to the river, then waded the horses along in the shallows, leaving no trace for the Arapaho to follow. A couple of hours after their exit on the opposite shore, they stopped in the forest for a noon rest.

* * *

The cawing of a noisy crow awoke Nate. He looked up through the trees and found the sun, which indicated it was two hours past noon. Nate couldn't believe his eyes. Two hours he'd slept; it seemed like only a few minutes. And where was Tara? He called her name twice but there was no answer.

Still rubbing the sleep from his eyes he picked up the packs, untied the horses, and started leading them over Tara's trail. It was not unlike her to venture off on her own once in a while, if she heard something, if she wanted to see a view, or was curious. But his thoughts raced as he picked up his stride. Something had to be wrong; she had been gone a while. It was small comfort to know that she had the rifle, but he tried to remember how many bullets were left in it.

Suddenly Nate stopped dead in his tracks. About a hundred yards in front of him, well-hidden in the brush, he made out the tops of lodgepole tepee frames. How in the world did he and Tara always end up in the same place as these people, he wondered. And now he was about to meet them for this was where Tara must be. She would've come upon it unexpectedly as he had.

He moved in closer to the group of tepees. He heard a sudden burst of laughter and talking and turned to see a pale-faced Tara standing silently with a hoard of jolly and entertained braves swarming over her. They had taken the rifle from her and now one young brave began to finger her light brown locks. She furiously slapped his hand away, drawing more laughter from them.

Nate dropped the packs and the horses' lead ropes and began walking towards the group. "Hey, back off!"

The startled braves whirled to face the intruder and their smiles faded away. The one with the rifle pointed it towards Nate, and all of them assumed a cautious stance. Nate raised his arms to show his hands were empty, a peaceable gesture that relaxed the braves just a little.

"Easy now, I'm not here to cause trouble," said Nate. "Anyone here speak English?"

A particularly stern-looking Arapaho stepped forward, his dark, muscular body dressed in leather clothes with painted designs.

"I am Nate Hunter, Eagle Shadow of the Northern Cheyenne."

"We have heard the Cheyenne speak of you, Eagle Shadow. But we did not know it was you who took our horses. We understand why the Cheyenne have such respect for you."

"Give her back the rifle," said Nate, pointing to Tara.

The English-speaking brave indicated to the other brave to do as Nate said, and when Tara had been given the rifle back, she rushed to Nate's side. Another one of the band went to retrieve the appaloosa and the pinto and lead them away.

"Why did you take our horses?" asked the brave.

Nate thought fast. "Well, I'm on a long journey to take this woman to her people. She is very important. But she couldn't walk much further, and when she saw your people on horses she begged me to take some for us."

Tara's jaw dropped but she said nothing.

The brave looked skeptical and Nate offered a smile. "Well, just look at her. I mean, could you say no?"

For the first time the brave's tough exterior cracked. "I see Eagle Shadow is a slave to a woman," he said with a laugh.

Nate feigned embarrassment, which turned to sheer discomfort when he saw Tara glaring at him. He quickly looked away from her.

"You can have the horses," the brave was saying, "if you trade something for them."

Nate nodded his agreement and went back for the packs. He opened them and began taking out articles for the brave to inspect. "I can spare one blanket, some food, a penknife. And how about this coat?" He held out Tara's red coat. "I'm sure your wife or daughter would like to have this."

Tara watched with a pang of regret as her coat was handed over, but she wanted the horses more so she kept silent.

"All that," said the brave. "And your gun." He pointed to Nate's Colt .45.

"Uh-uh," replied Nate. "Not the gun."

"Then give the bullets for it."

"The bullets are no good to you without the gun."

"We can use them to trade."

Nate impatiently emptied his gun and cartridge belt and gave the contents to the brave.

"These horses are some of our best. Give the bullets from the rifle also."

"They're not worth that much."

"No bullets from rifle, no horses."

Nate looked down at the ground and thought it over.

"Isn't there something else we can give?" asked Tara.

"No, he's not going to budge."

"Then don't do it. Let's just go." She looked on, appalled, as Nate emptied the rifle, discreetly leaving one bullet in the magazine, and delivered the contents to the brave's waiting hand.

The brave motioned for the horses to be brought back to Nate and Tara, who immediately gathered what was left of their belongings and mounted the horses.

They bid a polite farewell to the Arapaho and rode away from the camp. No sooner were they out of sight of the Indians than Tara pressed Nate. "Why did you do that? They know we have no ammunition. They might come after us."

"Naw, they won't do that." Before she could object he reached over and grasped her hand. "Besides, we don't need the ammunition. We're going to get home tonight."

Her spirits sufficiently boosted, she smiled at him. "Eagle Shadow, huh?"

"Yeah, that's me."

*   *   *

It was late in the day when Nate and Tara guided their horses through the thick forest on Mount Defiance. It wasn't merely by chance that they rode into their old meeting spot, the Grotto. With the fatigue from the long trip curbed by the rich, beautiful sight of the waterfall, the glistening pool, and the willow tree, they dismounted for a rest.

The calming effect of the Grotto wasn't enough for Nate; he had to be in it. He took off his holster, knife belt, and jacket and with a youthful yell of glee ran and dove into the pool. Amidst Tara's laughter he rushed back out again, shivering. But her giggling subsided when she saw him coming towards her with a roguish grin. Too late she jumped up and tried to run out of his reach, but Nate was faster, and with a victorious laugh he grabbed her and swept her off her feet.

"I'm not gonna suffer this alone," he declared amid Tara's screams. He mercilessly ignored her pleas to be put down as he walked to the edge of the large, flat rock and jumped in the pool with her in his arms.

Stiff from the shock of cold water, Tara stood and pushed the wet hair out of her face. She took to slapping the water with both hands and splashing him. A playful chase resulted, and shortly Nate caught her beneath the waterfall and they fell at the water's edge inside the cave.

Temptation grabbed hold of Nate and with no warning he smothered her lips with kisses. Running his hand underneath her dress and up her thigh, he declared, "You've got goosebumps." That sly grin returned. "We better get you out of these wet clothes. The sooner the better."

Laughing, Tara gave him a shove. "I haven't anything else to wear."

Nate raised his eyebrows and whispered, "I know." He drew her face close to his and locked his lips on hers. Afterwards he moved back and lay propped up on one elbow. "I have to ask you, I know your family used to like me, but what are they likely to say about us, together?"

"Well, they probably won't be happy I ran away, but they won't have any objection to us."

"Why not? I was a hired hand."

"My family's part Irish, and in some places Irish aren't well-accepted. We're not so quick to pass judgment on others." She laid her head on his chest and felt the soft touch of his hand around her neck, and she wanted to delay the future a little longer. "Let's not go into town tonight. Let's go back tomorrow." She looked up and watched his eyes for a response. The smile he gave her warmed her body all over.

"I was hoping you'd say that," he whispered in her ear so she could barely hear him over the waterfall. He rolled her over on her back, closed his eyes, and brushed his lips across her cheek until he met her lips, passionate and inviting. In Tara's arms he could shut out the world for one more night.

They made love in the cave and later on under the willow tree while their clothes dried by the fire.

There were no evil spirits in this forbidden place, thought Tara. Anything evil lay beyond its borders, and as she lay in Nate's arms in the darkness, listening to the waterfall and watching its constant splashes by dim firelight, she wished they would never have to leave.

Chapter 22

The next morning at dawn Nate and Tara were riding into the valley south of Mount Defiance. But Nate didn't head straight for the town. Instead he aimed his direction a little westward near where Elkhorn Creek formed the boundary of the Broken Bow.

They ascended a hill peaked with weeping willow trees, and at the top they looked down at several straight rows of white tombstones about five feet apart. Suddenly Tara realized why Nate had come to the cemetery. He had never seen the graves of his parents.

They remained silent as they wandered among the rows, glancing at the names on the faces of the markers. This site was a hauntingly tranquil and lonely place set aside for resting places for the dead and memories held precious for the living. Here on the southern slope of the hill where the willows swayed softly in the breeze, the graveyard was sheltered against the forceful north winds. It had seen many a winter's snow, spring flowers, summer's rain, and colors of autumn. But now the stillness was broken by the slow, hollow thumping of horses' hooves as Nate and Tara rode by, looking for a name on a piece of wood which stood for an entire life.

Finally Nate halted the appaloosa, swung a leg over, and slid off to the ground. Tara stopped and dismounted also and took the rein of his horse when he handed it to her. He wanted to be alone. He walked to two graves that were side by side and knelt at the foot in between them. While he cradled the rifle in the crook of his arm he studied the simple markers. On them were carved the full names and date of death of his mother and father. His mother's birth date was included on her marker; his father hadn't known his birth date.

To Tara, Nate seemed like a stranger, like she had just walked up and found him here. He looked very serene, totally unaware of anything but the graves.

His inner thoughts remained a mystery to her. Maybe he was remembering the horrors of that night when as the barns and homes of old Broken Bow had burned around him, he had watched his parents fall before Cheyenne hostiles. Or perhaps he was thinking of the period since then which had changed him from an ordinary, unknown ranch hand to a fugitive sought by two peoples, when his own fierce determination had driven him on at times when, because of weariness, loneliness, and persistent trackers, he wanted to surrender his life to fate.

But whatever went through his mind, only a trace of it was revealed when he spoke, in a tone that didn't seem to be directed at anyone. "It just doesn't seem like it's been two years." He arose, walked back, and took his horse's reins from her.

"They would be very proud of you, Nate," said Tara.

Nate's only reply was a smile, and by that Tara couldn't tell whether he was glad to hear those words or if she amused him. He put his arm around her waist and they strolled on down the path, leading the horses behind them.

There was one more headstone they had to look for and they found it at the end of the same row. They knelt on either side of the grave and read the granite marker, engraved with the words:

> In memory of
> Mark Lawrence Curtis
> Born - Jan. 14, 1847
> Died - Sept. 24, 1866
> Beloved son and brother
> Though heaven welcomed you
> with open arms
> you are never far
> from our thoughts

They silently pondered a few moments, each reflecting on their own, very different memories of Mark.

Their thoughts were interrupted when Nate heard someone coming and turned to look. Tara followed his gaze and soon saw Julie Curtis strolling up the rise from the direction of the town. She wore a blue calico dress and matching bonnet, which framed her blond shoulder-length curls, and she carried a bouquet of wildflowers. She was a most welcome sight for Tara.

"Julie!" Tara called out.

Julie looked up and was stunned into silence a moment. Then the flowers slipped from her hand, forgotten, as she ran to embrace Tara. "Oh, you're home at last. How we've missed you, Tara."

"I missed you too, Julie, ever so much."

Julie walked past Tara and stood before Nate, unsure of how to respond to him.

"Hello, Julie," he said with a smile.

"Goodness, Nate, I hardly know what to say. It's been so long."

He glanced at Mark's grave. "We're sorry about your brother."

"Thank you." She, too, looked at the grave. "This isn't the first time that Indian wars have affected our family. But hopefully it will be the last."

Nate bowed his head in shame for the sorrow that his people had caused Julie.

"I don't hold anything against you, Nate. I never did." She turned to Tara. "You know Mark wanted to be an adventurer. Now he's gone on ahead. We'll catch up." She went to pick up the dropped flowers and Tara helped her place them on the grave.

"Where have you two been all winter?" asked Julie afterwards.

"We stayed with an old trapper," answered Nate. "He lives not far from Milestone."

"Way up there? And where did you get these horses? They're beautiful." She stroked the face of the pinto.

"Nate stole them from Arapaho Indians," reported Tara.

Julie cast him a sidewise glance and flashed a teasing smile. "Horse thief, huh? You can get hung for that, you know."

"But Tara didn't tell you how I traded for them."

"Oh, yes," Tara added, "with just about everything we had."

They laughed together as Nate and Tara began leading the horses down the hill towards town with Julie walking in between them.

"We heard there was trouble here," said Tara.

"Yes, there was," sighed Julie. She looked from one to the other as she relayed the story. "After the battle last September the cavalry expected the Indians to want revenge. But there weren't enough Indians left to put up a fight. They would've had to catch up with the other bands of Cheyenne that moved out before the battle and get their help. And the cavalry knew that so they sent out soldiers to block their way. Some settlers volunteered too. Well, there was a skirmish and the cavalry didn't fare too well. Several men were killed and some Indians broke through and got word to the others. Then there was a rush to get ready for massacre attempts on the white settlers. A lot of Indians came and the two sides met just outside of town. There was another skirmish, more killings, but finally, the Indians saw that the cavalry was loaded for bear so they turned and ran. We've not seen them since. The cavalry says they've left the Territory for now, but everyone's still a little nervous."

"Was my father involved?" asked Tara.

"No. His only concern was for you. He could think of nothing else."

Tara winced. "Who among the settlers was killed?"

"Jake Litton, Zack Collins, and the two Manning brothers. Then over the winter Major Elliot died quite suddenly of pneumonia."

"How awful!" Tara shook her head.

"Yes, be glad you weren't here. There for several days the whole town was scared half to death. And we were grieving over Mark. Anyway, things are better now."

"Has anyone heard from my sister?" Nate eagerly asked.

Julie stopped dead in her tracks and clapped a hand to her mouth. "Goodness, how could I forget? You won't believe it, Nate. Lena's living here again."

Nate's heart skipped a beat. "She's here? Really?"

"Yes. And she's married."

"Married!" Nate echoed.

"Lena's married?" Tara was equally surprised. "Who is he?"

Julie started walking again as she explained. "His name is Ward Taylor and he's the middle son in the Minnesota family she stayed with, and he's quite wealthy. They were married in St. Paul around Christmastime and moved here soon after. We never knew anything of it until they got here."

"Where do they live?" Nate wanted to know.

"Ah, another surprise. They bought the Split Timber off of Mr. Sinclair."

"Papa sold the Split Timber? He had never planned to do that."

Nate was pleased that Lena had made out so well. He didn't realize he was smiling so broadly until he caught Tara glaring at him.

"You needn't worry, Tara," Julie was saying. "No one will say exactly what Ward paid your father for it, but it was several thousand dollars. Your father said that the ranch was getting to be too much for him to handle what with managing the store and all, and he couldn't pass up Ward's offer."

Nate was anxious to know more about his brother-in-law. "Where'd this Ward Taylor get that kind of money?"

"He used some inheritance money for several business investments, and I guess he pocketed a lot from those. And he held some position in his father's law firm. He was studying the law himself till he came here. I'm afraid he wasn't born for the frontier though. You can tell he's never done any real work. And you should see him trying to work cattle." Julie laughed as she pictured a scene in her mind. "Lena must've had a great influence on him. Apparently he was as excited as she was to come here. He has jumped into ranch work with both feet, I'll give him that."

The group soon found themselves at the edge of town. They avoided the bustle of Main Street and chose instead to walk along the backs of the buildings.

"Well, Julie, we've talked about everyone else," said Tara. "How are you getting along?"

Julie grinned smugly. "Oh, I can't complain."

"I know that look, Julie Curtis. Who's the object of your attentions now?"

"Captain Joshua Blaine."

"The captain? How did that happen?"

"It's all your fault. Two days after you two disappeared I paid him a visit to inform him that it was useless to look for you."

"Well, thanks!" Tara teased.

"No, I mean I told him you'd gone of your own free will and would come back when you wanted to. Anyway, he invited me to dinner that night and I suppose that's where it started. Now when he gets leave he comes from Fort Mason to see me."

"Then I must meet him next time he comes."

All talking subsided as they stood looking up at the back of the Sinclair home. Tara was suddenly filled with apprehension, and upon seeing her expression, Nate smiled sympathetically.

Julie spoke softly, as if trying not to intrude on their thoughts. "You go on in. I'll stable your horses."

They climbed the steps to the door and entered the kitchen. Nate leaned his rifle against the wall and followed Tara to the doorway of the parlor. There were the imported European rug, pale green striped wallpaper, the fine plush furniture, French oil paintings, and figurines and ceramics, all familiar icons of Tara's life, which now stood in stark contrast to her illuminating experience of the last few months. And there at the big oak writing desk working on the accounting books was Edward Sinclair.

"Papa," Tara called softly as she stepped down into the parlor.

Edward looked up and appeared stunned for a moment, then without a word he dropped his pen, rushed to his daughter, and embraced her as if he would never let go. "Thank heavens you're safe. It's an answer to prayer. Why did you go, Tara, why?"

"It's—it's kind of hard to explain. But I was in good hands."

Edward looked past her and for the first time saw Nate standing in the doorway.

Until now Nate had been content to watch the reunion unnoticed, but as his eyes met Edward's he wondered what the reaction would be. But Edward simply looked back at Tara and smiled.

Just then Margaret Sinclair entered the room from the store. "Who's there, Edward?"

"Mother, I'm home."

The strain of many months seemed to flee Margaret's face in an instant as she broke into tears and ran to Tara with open arms. "At last! Darling, you had us so worried."

Edward now stood before Nate with a displeased countenance that made Nate's palms sweat. "What am I supposed to say, Nate? You stole my daughter."

Nate drew in a breath and held it.

Tara broke away from her mother's embrace. "No, he didn't, Papa. It was my choice to go with him. In fact, he tried to talk me out of it and I begged him otherwise."

In the young man's eyes Edward perceived an independent, yet lonesome look and a hope for acceptance. "Well, he did take care of you all winter and bring you home safely." He remembered the last time he'd seen Nate, at the battle on Mount Defiance. "He had a chance to kill me once but he didn't. I suppose it's incumbent upon me to forgive you for this, Nate. You were on my side. Now I will be on yours." He extended his hand. "Welcome home at last."

With all doubt now removed, Nate stepped down into the parlor. He was the same height as Edward and met his gaze resolutely as they shook hands. "Thank you, sir."

While the younger children clambered down the stairs to see Tara, Margaret came forward to greet Nate. As her eyes met his she remembered that clear, penetrating look from long ago. Still, she saw him not as the sixteen-year-old she remembered coming into the store on his birthday to buy a Colt .45 with months of hard-earned money, but as a famed mountaineer whom she had heard about but not seen.

"You remember me, Mrs. Sinclair?"

Those ordinary words spoken so nonchalantly confirmed to Margaret that this was indeed the same Indian boy from the Broken Bow. "Oh, Nathaniel, of course I remember you," she said, giving him a motherly hug. "And it's good to finally see you again. You're more than welcome in this house."

"I'm much obliged, ma'am."

Tara went to stand beside Nate. "Mother, Papa, there's something I kept hidden from you for a long time, about seeing Nate. I helped him out when the men were trying to capture him. I took him things from the store. And when I heard the men in the store talking, I told him everything they said."

There was an uneasy pause and Margaret looked at her husband, then back at Tara. "We know."

"How did you know?" asked Tara in surprise.

"Julie was a great comfort to us when you were away."

"I believe I may have done the same thing myself under the circumstances," added Edward.

*　　*　　*

That evening Nate sat down with the Sinclair family and Julie to a dinner of roast beef and gravy, potatoes, peas, applesauce, and sourdough biscuits slathered with fresh butter, honey and fruit preserves. The long, varnished oak dining table with legs carved with scrollwork was adorned with a snowy white, lace-appliqued tablecloth on which sat two silver candlesticks holding lit candles, not the rough, homemade ones Nate was used to, but smooth, store-bought ones. There were seven places set with blue-flowered china, silverware polished till a reflection was visible, and sparkling crystal goblets, all family heirlooms that had been packed cross-country from Chicago with amazing success. The pastel blue linen napkins were rolled and tied with blue satin ribbons.

Although Nate wasn't sure what the point was of tying up a napkin like a lassoed steer, he was appreciative of the effort put forth in the welcoming celebration. It was like nothing he'd seen. He could count on one hand the number of times he'd seen the inside of the mansion on the Broken Bow, and he had never partaken of a meal with Sinclairs before.

"Don't be shy, Nathaniel," said Margaret. "Eat as much as you want."

Nate caught Tara's eyes and gave her a private, sort of cocky look, and she knew exactly what he was thinking. He had finally wangled a dinner invitation, and not from her, but from her parents. She acknowledged him with a smile.

Nate was glad Margaret Sinclair had been able to procure a clean red plaid flannel shirt for him to wear and had cut a couple of inches off of his hair. He looked breathlessly at Tara across the table from him. She wore a deep red brocade dress buttoned high up the neck with a cameo brooch, well-fitted to her slender waist, and falling in graceful gathers to the floor. Her hair was loosely twisted into a bun in the back with tortoise-shell combs, and a few stray curls framed her face. He couldn't take his eyes off her and was keenly aware of the edge of her dress touching his feet under the table.

"Well, Nate," Edward's deep voice began, jolting Nate from his trance.

"Yes, sir?"

"I remember you took a bullet in the arm last September. I had wondered how you were."

"I was all right, with Tara's help. She cut the bullet out."

Every jaw dropped as they looked at Tara, much to Nate's amusement.

"It was that man Jed who shot him, Papa," said Tara. "He did it on purpose."

Edward's eyebrows drew together. "That scoundrel. I don't know what happened to him. No one's seen him around here in quite a while."

Nate very subtly shook his head to Tara, a pleading message for her not to respond. But she never noticed.

"He showed up at the cabin where we were staying and robbed and beat Thaddeus. Nate went after him. There was a fight and Jed was killed."

Everyone at the table stopped chewing at the same time and stared soberly at Nate. He wanted to shrink under the table until Edward solemnly voiced his opinion. "A barbaric kind of justice perhaps, but it sounds like he had it coming."

The patriarch of the family had spoken and the subject would not be addressed again. Everyone resumed their meal, Nate last of all.

"So, Nate, I'm sure you'll want to visit the Split Timber first thing in the morning," said Edward.

"You bet. I'm looking forward to meeting this brother-in-law of mine."

"Oh, Ward?" Edward laughed. "He's a little bit different, but I think you'll like him. What are your plans now that you're back?"

"I'd like to find work on a ranch if I can."

"Well, I don't own any more ranches, unless you consider that piece of land called the Broken Bow. But I think I know who can help you. Ward Taylor needs a good foreman to oversee the work on his spread."

Nate stopped chewing in the middle of a bite of beef and stared at Edward.

"I know it's a bigger responsibility than you're used to, but any foreman is better than none. They've gone through three already. They're in between again and trying their best to keep things somewhat organized. But with spring roundup approaching it will be hard."

Nate couldn't help but smile at the obvious. "So that means my little sister would be my boss."

Edward laughed. "Officially, yes. But you'd be the one running the operation, making decisions, and of course, you'd get to holler at the hands. And, if you squeeze him hard enough, you might be able to get a good wage. What do you think about it?"

Nate felt a surge of self-confidence. After all, the way to gain experience was by trying and doing. Then there was the look in Tara's eyes across from him. She knew as well as he that this would be only one step away from fulfilling his plans of starting his own ranch. "I think it's a good idea, if they'll agree to it. What happened to the other three foremen?"

Edward chuckled. "I think Ward tries too hard to get involved in the daily tasks."

"Let me warn you, Nathaniel," said Margaret. "Your sister will seem different to you than when you last saw her. Remember, she spent a year and a half in a big city and had a lot of adjusting to do. She attended school and was at the top of her class. She's a grown woman now and very lovely. You can be proud of her."

"Yes, ma'am, I'm sure I can."

*   *   *

The white ranch house at the Split Timber was two-story but not nearly as large as the one that used to stand at the Broken Bow. When the Sinclairs owned it, only caretakers and guests occupied it. Now as Nate stood looking up at it, it had the same stone base he remembered but sported freshly painted brown shutters. The planters around the front were well-kept and filled with rose bushes not yet in bloom.

Nate, Tara, and Edward tied their horses to a hitching post in front and walked up the steps to the porch, which ran the length of the house. They paused at the big oak door and Edward knocked. Nate held his breath, waiting for Lena to open it, but to his surprise a maid answered. She was a heavy, middle-aged woman and was wearing a plain gray dress and white apron and holding a turkey-feather duster.

She smiled broadly, showing a couple of missing teeth. "Why g'morning, Mr. Sinclair."

"Good morning, Myra. Is Lena here?"

"She shore is. Y'all step right on in and I'll git 'er for ya." The guests entered and Myra hollered to the back of the house. "Miz Taylor, y'got company!" There was no answer. "When she's a-workin' on her blanket loom it's hard to tear 'er away, but she heard me and she'll be a-comin'." She continued her dusting while the others patiently waited.

It was Nate who did the most observing. He had only been here once five years before when the hired hands of both of the Sinclair ranches had collaborated for a Thanksgiving celebration. The interior of the house looked much the same as he remembered it. The ceiling of the parlor in which they stood rose up the full two stories, and stairs along the right wall led to a balcony overlooking the parlor. The room was filled with cedar wood furniture that had been polished to a sheen, and Edward pointed out that it had been custom-made in St. Paul.

From one of the back rooms Lena appeared. She was wearing a tan dress with sprigs of pink flowers, and her long hair was braided and pinned up in the back.

"Mr. Sinclair, how nice to see..." Nate stepped into her view. By her look she obviously was not prepared for such a sight this day. But it was not a time for questions. He breathlessly called her name and they ran to each other, meeting in a tight hug.

"I'm back, Lena," said Nate after which he kissed her cheek. "I finally came back."

"Oh, Nate, I came here so excited about seeing you, and they said you were gone and no one knew where you or Tara were." She laughed. "I knew you'd come home, but I never dreamed you'd be walking in my front door this morning!"

"I never dreamed it either until yesterday. I thought you would still be in Minnesota." He stepped back to admire her. "Just look at you, Lena. You're so pretty."

"I suppose the Sinclairs told you about Ward and me?"

"Yes, and I'm happy for you."

Myra the maid, watching all of this with wide eyes, asked, "So this here's that brother of yours?"

"Yes, Myra."

"Well, son-of-a-gun." She looked Nate up and down in a manner that made him uncomfortable. "I hope we'll be seeing plenty of you."

"We certainly will," laughed Lena. She turned to Tara. "I'm glad you're back, Tara." They hugged and Lena narrowed her eyebrows at her. "What sort of lies did my brother tell you to win your attentions?"

"I think you could say we both told a few," Tara replied with a smile. "Congratulations on your marriage, Lena."

"I wish you could've been there for the wedding. It was beautiful."

"Where is Ward?" asked Nate.

"He's doing chores. He should be in any minute now. Myra, would you fix some coffee for us?"

Myra exited the room and Lena seated her guests in the parlor. She did indeed seem different as Tara's mother had said. She was refined, moved with grace, and looked every bit comfortable in a dress. Her new manner seemed natural, not pretentious or confining.

"I told your brother about your job opening for foreman," said Edward. "He's interested."

"You, Nate?"

"Well, don't look so surprised."

"I'm sorry. I guess I'm just not used to thinking of you that way. But I suppose you'd make as good of a foreman as any."

They heard someone bounding up the porch steps outside.

"Here comes Ward now," said Lena, standing up.

The door opened and in came Ward, perspiring and quite tired for such an early hour. He slammed the door, hung his hat on a nail, and looked at Lena. "Honey, why couldn't we have started a nice little chicken farm." Using his hands to indicate the size of a chicken, he continued. "They're small, more manageable, and if one becomes difficult you just twist its neck and eat it for supper."

Nate and Tara both looked away to hide their smiles.

"Ward, I'd like you to meet someone. He wants to be our new foreman. It's all right with me."

Ward sighed. "Lena, I wish you'd leave the hiring and firing all to me." His expression softened as he looked from Nate to Lena and back again, noticing the obvious resemblance. "You must be Nate."

"And you're Ward Taylor," said Nate.

"Well, I see we need no introduction," laughed Ward, extending his hand and shaking with Nate. "This is a surprise. I've heard so much about you."

"I've heard a lot about you too."

"I'm not even going to ask what it was."

He seemed very pleasant, but just as Nate had imagined, he looked like a city man who was only visiting the ranch, quite like the Chicago relatives of the Sinclairs who used to visit the Broken Bow and carry on as if they were there to watch a show. The hands all sneered behind their backs and imitated their highfalutin ways.

Ward's work clothes consisted of a white shirt and black pants held up by gray suspenders, what most ranchers saved for Sunday wear. His weather-tanned face was obviously supposed to be fair-skinned, and he had blue eyes and curly brown hair.

"I am a respecter of tradition, Nate," Ward began, "and I would've come to ask you for Lena's hand. I felt bad that that wasn't possible. Then she told me she made her own decisions anyway."

Nate looked at Lena with raised eyebrows, then he smiled back at Ward. "That's true enough."

"So what kind of wages would you expect?" Ward asked.

"Eighty dollars a month plus room and board."

"Eighty dollars! You've got to be kidding."

Nate ignored his shock. "I got my own horse. I'll train him myself."

"And you'll stay here in the house," added Lena. "We have an extra room upstairs."

"Now wait just a minute, everyone," declared Ward. "With all due respect, how do I know you're worth eighty dollars?"

"Mr. Sinclair told me a little about your operation on the way over here. You need to hire more hands. During roundups and trail drives you should have one for every two hundred fifty head of cattle."

"I was told that one for four hundred was enough," Ward countered.

"That's what most ranchers think," replied Nate. "But to avoid sloppy handling and keep tighter control—and I can tell you're a man of control, it's one for two hundred and fifty. And another thing. It's not practical to catch wild mustangs and break them. It's too hard and it takes too long. If you do a little shopping you can find good, trained mounts for fifteen dollars a head. And you don't have to employ a bronc buster."

Everyone's eyes were on Ward to see if he was duly impressed.

"Well, up-front it sounds like all you'll do is cost me money," said Ward.

Nate shrugged and started towards the door. "Suit yourself."

"Wait a minute. I wasn't through yet." Ward paused and took a deep breath. "I know about your background in ranching. It's a lot more extensive than mine. I will pay the extortion money. And I will give your advice a try."

*   *   *

The gathering dusk of that evening found Nate walking alone with Lena. Tara and her father had gone back to town hours before. He had waited for a moment like this and hoped that somehow they could bridge the gap that had separated them for nearly two years. He wanted to know for sure that she was the sister he knew and loved, that the city and life with Ward Taylor hadn't taken that wild, carefree spirit from her and locked it away in an inaccessible place.

The evening was quiet except for the chirping of crickets as the two of them walked by the corrals. In one, a sleek black stallion pranced back and forth, his nose testing the wind for signs of mares. Scattered about were a few oak trees, their ghostly figures silhouetted against the sky, where stars were popping into view one by one.

"Hard to believe you two bought this place all yourselves," said Nate as they sat down on the back end of a wagon partially filled with hay.

"Sometimes I think we bit off more than we can chew. But Ward is determined to make a go of it and so am I."

Nate hesitated. "How is it that you ended up with him? He's not like you at all."

Lena smiled and nodded. "I know Ward came as a surprise to you, and it's true he doesn't seem to fit in here in Montana. But he's a good man, Nate. He really is. Things were kind of hard for me in St. Paul. A few people didn't take kindly to an orphan Indian girl among them. There were some threats, even against the Taylor family. But Ward always stood by me, more than anyone ever did before. There were some boys at the school who..." Her voice caught for a moment. "They would've had their way with me, and Ward just appeared at the right time."

Nate's eyebrows drew together in concern but he let her go on.

"He sacrificed friendships for me. I felt guilty. I wanted to come back here, but I didn't have anything to come back to. Then Ward asked me to marry him." She shook her head. "Poor Ward, he didn't think I'd say yes. But he said he'd bring me back here and talk to Mr. Sinclair about the ranch."

"So you married him for the money, because he takes care of you."

"No, not for the money. Because he was always there for me. He became my friend."

"Do you love him?"

"Being with him here, working together, I have come to love him."

"Have you, really?"

"Yes."

Nate was satisfied with the certainty of her answer and he viewed Ward a little differently now. He also had a different view of her life experiences since bidding her a sad and hurried farewell in their barn on the Broken Bow. Her life in the city had not at all dulled her spirit; rather, it had toughened her in ways Nate had neither expected nor wanted. But she was not fragile and he knew he didn't need to worry about her.

"Isn't it strange how things happen?" said Lena. "I mean, about you and Tara Sinclair, the boss's niece whom you couldn't stand the sight of?"

Nate laughed and bowed his head bashfully. He still found it hard to talk about his own affairs of the heart with his sister.

"Come on, admit it. You're smitten. You're clay in her hands."

"Now quit it."

"Are you going to marry her?"

169

"Yes. We haven't told her parents yet, although I'm sure they suspect it. If they hadn't been so relieved to see her alive and well yesterday I think her father would've strangled me."

"Probably rightfully so," teased Lena. In the moments of quiet that followed, she studied his profile in the starlight. "I can't imagine what it was like out there for you, living in the mountains while Indians and white men both tried to capture you."

"Yeah, our lives did take different paths, didn't they?"

"Did you ever see or talk to any of the Cheyenne?"

He nodded. "I was in their camp one day." He saw her watching him intently and sensed her burning desire to know something of these people who had altered her life so dramatically. "They were friendly at first and treated me with respect, but they were cautious and so was I. There was a certain tension in the air the whole time. We weren't able to get past that." He found himself relating the entire story to her, of how he had entered the camp with the intention of getting Tara released, how the negotiations broke down because of Beartooth's deception. He talked about how he felt upon learning that the Cheyenne's demands were much bigger, the problem ran much deeper than he could control, how he became crazy with anger and got thrown out of the camp with a sentence of death by evil spirits. It was the most he had ever said about the incident to anyone, and he wasn't sure if it was Lena's need to hear it or his need to talk which drew it out of him.

"It's hard, isn't it," she said when he was finished, "making enemies of our father's people."

He lay back on the hay with his hands behind his head. "Yeah, but I don't hate them. Some of them are good people and some are bad, no different than the people in town. But if I could live out my life here without them ever knowing that I'm still alive, that would be fine with me. Somehow I don't think that's going to happen."

"Oh, speaking of people knowing you're alive, there's a cavalry soldier who comes here sometimes asking about you, if I've heard anything from you. He's a friend of Julie's."

Nate sat up in the wagon and thought. Yes, Julie had mentioned a captain. An incident fleeted across his mind but he quickly banished it. "I don't know what he wants." And then as an afterthought, "Has he talked to the Sinclairs?"

"I don't know. I don't think so."

Her answer didn't exactly give him the peace of mind he was looking for, but there was nothing to be done about it now.

"Shall we go in and fix up your room now?" asked Lena.

"Definitely. I'm so tired."

"Well, you'll be able to sleep in no time. Let me warn you though. You better look out for Myra the maid. She sometimes sleepwalks."

Chapter 23

Nate fell back into ranch work as if he had never left it. He had taken over his duties at the first of spring roundup so his time was devoted to rounding up range cattle, branding new calves with the Split Timber brand, which was the letter T split down the middle, running tallies on the herd, and riding fence lines to check for damage by winter storms.

He quickly established his position among the ranch hands, none of whom he had been acquainted with before. They knew nothing of him or his past, but he earned the respect of every one of them, often with humor and reserved friendship.

He found that the most difficult thing about his job was balancing what he knew to do with what Ward wanted. He understood Ward's desire to learn about ranching and he was willing to accommodate him, except when doing so would upset the organization he was working so hard to create. He discovered that the hands did not have much respect for Ward, and so he used his position to keep Ward from dealing directly with them.

By the summertime Nate had succeeded not only in running a smooth operation on the ranch, but also in gaining Ward's confidence and convincing Ward to back off a bit and allow him to do his job. Ward didn't even balk at handing Nate a hefty wad of money to take to distant ranches to find trained horses, negotiate their purchase, and bring them back to the Split Timber.

Throughout his long days of exhausting work Nate kept his eye on his secret goal. He wanted a position like Ward Taylor's. He wanted to hand the wad of money to someone and call the horses his own. He wanted a herd of cattle to wear his brand. So he found time whenever he could to spend with Tara, to renew his enthusiasm and remind him of the reason for his goal.

Tara wasted no time in idleness either. Her father paid her weekly wages for keeping the accounting books, stocking shelves, and working the counter in the store. She sorely missed being with Nate all the time, day and night, but she kept this to herself. Such things were not discussed among her sort of people. So she found distraction in the steady stream of customers, both familiar and unfamiliar, who did business in the store.

*   *   *

By August Nate decided it was time to make his next move. So one day when he was riding in from the range and spied Tara's father leaving the house, he called to Edward, who responded by waving and coming over to him.

"Did Tara come with you?" asked Nate as he dismounted.

"No, but she said to tell you hello if I saw you."

"Got time to talk a minute?"

"Certainly."

Nate led his horse into the barn and tied him in a stall.

Edward followed and asked, "What's on your mind?"

"I want to ask your permission to marry your daughter. I've been saving up my money and I can provide for her. I can't give her all that you can yet, but I'm going to start up my own ranch as soon as I can. She'll have a good home."

Edward scratched his head. "You and Tara have already talked this over, haven't you?"

"Yes."

Edward looked thoughtfully at Nate for a long time and Nate stared right back. He hated this long silence for it could only mean that Edward had to contemplate his answer.

"Nate, you know I think highly of you. And it pains me to say this but I have to say no for the time being."

Nate was shocked at this unexpected answer. "What do you mean no? Why?"

"I don't want to tear down your hopes now that you're home and you're with your sister and you've got a good job. But the fact is, you're still not free of the Cheyenne. Even though they're long gone for now, whenever I see you I remember them. And I'm afraid of what would happen should they find you."

For a while Nate wasn't sure how to respond to this. "So I'm a constant reminder?" His irritation became evident. "Well, tell me what to do about that, Mr. Sinclair. Am I to be branded for the rest of my life because of what happened one unfortunate night?"

"Now give me a chance to explain—"

"No, you let me explain. Every single thing I do, I do for Tara. I love her, and I would never put her in danger—"

"I know, Nate. I believe you. Now listen—"

"Don't give me that." Nate turned away in anger. "If you believed me you wouldn't stand in our way."

Edward laid a hand on Nate's shoulder and whipped him around. "Damn it, you're going to shut up and listen to me, you understand?"

Nate calmed down, his anger replaced by astonishment. "No one's ever talked to me like that before, Mr. Sinclair, except my father."

"I'm sorry. I didn't mean to do that."

"No, it's okay. Maybe that's what I've been needing." He sat down on a bale of hay with his head in his hands. "It's just that I can't seem to get away from my past. Why should it now interfere with mine and Tara's plans?"

"I just don't want Tara in any more danger than she's been in already."

"After I nearly got myself killed trying to rescue her, spent a winter in the mountains, and brought her home to you safe and sound, you're trying to tell me that I can't protect her? Mr. Sinclair, I would lay down my life for your daughter."

"But I don't want you to have to. And it wouldn't do any good against a whole tribe of Indians. How do you know that the same thing wouldn't happen to you and Tara that happened to your folks on the Broken Bow?"

"It wouldn't happen," Nate mumbled.

"How do you know that?"

Nate hung his head in shame. Edward had him cornered. "I don't know," he answered softly.

Edward gripped his shoulder. "It's not just Tara I'm worried about. It's you too, Nate. You're like a son to me. Now I'm not dumb. I know what you'll want to do. If you asked her I'm sure Tara would elope with you. You don't really need my permission."

Nate shook his head. "I don't want to do that. I've always respected you, Mr. Sinclair. And I want your blessing."

"Then be patient. I would be proud to have you as a son-in-law. We will work something out."

"I'm gonna see to that."

"I believe it," chuckled Edward. "You know, you've grown up to be just like your father."

"Have I? Sometimes I wish I'd never been born Cheyenne."

"That's not like you, Nate."

"How do you know what I'm really like?"

"Maybe I don't, but I know that you have the advantage of being able to see both sides of the fence. None of us can do that. If we could this would probably be a more peaceful place."

"Then how come people look down on me as an outlaw, a traitor? Answer me that."

"Because you are part of two worlds. I believe that deep down some people envy you because you can walk the line between confidently. There is no question in your mind of who you are or which world you stand for because you stand for both. The only conflict you have is from other people who don't know who you are."

Nate pondered Edward's words. He was no longer angry, just feeling slightly misplaced in the world. Why was he such a perilous person to be around?

As Edward mounted his horse, he smiled down at Nate. "Why don't you go up to the house? There's someone there who says he wants to meet you."

Not feeling like meeting anyone, Nate plodded to the house and entered the parlor to find Lena and Ward seated with Julie and a uniformed cavalry officer.

173

Immediately Julie stood. "Nate, I'd like you to meet Captain Blaine. Josh, this is Nate Hunter."

The captain and Nate stood before each other to shake hands. "Good afternoon, Captain," said Nate, "and welcome to the Split Timber."

"Thank you," said the captain.

Even as Nate eyed the double bars on the captain's shoulder straps, he had a sinking feeling this was not to be a social visit. Captain Blaine's visible uneasiness didn't escape his attention either. This was turning out to be a bad day for Nate all the way around.

Captain Blaine glanced at the others. "Would you mind leaving Nate and me alone for a moment please?"

Ward rose but Lena stayed put, sensing something was amiss. "This is my home and I will not leave the room."

Ward sat back down and he and Julie looked at the captain questioningly.

"Very well," said Captain Blaine. He pulled his gun and leveled it at Nate. "I must ask you to hand over your weapons please."

"What?" gasped Lena.

"Josh, what are you doing?" asked Julie in alarm.

The captain's eyes remained fixed on Nate. "I have orders to place you under arrest for the murder of Lieutenant Sam Wyatt."

Nate met Captain Blaine's gaze with contempt as he unwillingly removed his gunbelt and laid it over the captain's waiting hand.

"Josh, does that have to be done this way?" Julie asked.

"When you wrote and told me Nate was back, it was my duty, of course, to inform my superiors. This is not of my choosing but I will carry out my orders." He turned his attention back to Nate. "You will return with me to Fort Mason immediately. If you agree to cooperate I will not shackle you."

Nate narrowed his eyes in disgust. "I will cooperate, Captain."

Ward stood up. "Nate, did you kill that man?"

"Yes, I did."

"It was in self-defense, wasn't it?" asked Lena.

Nate looked squarely at her. "I swear, Lena, he would've killed me." He started to name Tara as his witness but thought better of it. He didn't want to drag her into this in front of the others.

*   *   *

The following day Nate and Captain Blaine started for Fort Mason, on a trip devoid of much conversation between them. Although there were no shackles or binding ropes, both were fully cognizant of their roles as soldier and prisoner and behaved accordingly.

A day and a half of riding over hills and prairie brought them to the big log stockade guarded by a watchtower at each of the four corners. The inside was very spacious with most of the log cabins built into walls around the edge. The commander's quarters were at the opposite end from the gate. In the middle was a flagpole flying the United States flag, visible outside above the fortress walls.

A private meeting held that evening between Captain Blaine and Colonel O'Brien excluded Nate, who spent the night in a tiny, musty jail cell by himself. He was summoned to see the commander the following morning. He entered the colonel's office filled with apprehension cleverly veiled with confidence. He stood before the colonel's desk, head held high and looking down on the large, bald man with brown hair on the sides, light blue eyes, and thick mustache.

"So you are Nathaniel Hunter," said Colonel O'Brien, studying in detail the man in weather-toughened buckskin.

"Yes, sir."

"Sit down, please."

Nate sat in the chair the colonel indicated and Captain Blaine sat in another beside him.

"So tell me about the shooting."

Nate reluctantly took himself back to that night ten months before. "I was with Tara Sinclair on Mount Defiance after we got away from the battle. We split up. She was going to the bottom of the mountain where she was to meet some soldiers. I was leaving the Territory, heading for Canada. But I decided to follow her to make sure she made it safely. I heard her scream and went to her. She was very scared and crying. That soldier also heard it and came looking for her. He saw her with me and thought I was..." He took a deep breath. "He accused me of trying to molest her. I wasn't, of course. He didn't know that we were friends. He knew who I was, though, and I guess he thought I was on the Indians' side. I said I was innocent and Tara was free to do what she wanted. He wouldn't listen but said he'd give me one more chance to surrender to him before he killed me. I said again that I hadn't done anything to her."

There was silence as Nate stared out of the window behind the colonel's desk. But he was not seeing it. He was recalling what he had done with dread. His voice was barely audible. "I don't know why he felt threatened, but I saw him reach for his gun and I pulled mine... . I was faster."

"Did you realize at the time that what you did was a capital crime?" asked Colonel O'Brien.

"No. I know he meant to kill me and I was protecting myself. I didn't want trouble. I warned him not to draw."

The colonel looked at Captain Blaine. "What do you think of this, Captain?"

"Well, Lieutenant Wyatt was a little trigger-happy. We all knew that about him."

Colonel O'Brien switched his attention back to Nate. "You really consider yourself innocent?"

"Yes, sir. I believe it's only natural for one to defend his own life, even if it is against the United States Cavalry. I'm sure you would do the same if you were up against a Cheyenne Indian."

"Of that I'm sure. Then again, it all depends on which person is in the wrong."

Nate was growing tired of the colonel's attempts to corner him. It seemed to be some sort of test. "I think you and I both know that I wasn't in the wrong."

Colonel O'Brien chuckled. "I see you are exactly the way Captain Blaine says your friends perceive you. You judge people beyond their words."

Nate looked over at Captain Blaine and the captain read the question in his eyes. "In the days after you and Tara ran away, I talked to Julie a lot. It was fortunate that she knew you so well and was able to tell me the kind of person you are, someone who is unlikely to kill in cold blood. Bearing this in mind, I and some other officers held a meeting and decided that, upon hearing your own explanation, we may not hold you accountable."

Nate was skeptical. "The testimony of one woman managed all that?"

"Definitely not, but it helped."

Colonel O'Brien added, "We concluded that the sole reason we had men up there on Mount Defiance that night was to rescue Miss Sinclair and see that she was safe. Well, it seems that you took care of that as well as or better than any of us could have. Also, we never even considered that she wouldn't want to come home. If she chose to go with you that was her own personal affair and had nothing to do with us." The colonel glanced at Captain Blaine and continued, "I am willing to negotiate a pardon for you."

"Thank you, sir," said Nate, relieved. He was eager now to go home and continue his simple, law-abiding life where he left off.

The colonel had other ideas. "The main reason I had you brought here is, as you know, we've had trouble with the Cheyenne for a couple years now. White settlers from here to Timber Fork live under the constant shadow of Indian threats. There are rumors that the Cheyenne are now staying in a valley maybe seventy, eighty miles south of here. We want very badly to form a peace treaty of some kind with them. But we need an unbiased mediator. That's where you come in. We feel that your involvement is essential in bringing about this compromise."

Nate looked sternly at Captain Blaine. "You kept this from me all during our trip here. Why?"

Colonel O'Brien replied, "Captain Blaine did not know about this until last night."

"So you brought me here to use me, did you? Do you really think I'd be so willing to jump in and bring about a treaty that, no doubt, would be mostly for your benefit and not the Indians?"

"I didn't just think you'd be willing, I expected it."

"Well, you expected wrong. I've been involved with them too much to want to stir them up again. They don't even know I'm still alive and that suits me just fine. My life is more peaceful now than it's been for two years."

"I guess I had you figured wrong then," said Colonel O'Brien. "Somehow I thought you would want peace with the Cheyenne too, after all they put you through."

"Colonel, they've put me through more than you probably know. Do you think for a minute that I don't want peace just as much as you, even more? It was my home that was burned to the ground and my father who was killed by his own people. My mother died in my arms. And what about that senseless battle last September? My best friend died from an arrow in the chest. You think I didn't ache to see peace then? You bet I did. Even as I took down braves with my own gun I wanted it. But you can't have peace with a people like that. They have no desire for it. They've had promises broken too many times by white men who think they're nothing more than wild and worthless savages."

"I sympathize with them," said Colonel O'Brien. "It was never my wish that the Indians be treated like they have. I realize this was their land first but I truly believe that they and the white man can share it in peace. It will take sacrifice on both parts, I know, and I'm prepared for that. Now I understand your feelings, Nate, but this means very much to a lot of people." His eyes bore down hard on Nate. "I strongly urge you to consider my request some more."

"I already have. My answer is no."

"Then Captain Blaine, return Nate Hunter to the brig."

"What?" asked Nate, stunned.

"I think you misunderstood," said Colonel O'Brien. "I was willing to negotiate, but apparently you're not."

Nate pointed an accusing finger at the colonel. "You are blackmailing me. You, an officer of the U.S. Cavalry."

"I am giving you the opportunity to help yourself." Colonel O'Brien carefully took a cigar from a carved redwood box on his desk, stuck it in the side of his mouth, and lit it. "I hear that you hope to marry into the Sinclair family. Your murder conviction would make a nice scandal for them, wouldn't it?" He leaned forward. "And I would see to it that it did."

Nate was seething.

"And I suppose your little fiancée would love coming to visit you in a dirty, stinking prison, just before your hanging."

Nate glared at Captain Blaine, waiting for him to respond, but the captain would only look down at his lap. "You're just going to sit there and let him issue

177

an immoral order?" Still no acknowledgment from the captain, and Nate made no effort to hide his disgust. "Well, I can see how you became a captain." He fought the urge to fly out of his chair and lay into both of them, but a quick review of his options told him it would serve no purpose. He was in enough trouble with the cavalry and there was no higher officer to whom he could make his plea. And he couldn't risk the scandal for Tara's family. He gripped the arms of his chair and swallowed his pride. "I will be your mediator, Colonel."

Colonel O'Brien clapped his hands. "Splendid! We can send a contingent with you and—"

Nate held up one hand. "No soldiers. I stand a better chance of winning their trust if they see I'm on my own. And I'm sure there's no need to tell you how I detest the sight of soldiers right now."

The colonel shot him a displeased glance but didn't press the subject further. "When can you leave?"

"Soon. I'll be returning to Timber Fork first. I have a couple things to tie up there."

"Very well. If you can help us procure a signed treaty your pardon will be in effect the same day. Captain, restore Nate's weapons and horse to him, to show our good faith."

* * *

Sitting on his horse outside the fortress walls, Nate contemplated his prospects. He was free of the cavalry and Mr. Sinclair wasn't going to tell him what to do either. He would go back to Timber Fork, marry Tara before anyone knew what was happening, and light out for other parts. But where? He thought about Mark Curtis. Mark had seemed to think California was a good place. But even as Nate made his plans, he knew that an irritating sense of duty would prevent him from putting his own desires ahead of the expectations placed on him.

"Damn it," he muttered to himself as he kicked his horse into a trot.

Chapter 24

"You want us to have peace with the Indians before you'll let Tara marry me," Nate said to Edward Sinclair as they sat in the Sinclairs' parlor. "So I'll go to the Cheyenne and negotiate with them."

"I'm not so sure that'd be a great idea," said Edward. "That's a monumental task. There's been so much bloodshed that I think peace is a long ways off."

"But if anyone can do it, it would be me. Remember how you said I walk the line in between?"

"Nate, think about what you're doing. You're making a rash decision for the sake of my granting permission to marry Tara. You may be throwing yourself into danger if you visit the Indians again. Your feelings for Tara are blinding you to the risks involved."

"I'm not blinded to anything, Mr. Sinclair." Nate leaned forward in his chair. "If anything, my eyes have been opened by this. The white settlers aren't going to go away and neither are the Indians. We don't have a choice but to make friends with them. I have to at least try." Though the cavalry had provided his initial incentive, Nate had become convinced of the necessity of his mission. Coming back from Fort Mason, he had known that Edward Sinclair would be the hardest to convince of the wisdom of this endeavor, but now he sat in the parlor ready to bargain.

Edward studied him scrupulously. "How will you do it though?"

"I don't know yet. But the time is right. The cavalry wants to have peace and they're willing to compromise. All we have to do is bargain with the Indians and come up with the compromises." He paused. "It's either that or I take Tara and move away somewhere where there's no threat of trouble. I don't think you'd want that."

"You're right. I wouldn't."

"Well, neither would Tara. She's done more for me than you'll ever know. I don't want to repay her by taking her away from her home. I do want to give her something that will show her how grateful I am to her, something she'll never forget. And I know what it is I want."

"What's that?"

"The Broken Bow." Upon seeing Edward's skeptical look, Nate queried, "The ranch is for sale, isn't it?"

"Well, yes, but—"

"You can't refuse a buyer, Mr. Sinclair."

"But you don't have any money to offer."

"You don't need it right away. I could pay you a percent of my earnings every year until I've paid off however much you want for it. And it will still be in your family."

"Would you really want to live there again after what happened?"

"I had just as many good times there. It was my home. I don't hear the war cries anymore, and I don't see the flaming torches. I see only the future and a chance to give the Broken Bow back its place as the pride of the Territory."

Edward leaned far back in his chair and scratched his chin thoughtfully. "You'll need cattle, horses, and people to work them."

Nate nodded. "In time it'll all come together. That ranch is going to be great again someday, Mr. Sinclair. You'll be proud."

"All right then, if you can calm down the Indians, we'll work out a deal on the Broken Bow."

Nate had to restrain himself from jumping up and shouting his triumph to anyone within hearing distance. "Do you mind if I have that in writing?"

"Don't tell me you don't trust me," chuckled Edward. He took a piece of paper from one of the small shelves of his writing desk, picked up a pen, and dipped it in the inkwell. Halfway through the note he stopped and looked at Nate. "I don't think Tara should know about this yet. I don't want her to get her hopes up."

"I wasn't planning to tell her. I wanted to surprise her with it. I guess I still have to prove myself to you too. Don't worry, I will."

* * *

That night following supper at the Split Timber, Nate laid out his plans for Lena and Ward. "I'll finish out the week here and leave Saturday."

"Are you going all by yourself?" Ward asked before taking a sip from his glass of brandy.

"Of course not. I'm going to take a representative for the white man."

"And who might that lucky person be?"

Nate looked at Ward's unsuspecting face and smiled mischievously.

"Now hold on just a minute!" declared Ward. "If you think you're getting me tied up in this you've got another thought coming."

"Why, I wouldn't leave you behind, Ward. I knew you'd jump at the chance for political power. It'll be just like being a representative for government in the big city, only you'll be dealing with Indians."

"I don't think it's such a good idea though," said Ward, sick at the thought of facing Indians after what he'd heard about them.

"I know just what you're thinking," Nate said, "but you don't need to worry about being a burden to me. Besides, if I don't get this thing done right, I may be headed out of the Territory. You don't want to see that happen, do you?"

180

"Why wouldn't I? There are some rather nice places elsewhere."

"Ward, shame on you!" scolded Lena.

"I was kidding, honey." His smile quickly faded. "But I am not going to walk into that Indian camp. One look at a city man like me and they'd scalp me for sure."

"You'll have to face me if you don't go, and I can't promise you'll fare any better," said Lena.

"Never mind, Lena. I can't tell Ward what to do. He's the boss."

"Come on now, Nate," Ward began. "I'd love to help, but—"

"As long as there's no risk involved," replied Nate. "I spend two years out in the mountains, then as if it's not enough that I have to get myself on my own feet I have to come over here and get you on yours. I've been all summer bringing your ranch up to snuff. It's now competitive with any ranch in the Territory. And you don't even want to dirty your shirt for me."

Ward shifted uneasily and took an extra-long swig of brandy. "I guess I do owe you one. All right, I'll go."

"Wonderful!" exclaimed Lena.

"Can I take my brandy with me?"

"You better. You may need it," replied Nate.

Chapter 25

At dusk on a warm mid-August evening, Tara stood alone in the barn behind the store, petting Molly's velvety black muzzle and feeding her a carrot. The orange of the setting sun shone through the open door and reflected on the golden hay. The light in the barn suddenly dimmed, and Tara turned to see Julie standing in the doorway. The sunset behind her silhouetted her petite frame and blond curls.

Tara smiled and looked back at her horse. "I've been neglecting Molly. The poor thing probably thinks I forgot all about her."

"She misses you riding her." Julie walked over to the stall where Tara stood and began stroking the horse's neck. "You know, Tara, you're different than before you went away with Nate. The mountains did something to you, something good I mean. There's hardly anything of the city girl left in you."

"I feel different," replied Tara, glad to finally have this conversation with someone. She looked past Julie at the mountains visible in the distance beyond the open barn door. "It's beautiful out there, Julie. I don't mean just physically beautiful. It's dangerous, but there's beauty to be found in the danger. It's almost like..." She struggled to find the right words to express herself while Julie listened, fascinated. "...like when you overcome the danger you earn the right to be there."

"Even with everything I've done," said Julie, "living way out in the Oregon country and all, you've experienced something I know nothing of. You've become more like him." She smiled with admiration. "I like it."

Tara considered that a high compliment, and coming from her best friend, it meant the most of all.

Julie's exuberance faded. "We're moving to California, Tara, leaving the end of this month. My pa finally talked my ma into it."

Tara stared at her in disbelief, wanting her to be teasing, wanting her to say she wasn't going. "Julie, I... I don't know what to say."

"I know." Julie tried to hide the difficulty of breaking this news with smiles and laughter. "But you know how my pa is. There's always a better life for us somewhere else. He says we need to make it to Oregon before winter sets in, then we'll follow the coast on down." She felt a lump rising in her throat and hurriedly thought of more to say. "Can you just imagine how excited Mark would have been?"

But Tara was not listening. "I had hoped when you came back from Oregon I'd never have to say goodbye to you again."

Julie turned and, with her hands clasped behind her, strolled a few feet, idly kicking at clumps of hay. "Oh, you've got Nate now. You'll be getting married. You won't miss me."

Tara shook her head. "I'll miss you. Every time I go riding to places we used to go, or go sleigh riding in the winter, or when there's a dance I'll miss you."

At the same moment they began to cry and reached to embrace each other. When they let go Tara wiped her eyes with the back of her hand and asked, "What about your captain?"

"Oh, that's not really so serious. I think it'll be good for me to get away."

Tara sensed there was something amiss that Julie didn't want to say. "I know you don't want to go and leave him, do you?"

"It will be best for Josh and me both in the long run."

"Why would it be best?"

"Because of what happened when I was in Oregon." Tara was watching her expectantly. "There was a handsome cavalry soldier at Fort Brooks, Lieutenant Jonathan Foster. I first saw him when he rode by our farm one day and stopped to help us catch our milk cow that had gotten loose. After that whenever Ma needed anything from the store at the fort I offered to go, just so I could try to run into him." She smiled. "It worked pretty well and soon we were seeing each other steadily. Once when he was to be transferred he even arranged to stay at Fort Brooks. I never knew how he did that." The faraway look left her face. "I really loved him, Tara."

"What happened?" Tara breathlessly asked.

"He was killed in the last raid."

"Oh, how awful for you," whispered Tara. "In two years you've never mentioned a word of it to me."

There were new tears forming in Julie's eyes. "I tried so hard to forget. Anyway, Josh reminds me of him, young and ambitious, a soldier through and through."

"How are you going to tell him?"

"I don't know yet. Next week I'm going with Pa to Fort Mason to outfit a wagon for the trip. I'll talk to him then. I was wondering if you'd come with us so we could spend a few days together."

"Of course I will."

*   *   *

When Nate walked into the Sinclairs' store the next morning, he headed straight for the counter where Tara was helping a customer. He winked at her and smiled. Nate looked to see who was standing next to him. He was a young man with sandy-colored hair. For Nate the memory of him went back a ways.

He remembered when the boy had banged on the door of the Hunter cabin and frantically informed Nate's family that Indians were on the warpath and headed for the Broken Bow. He looked older now. He was more brawny and had a mustache.

"Andrew Matheson!" Nate exclaimed. "I never knew if you were still alive after the massacre."

"I got away with my brother, spent some time in Dakota," Andrew solemnly explained. "What are you doing here, Hunter?"

Nate steeled himself for the coldness of his attitude. "I'm living here, working."

"So the rumor I heard is true. Somebody should've run you outta the Territory a long time ago, Nate."

"How could you listen to people's idle talk? We used to be good friends, Andrew."

"That was in the innocent old days before you started causing trouble. Now no one's mind can rest thinking about Indians attacking us."

"And you blame me for that?"

"You bet. You'd best clear outta here before anything else happens. I have a wife and baby son now and I don't wanna lose them because of you." He turned to the stunned Tara. "And you're an Indian lover now, I hear. What's happened to you, Tara? You would mix your blood with his?"

In a flash Nate grabbed him by the collar and shoved his back against the counter. "You don't talk to her that way."

"Oh yeah," replied Andrew through gritted teeth, "you were always touchy about insults to your Cheyenne blood."

Nate no sooner let go of him than Andrew balled up his fist and skimmed Nate's jaw with it. A fight erupted in spite of Tara's protests.

The two paid no attention to anything except the power of their punches and didn't even seem concerned when Andrew was knocked against a shelf, causing a lantern for sale to fall on the floor and shatter.

"Now see what you've done!" Tara shouted. The sight of Nate fighting was a familiar one these days due to people like Andrew who wanted him out of town. Tara was just glad that there was no jail around for him to be locked up in.

After a while of rolling on the floor, Nate pinned Andrew down and socked a couple of blows that dazed him. Effectively beaten, Andrew conceded the fight and made a hasty exit to preserve what pride he had left.

His cheekbone bruised, Nate stepped up to the counter and slapped some coins down. "For the lamp. You don't need to thank me for defending your honor."

"You can joke at a time like this," Tara hissed.

"Tara, this is my life. I have always lived with the knowledge that some people hate me because of my heritage." At this she simmered down, and he continued. "We need to talk. Meet me out back at the barn."

In the barn he sat on a bale of hay and she paced back and forth, both trying to calm their emotions.

Finally he collected himself, looked wistfully out at the mountains, and began, "We fell in love in the wilderness where there are no class distinctions, no rules of society, no one looking on. But we came back, as we knew we had to sooner or later. Now we're in a different kind of reality. Your family is well-respected, and you marrying a half-Cheyenne..." His voice trailed off, and he could not look at her as he continued, "I must give you the opportunity to back out of our engagement if you want to."

Tara stopped pacing and beheld him in disbelief. "Why would I consider that?"

"This is just a little frontier settlement, but your family has a position in society here and across the whole blame Territory." He shook his head hopelessly. "I can't match that."

"Do you have any idea how many people told Jerome Sinclair he could never make a go of a cattle ranch out here, that they'd never make it through the first winter, or how many people berated him and my father for turning their backs on their businesses and bringing their wives and children out here to this frontier? My family did not attain to this position by living by other people's rules. You taught me yourself to see beyond people's mere opinions of what we should or shouldn't be."

"Tara, my mother was an outcast, *even among her own family,* when she married my father. If I love you, I cannot with a clear conscience ask you to make such a sacrifice for me."

Tara moved closer to him and her eyes bore deep into his. "Did your mother have a happy life with your father?"

"Yes," he replied softly.

"Did she love you and Lena?"

"Yes."

"And so shall we be happy with each other. And so shall we love our children and teach them to respect themselves and *all* other people."

He felt grateful to her for her sobering perspective. She had stepped into the unknown with him before and survived, even flourished, and she would be up to the task of building a life with him too, he decided. "Okay then."

*   *   *

185

On Saturday Ward and Nate arose before daybreak to begin their journey. They packed food, ammunition, blanket rolls, and rain slickers. At the barn they dropped the supplies in a heap and led their horses from the stalls.

Lena appeared and, without a word, led her own horse from its stall and began to saddle it. She looked like the Lena of long ago, wearing a riding skirt, checkered shirt, and boots, with her long coal-black hair hanging loosely down her back.

"What do you think you're doing?" asked Ward.

"I'm going with you."

"That's completely out of the question," Ward objected.

"I am going. I want to be involved."

Ward appeared utterly horrified and looked to Nate for help. "Tell her, Nate."

Nate had already been questioning her motives. "The massacre's over and done with, Lena. This trip has nothing to do with that."

"I know," she insisted. "But I have an interest in this too. It's important to me."

Nate regarded her thoughtfully, then offered a smile. "We're glad to have you along."

Ward was flabbergasted. "And what about the ranch?"

"Our able-bodied hands can manage," replied Lena. "Nate said Josiah was the best one to cover for him while he's gone. I've already talked to him."

The matter seemed to be settled and preparations continued silently until Nate looked up to see Tara standing in the doorway.

"Papa said I should come out to say goodbye to you," she said. "He said you were going away for a few days. Is this another horse-buying trip? I thought the Split Timber had enough horses now."

Nate wasn't sure how to answer. He hadn't wanted to tell her the purpose for this trip. He looked at Ward and Lena and they understood his subtle message and left him alone with Tara in the barn.

"Ward and I have some business to take care of. You'll likely be at Fort Mason with Julie before we get back."

"What are you going to do?"

Nate continued to tighten the cinch on the appaloosa's saddle. "We're going to the Cheyenne to start peace negotiations between them and the white settlers. The cavalry wants to make a treaty." He finished the cinch and petted the horse's neck. "It's also a chance for me to clear up things between them and me."

"How can you possibly think of doing such a thing?" she asked, her face etched in worry. "You know how they treated you."

"I expect our discussion to go a lot better this time, now that they don't have you to bargain with."

"Isn't it enough that you're free among the white settlers?"

186

"No. This town is not at all the same as two years ago. I used to have friends here and now they hate my guts. And I've drug you down with me."

"We don't have to stay here. We can go where no one knows us."

"We're not going to run from our problems again. I don't want there to be anyplace we can't go and hold our heads high. You never complain but I know that people say things to you because of me. They make snide little remarks. You put up with it but I can't. Every time I go into town I get in a fight with someone who used to be a friend. I have a chance to redeem myself with these people now, and I must take it."

"But Nate, this is dangerous for you. I'm begging you not to do this." He was visibly bothered and began to pace the floor. "Please listen to me," she continued. "The Indians will—"

"Tara, the cavalry's going to try me for murder," he blurted out. "They're forcing me to do this for a pardon."

"Oh, no," she breathed when she had overcome the shock. "It was self-defense."

"They know that."

"Why didn't they want to talk to me? I was there. I will tell them the truth."

"The truth doesn't have anything to do with it. They're going to hold this over my head to get me to do what they want."

Tara narrowed her eyes in disgust. "Oh, how could Julie have anything to do with that man?"

"It's not his fault. All he does is follow orders. He's just a puppet in a uniform." His mood softened as he gripped her shoulders. "Oh, Tara, there's more, much more, and I'm so tempted to tell you everything but I promised I wouldn't. Just believe me when I say I'm gonna make you so happy when this is all over."

"I believe anything you say. But that doesn't stop me from worrying about your safety. How do I know you'll come back?"

He looked into her anxiety-ridden face and his heart went out to her. He reached behind his neck and untied his Cheyenne beads, something she had never seen him do before. Gently he took her hand and placed the beads into it. "I'll come back." He put his arms about her and softly kissed her. "I love you," he whispered in her ear.

Tara clutched the beads in her fingers and held him tightly. "I love you too. I'll be waiting for you."

When they had finished securing the last of their gear on their saddles, Nate, Lena, and Ward mounted up. "When you get to Fort Mason," Nate said to Tara, "will you tell Colonel O'Brien to be ready for some word from us?"

"I have no respect for that man, but I will do as you say."

Nate turned pensive as he looked down at her. "Let me see your smile one more time."

She knew he was worried too, and she obliged. He leaned down and, sliding his hand around her neck and drawing her close to him, he kissed her long and hard.

"Don't worry if the negotiations don't work out," said Tara afterwards. "Just take care of yourself and come back to me."

"I will. Nothing will stop me."

It was six o'clock and turning light when the three horses galloped southeastward. Saturday's journey took them through hills and forests and onto some flats. The first day was hot, but the second day it clouded up and they descended a ridge in a downpour. It rained heavily throughout the day, making travel difficult. Rocks were slippery and in open places the mud was thick. Nate, Lena, and Ward were drenched to the skin but they never stopped once. That night as they huddled under a rock overhang and ate cold cornbread, they wondered if the next day would bring more of the same.

"Myra never could make decent cornbread, even when it's hot," complained Ward, throwing his piece aside in disgust.

"You just threw out your supper," Lena casually told him.

"I'm not hungry." Ward slouched down and pulled his rain slicker around him more. "You know whose fault this is, don't you?"

"Okay, so I took you out of your comfortable house and made you a trail goat," said Nate. "So what? It's good to do something like this once in your life."

"That's right, once. And if and when I ever get home, I'm never going to do it again. Is that clear?"

Nate chuckled as he leaned against the rock and closed his eyes. "I couldn't care less what you do when you get home, Ward. Just so long as you make this trip."

Ward grunted as he went to his saddlebag and pulled out his ever-present silver flask of brandy and took a healthy swig. "This is ridiculous. A representative of the white man. I bet you don't need one of those any more than you need the president of the United States along."

There was no answer. Nate wasn't sure why he wanted Ward to come along either, except that it just somehow seemed right for Ward to learn something of the Hunter family's heritage, firsthand knowledge that he couldn't have gained in the city.

During the night the rains subsided and the stars came out one by one. The next day dawned clear and sunny, and the group hoped to make up for time lost the previous day.

That morning, the third day of their trip, they were crossing a sizeable clearing when suddenly Nate vaulted from his horse, having spied the remains of a bonfire. He knelt down, and from the still-wet ground he picked up a damp but charred piece of wood. He held it up along with a couple of gnawed-off rabbit bones for Ward to see.

"How do you know it's even from an Indian camp?" asked Ward. "Anybody could've stayed here."

Nate looked down again and his keen eyes picked out a tiny brown bead lost from a moccasin or piece of clothing. "And leave this?" he said, picking it up and rolling it over in the palm of his hand. "I doubt it."

"When do you suppose they were here?"

"Well, there weren't any fires burning last night, that's for sure. Must've been the night before." He dropped the articles and stood up excitedly. "I heard they were in the Territory but I hadn't expected to find them so soon. I'll venture to say we catch up with them tomorrow."

Ward did not share Lena and Nate's enthusiasm but chose not to say so.

They continued on their way, led on by vague clues, until they made camp that night, confident that the following day would see them in Red Feather's camp.

They were on the trail before sunrise the next morning, and by the time noon rolled around they were coming out of the mountains to a great, round valley. There they stopped on a large, flat rock to rest the horses, and Nate stood up in the stirrups to see what was ahead. "Ward, Lena, look!" he exclaimed, pointing.

Ward held up a hand to shade his brow. "I don't see anything."

"Yes," said Lena. "Way in the distance, about twenty miles." And there where she pointed were several thin, faint strips of smoke rising to the sky from bonfires. "You think it's Red Feather's band, Nate?"

"I know it is. I can feel it."

They guided the horses into the valley and began to follow the lines of smoke. At times they were in plain sight; other times a hill blocked their view. But each time they saw the camp it was closer. By sundown they were only a couple miles away but decided to wait until morning before going into the camp.

* * *

Tara sat waiting in Colonel O'Brien's office while an orderly went to get him. The ten-minute wait only served to contribute to her feelings of irritation and dislike for the man she'd never seen before. Upon his entrance she tolerated his polite smile and apologies for the wait and let him get settled at his desk before she relayed her news.

"Nate Hunter is on his way to visit the Cheyenne, along with his sister and brother-in-law. They hope to talk the Indians into meeting with you. He said to be waiting for some word from him soon."

"Good. I'm sure if anyone can do this he can."

"Yes, well, he told me to tell you and I've done so."

Colonel O'Brien looked down at his desk and smiled. "You don't like me, do you?"

"I don't approve of your methods. And I did some checking on you. I know that you're from Boston, and quite well thought of in your hometown. I'm prepared to write a letter to your town's newspaper and tell them all about you."

"Miss Sinclair, I don't know what Nate told you, but he murdered an innocent soldier. And aren't you at all concerned about the scandal that could result when everyone knows that you were alone with Nate on the mountain that night?"

"Colonel, everyone in Timber Fork already knows that I was alone with Nate on the mountain that night."

The colonel held up an index finger. "But they don't know about the murder. That's been kept quiet. Of course, if there's a trial that would have to change."

"And I as the only witness would have to testify. He couldn't be convicted because my integrity would not be questioned." She stood up and offered a polite smile of her own. "But I don't think there's going to be a trial because, unbeknownst to Nate, I just apprised my father of the entire matter, and if you try to carry on with this mockery of a trial, he will appeal to the governor of the Territory. I think the least you could expect is a court martial and to be stripped of your rank. Won't the hometown folks be proud."

She left him there, sulking in his humiliation. He hadn't counted on any member of the Sinclair family being so loyal to Nate.

* * *

As the sky lightened and stars began fading, Nate and Lena dragged Ward from his bedroll and shoved a cup of coffee into his hand.

Soon after hitting the trail they rode into the camp. As they walked the horses by, the people stared curiously at Ward with his white shirt and black pants. Ward took it boldly and Nate was pleased and surprised. Near the center of the camp in front of his tepee was Red Feather himself, standing beside his small fire.

The chief and Nate saw each other at the same time, but Red Feather's face held no expression. He simply watched the three of them ride up and dismount before him. His unblinking eyes stared hard at Nate who returned the gaze, remembering the face of the noble chief who only a year before had had him thrown from his presence in a pang of fury.

Ward was overly eager to gain favor with Red Feather. "Chief, my name is Mr. Ward Taylor and I'm pleased to make your acquaintance, sir."

The chief ignored him. His first words to Nate were nothing like his last words to him when Nate had been his prisoner. He spoke with newfound respect.

"I sent you to the Sacred Mountain to die but you return alive. The Wise One Above smiles on you, Eagle Shadow."

"Yes, he does, Red Feather. And he sends me to you now in the name of peace to make talk."

The chief called to a nearby young boy. "*Me'kono*," he said, and the boy responded by running about the camp to summon the chief's council.

"This is my sister Lena," said Nate, "and this is her husband Ward."

Red Feather turned to Lena. "Why have you come?"

"Ward and I have come far to meet you. I will be part of the peace talks."

The chief looked at Nate to see if he was going to allow his sister to have that much say in what would happen, but Nate stood silently, affirming his consent and subtly challenging the chief to defy him.

Red Feather beckoned his visitors to enter his tepee where they were invited to sit on blankets opposite him. Soon the chief's council filed in and took their places around the perimeter of the tepee. Nate recognized Beartooth, and one look from him told Nate the hostility Beartooth had displayed the year before had not subsided.

They all looked at Nate expectantly. "What is it that Eagle Shadow has come to tell us?" Red Feather inquired.

"You and I, Red Feather, have been against each other for a long time, and I want to end that."

"What do you want from us?" asked Red Feather.

"I'm going to marry soon. Tara Sinclair, you know who she is. We're going to live on a ranch near Timber Fork. I want assurances from you that you will leave us in peace."

The chief's face was rigid, but it was Beartooth who answered. "The white man turned your father's heart against us. He passed his poison blood on to you. Now you will marry a white woman whose family is among our enemies. The children you bear will be more poisoned than you. They will add to our enemies."

"That is not true," declared Nate. He glared at Beartooth. "What do you know of me? My children will be taught nothing but respect for the Cheyenne, just as my father taught us. Yes, he did fight against your braves when you attacked the Broken Bow, but he was defending his family and those who were always good to him, just as I would do."

"And what were you defending when you killed some of our people many moons ago on the Sacred Mountain?"

Nate's heart nearly stopped. Beartooth had fingered him as being present at the battle on Mount Defiance and fighting on the opposing side. Now he was on the defensive and faced with the harsh realization that he must secure his own position with the Cheyenne if he was to mediate negotiations with the cavalry. He turned to Red Feather. "It was an act of war. You lost some braves. I lost a close friend. You lost some fighting men. I lost my family on the Broken Bow. Now we're even. But I'm here to ask you for peace. I will not fight you ever again if you will promise me that."

Beartooth eyed him with disdain. "An act of war you call it. But you only wanted the white woman, and she caused you to fight against us."

"And you're jealous because you would've had her for yourself," Nate hissed.

Ward and Lena both noticed that the taut situation threatened to become overwhelming.

"Nate, please," said Ward under his breath. "Let's collect ourselves here."

The voice of calmness and reason was manifested in Lena, who addressed the chief directly. "Red Feather, I was away from the Territory for a long time, but I know about what has happened. My brother is a good and very honorable man. I stand by every word that he has spoken. In spite of what happened at the Broken Bow, in spite of what happened at Mount Defiance, he has struggled to maintain his respect for our people. I think he deserves the utmost admiration from you. If he was not honest, if he did not want to be your friend, why would he have even come here today to talk to you?"

Red Feather nodded in agreement. "I believe all of your words are true, Eagle Shadow. We will promise peace for you and the woman. But, like Beartooth, my heart is sad. You could have been a strong part of our people. You could have made a good ally for us."

Nate recognized the opportunity for his next move and he jumped on it. "You don't need me as an ally. I came here also to make peace between you and the whites. I bring with me a white man. He represents many who would like to be friends with you and your people. The soldiers at the fort asked me to come to ask you to meet with them." He paused and offered a smile. "You see, I can do a lot more good speaking for you than fighting for you."

The chief looked at his council and translated Nate's words for them. The discussion was short and Red Feather looked grim. "My braves feel no friendship for the white man who took our lands. We will make peace with you but not his kind," he said, pointing to Ward.

"Sir, I'm sorry," said Ward, "but I don't believe I'm familiar with the particular property you refer to."

"Never mind that now," ordered Nate under his breath. "Red Feather, I don't know everything about your situation or the land, but I know that the soldiers want to try to make it right. All I'm asking is that you meet with them and talk."

"How do we know you won't bring the soldiers here to kill us?" asked Beartooth.

"You don't, Beartooth. You just have to trust me. I know Red Feather does, and there's no reason you shouldn't."

A few moments of uneasy silence followed; none of the Indians seemed willing to budge.

Finally Lena spoke up. "I've already told you of my trust in my brother. It's for you to decide if you share that trust. But I know that he is asking a lot of you. I'm sure he would be willing to give something in exchange for your trust and for your agreeing to meet with the soldiers. What do you need that he could give?"

Again Red Feather addressed his council. It was already apparent that he responded to Lena's diplomacy much more readily than Nate or Ward could have anticipated. When he looked at Nate again his expression was softer. "You say you're going to live on a ranch. You could give us some good horses. More horses would make us hunt better and give us more to trade with."

Nate was so ecstatic that he was making progress with the Indians that he did not consider the fact that he had no horses currently except for the appaloosa. Ward's disapproving frown reminded him of it.

"My ranch is new, but I will work hard, and as soon as I can pull together a string of horses and have some to spare, I will certainly share with you."

"I will talk with my council again about your words. We will come to you when we are finished. You go and make your camp next to ours."

With their camp set up, Nate and Lena sat with cups of coffee while Ward paced back and forth. "What's eating at you?" asked Nate.

"That chief had no regard for me whatsoever. And if his cooperation has to be bought off with horses, I don't think this thing is going to go anywhere. We shouldn't have come."

"That may be true of you, but it's a good thing Lena's here. She got the chief to soften up and work with us."

"Well, it's as clear to me as the nose on my face that Beartooth is the main obstacle to any progress," Ward answered indignantly. "Somebody needs to lay him out flat, and if you're afraid to do it, I will."

"Oh, simmer down, Ward. You fight Beartooth and you'll be the one laid out, in a coffin."

"Okay, maybe that's not the best idea. But here's what we will do. We will get that chief off by himself, away from his council, and talk to him that way."

Nate stood and pointed his finger in Ward's face. "You may be the boss at home, but you are not the boss of this trip."

"But Beartooth's only intentions are to muddy up the water and—"

"The hell with Beartooth's intentions!" Nate fired back. "You are not Red Feather's favorite person to begin with, Ward. You could single-handedly botch up this whole thing right now, and if you do that you'll be sorry you ever knew me."

"Quiet!" demanded Lena loud enough to startle them both. "Maybe we should draw up a peace treaty among ourselves first."

Their argument effectively silenced, Nate looked over at where some curious Indian children had gathered to watch. He smiled, a gesture to show them that all was okay. But he suddenly felt silly and turned away.

"So how did you know just the right stuff to say, Lena?" asked Nate.

"I listened to Ward's father every day when he came home from the law office. He always talked about his cases, how he listened a long time to gather information before saying anything, how he negotiated settlements for big companies. It was very interesting. He always said that the way you worded things is what counted. By referring to you as my brother instead of by name, it made you seem more personable, more trustworthy."

"She's sharp as a tack, isn't she?" said Ward proudly.

Nate, still a little put out with Ward, grumbled, "You don't have to tell me. I always knew that."

The sun was directly overhead when Red Feather and Beartooth walked into their visitors' camp. Lena, Ward, and Nate quickly rose to meet them.

"We have made a decision," announced Red Feather. "Eagle Shadow will take my message to the chief of the soldiers. The message will tell them to come to us in peace to make talk. Beartooth will go with you. He can tell the soldiers in his own words that we are ready for talking."

Nate had an uneasy feeling in the pit of his stomach. He didn't trust Beartooth after the events of the year before when his dishonesty had been the spark that ignited a battle. And he knew very well that Beartooth didn't want to make friends of the whites. But Nate saw no way to object now without offending the chief. There was too much hanging in the balance. "All right, we'll leave in the morning." As an afterthought, he added, "We'll leave Lena here as collateral, to make sure we come back."

Red Feather nodded and he and Beartooth returned to their own camp.

"You're leaving me here as what?" asked Lena when they had gone.

"You wanted to help," replied Nate. "Don't let Red Feather change his mind while we're gone. Keep the idea of peace alive in him. He listens to you." He turned to the worried Ward. "This really is the best way."

Ward nodded, to Nate's great relief.

At daybreak the following morning, while Ward saddled the horses, Nate and Lena visited Red Feather's tepee. On a thin roll of birch bark Nate scratched in knifepoint a message in English from Chief Red Feather to the commander at Fort Mason. He was also given an eagle feather, the chief's signature, to accompany the message.

Afterwards Lena smiled graciously at the chief. "Chief Red Feather, I'm sure you agree that my brother is doing a great thing for our people. Such a thing must be worth a price to you. What do you think you could give him?"

"You are right," concluded the chief. "Eagle Shadow, we have already promised you peace. We now give you our friendship also."

"And protection from any enemies?" Lena ventured. "The soldiers he will bring here have given him trouble before. Perhaps an agreement that they will not harm my brother should be part of the peace talks."

"We will not make peace with anyone who would do harm to Eagle Shadow." He gave Nate a true look of admiration such as Nate had never received from him. "You are honored to have such a wise sister."

"Yes, thank you," Nate agreed. When they had returned to their own camp, Nate couldn't hold in his laughter. "You are amazing, Lena. Just yesterday you had me giving him horses for the same thing!"

*   *   *

Shortly afterwards, Nate and Ward bade Lena farewell and, along with a pensive Beartooth, rode away from the Indian camp.

Chapter 26

"He's gone!" exclaimed Ward as he shook Nate awake on the second morning of their trip. "Beartooth's gone. He must have left during the night."

Nate sat up and looked at where the warrior had laid out his blanket the night before, but the spot was barren and Beartooth's horse was gone too. "The sneaky coward!" he muttered.

"Shall we go after him?" asked Ward.

"No, he's probably halfway back to Red Feather's camp by now. And I say good riddance."

Ward's eyes widened. "Did he take the chief's message?"

Nate smiled mischievously as he pulled the birch bark from inside his shirt. "Not likely."

*   *   *

It was late on the third day of their trip. Knowing they were just hours away from the fort, Ward and Nate pushed the horses on at a fast pace, eager to make it out of the woods and onto the plain where the fort was located before darkness overcame them. As the warm afternoon sun moved through the sky it made spots of light and shade on the forest floor. The lighted spots were beginning to fade in the early evening when Nate and Ward guessed that it was only about five or six miles further to Fort Mason.

Nate's inner self was telling him to beware of something. The feeling had emerged over the last hour and was growing progressively stronger. He'd been hearing sounds in the woods, like something moving through the brush, following them. It was barely audible and Ward missed it altogether. Nate said nothing; it could've been small animals. But he knew from past experiences never to ignore that feeling. He felt to make sure that his rifle was handy.

They came to a big clearing which sloped down from the woods all the way around. In the center was a small pond. There wasn't much in the way of cover, but the horses hadn't had water most of the day and Nate and Ward's canteens were dry. Nate stopped his horse and studied the atmosphere, looking, listening—nothing out of the ordinary. They guided their horses into the clearing and began to cross.

Dusk crept in as they rode, and they hurried the horses faster. When they neared the pond, Nate heard a flutter in the brush on the other side. He turned his head in time to see three birds take flight, startled by something. He reacted with lightning speed. "Ward, it's an ambush!" he shouted as he jerked his horse to a stop, slid his rifle out of its sheath, and jumped to the ground.

They fled to the woods, using their horses for cover, while a band of six men led by Beartooth appeared from all directions in a blaze of gunfire. Once in the camouflage of the woods they turned back to retaliate and the attackers did not give chase so eagerly. The two sides fired back and forth to no avail until Ward shot and killed one of the assailants with his rifle.

"Would Beartooth do all this just to get the message?" asked Ward in between volleys.

"It's not the message he wants," replied Nate as he crouched behind a tree to reload. "Beartooth is here to kill me." His fingers flew as he shoved rounds into the magazine. Only Nate fully understood the gravity of the situation. They were up against the chief's best tracker and fighter, and if anyone of Red Feather's band could match Nate for stealth and cunning, it was Beartooth.

Most of Ward and Nate's shots were wasted for the enemy stayed well-hidden. Finally Nate caught a figure out of the corner of his eye, flitting from one tree to another across the clearing. He swung his rifle into position and fired. Now they were outnumbered by only two to one.

"I need to move around the side of the clearing," said Nate, "and see if I can pick off these men one by one. Can you handle this side by yourself?"

"Yeah. I used to be a sharpshooter for sport. I won first place at the county fair last year."

Nate wasn't sure if that was comforting or not. "Well, this ain't the fair."

He darted from tree to tree, thoroughly checking around him as he went. He followed the sound of gunfire until he came upon one of the attackers. He laid his rifle on the ground, pulled his Colt, and crept up behind the unsuspecting man. In one fluid movement he jumped the man, grabbed hold of his collar, and cocked the hammer of his gun behind the man's head.

Completely taken by surprise, the man whipped around, scared speechless. Now it was Nate's turn to be surprised. "Andrew!" He kept his gun trained on Andrew's forehead. "What the hell are you doing firing on me and Ward? What did Beartooth tell you to get you to do this?"

Andrew swallowed hard. "He said you were trying to rally the Indians to attack white settlements."

Nate didn't have to ask if Andrew still believed that; it was clear that he did. Releasing the hammer of the gun, Nate slammed the barrel against Andrew's cheek, knocking him to the ground with a grunt of pain. "You be grateful for that wife and son you have," snapped Nate, "because if it weren't for them I'd kill you now. Go on, get out of here and don't look back or I will kill you!"

Andrew scrambled to his feet and fled, and Nate was confident he was out of the fight. He retrieved his rifle and continued making his way around the edge of the clearing. He found a place where he could be more effective and set to work attempting to make the odds more even for him and Ward.

Nate soon realized that he hadn't seen Beartooth for a while. He checked the location of the other three men, but Beartooth was not among them. Suddenly he heard a subtle moccasin step behind him and stiffened with dread. He turned to look into Beartooth's menacing eyes several feet away in the gathering darkness. Nate instantly saw that there was no mercy or loyalty in him; he stood poised like a cougar ready to pounce on his prey. It was the consummate face of evil.

As Nate saw Beartooth's gun barrel being raised he instinctively went for the trigger of his own rifle and jumped aside to throw off the warrior's aim. But Beartooth had gotten the head start and his shot did not miss target. Nate felt a hard blow to his left front side just under the ribs and he was violently twisted backwards and slammed into a tree trunk. With the wind knocked out of him, the rifle slipped from his grasp and he sank to his knees. He clutched his side where he felt the bullet go in and struggled for a breath. When a moment later his wind returned, it was accompanied by a rush of sharp pain and he clenched his teeth to fight it. As he doubled over and slowly lay down, he realized he was now utterly defenseless, his very life in Beartooth's hands.

In a haze he saw Beartooth coming closer. The brave was going to count coup on him, and he braced himself. Beartooth jammed his foot into Nate's injured side. "No, don't," Nate groaned as he weakly tried to push Beartooth's foot away. He heard something crack inside him and blacked out for a few seconds. When he opened his eyes again he saw the enemy still standing over him. He realized Beartooth intended to stay there and watch him die. Nate mustered his resolve. This wasn't going to happen this way, he decided. He couldn't let Beartooth win. He closed his eyes and stilled his breathing to nearly nothing. The sting of the bullet pierced deep into his insides and burned like a raging fire. He felt warm blood trickling down his side. For a moment, as he lay on the edge of consciousness, he wasn't sure if he was really dead or just pretending to be.

Time passed excruciatingly slow until Nate chanced to open his eyes. Beartooth had gone, but Nate limited his movement until he could be sure he was alone. His first thought was to get back to the fighting; he couldn't leave Ward to himself. But as he started to rise he was startled by the sight of one of the shooters lying on his stomach about twenty feet away. The man was using a revolver to fire in Ward's direction. Nate wanted to take him out with his gun, but if Beartooth was still in the area, a gunshot from Nate's position would give away the fact that he was still alive.

Carefully he pulled his knife from its sheath, aimed with precision at the man's back, and drew back his arm. The knife hurtled through the air and found its target with a powerful thud. With a grunt of pain the man arched his back and tried to reach for the knife. But Nate was on top of him then, yanking his knife out of the victim and replacing it in its sheath. With all of the fury of a wounded animal, Nate wrenched the man's gun from his hand and smashed it against his head, knocking him out instantly.

Next he was on his feet and running. The wound doubled him over and he stumbled a couple of times before reaching the limited safety of a big spruce tree. There he fell to his knees and, supported by the tree trunk, began extracting bullets from his cartridge belt and loading them into the gun he'd just taken from the enemy. He knew his strength wouldn't last long and he needed both of his weapons to be ready. When the chamber was full he stuck it into the waist of his pants and pulled his own Colt, which was already loaded.

He saw one of the attackers moving through the brush northeast of his position and fired. The bullet grazed the man's leg and he fell. But he quickly rose again and moved behind a tree, still a part of the fight, still a threat. Nate trained his attention on the man and soon emptied the Colt. He holstered it and drew the gun at his waist. He fired a few more times but his senses were dulled and his aim was way off.

He couldn't hold up much longer. The pain was intense and he was losing strength rapidly. He felt himself almost fall and grabbed the trunk of the tree and held on.

He suspected Beartooth had long since left the area, thinking Nate dead and his objective complete. But there was still the one persistent shooter whom Nate had wounded. But Nate couldn't do any more good in his condition and he had no idea what had happened to Ward. He wondered if Ward was still alive. He shook his head, trying to clear the cobwebs from his mind. Of course, Ward must be alive, he thought. Why else would the attacker still be trying to shoot at him?

He tried to fire his gun again but it only clicked. The chamber was empty and he was too weak to reload it. He dropped the useless weapon on the ground and thought of Tara and his promise to get back to her. How he longed to be in her arms, to feel the soft touch of her hand on his sweaty brow, just to be with her. But that seemed so far away now.

He could feel a steady trickle of blood sliding down his waist and he stuck a hand inside his shirt to hold against the wound. His vision blurred, and suddenly everything started spinning around him, his hand slipped from the tree trunk, and his weight began to fall forward. He was unconscious before he hit the ground.

* * *

Ward heaved a great sigh of relief. After several unsuccessful volleys he had finally decided to quit firing and hoped the enemy would think he had run from the fight. It worked and now he stood alone in the forest. The smell of exploded gunpowder hung in the air and there were two bodies lying at the edge of the clearing, evidences of the ordeal that he had survived unscathed. He saw his faithful horse standing patiently nearby and he hurried over and mounted up, eager to get out of the woods. But he was beginning to worry about Nate. A quick check of the surrounding area turned up no sign of him, so Ward began to ride around the edge of the clearing. He found Nate's rifle and his feeling of dread deepened.

He heard a noise in the bushes behind him and whipped around. From out of the bushes wandered Nate's horse, the stirrups swinging against its belly. Ward picked up the loose reins and led the horse along while he kept searching. Then through the darkness ahead he barely caught sight of the form of a person lying motionless on the ground. As he rode closer, the wind blew the trees, and through an opening in the umbrella of foliage the moon shone through. It dimly lighted the spot to reveal the buckskin leather-clad body with the locks of black hair on the head. "Oh no," whispered Ward.

He vaulted from his horse and rushed to kneel beside him. Carefully he grabbed hold of Nate's shoulder and waist and turned him over. He opened Nate's jacket and was stunned to see the whole left front side of his shirt stained with blood. Ward turned his face away in utter despair, realizing that he must bear the tragic news to the Sinclairs and Lena.

"Ward," whispered Nate.

Ward looked back at him, not sure if he'd heard right.

Nate opened his eyes halfway. "It's good to see you're still alive."

Ward relaxed and smiled his relief. "You too, partner, you too."

"It was Beartooth," panted Nate through gritted teeth. "It's my fault. I should've been more careful."

"Never mind that now," said Ward as he felt around Nate's waist. "Did it go all the way through?"

"No. I've got broken ribs, and I've lost a lot of blood."

Ward sank back on his knees and shook his head. "Listen, we're only a few miles from the fort, but tell me what to do, Nate. Should I go on ahead and bring somebody back here?"

Nate vehemently shook his head. "Just get me to the fort. There's a doctor there." He clenched his fists and bit down on the leather sleeve over his wrist.

"Do you think you can sit a horse?" asked Ward skeptically.

"Yeah."

Ward went to his saddlebag, pulled out an extra shirt, and brought it back. "We need to stop the bleeding first," he said as he helped Nate sit up and lean against the tree. He opened Nate's jacket and shirt enough to insert the clean shirt and wrap it around his waist and tie it.

With his perspiration-drenched body exposed to the air, Nate began to shiver, a condition that worsened until he was shaking violently down to his insides. When closing his jacket provided no relief, Ward fetched a blanket from his saddle and threw it around his shoulders. Ward then reached deep into his saddlebag for his flask of brandy. When he turned back to Nate again he found him with his head hung down, his chin resting on his chest. He quickly put a hand on Nate's forehead and raised his face. Nate's eyes were closed and his countenance pale.

Opening his eyes just barely, Nate whispered, "Don't let me die, Ward, please."

His deteriorating condition greatly alarmed Ward, who kept it hidden and remained calm. "I won't, but don't you quit on me. Here, this is all I got, but it might ease the pain."

Nate grabbed the brandy with a trembling hand and drank.

"Keep that with you," said Ward as he positioned Nate's horse next to him. With his arms under Nate's shoulders he helped him struggle to his feet and climb up to the saddle. Nate hunched over, almost in a lying-down position, and clutched the mane.

"Hang on tight to the saddle. I need to get you to the fort as fast as I can." He strapped Nate's weapons to his own saddle and mounted up, then he picked up the reins of Nate's horse and began leading him eastward.

Some time later as they rode across the plain, the shape of the fort finally loomed in front of them against the backdrop of the stars. "We're here," Ward gladly announced. There was no answer but he saw that Nate still had a tight grip on the saddle. The gates at the entrance had been closed for the night but a guard in the gate tower called to them to identify themselves.

"I am Ward Taylor and you've got to let us in! There's a man here that's been shot!"

The guard called to a man on the ground who opened the gates. Ward and Nate rode across the darkened grounds to the hitching post in front of the commander's quarters. Just as the horses stopped, Captain Blaine and Julie showed up.

"Oh, Ward, it's you," said the captain. "The guard at the gate said somebody here was shot."

"It's Nate. He's pretty bad."

Nate lost his grip on the saddle and started sliding downward. Captain Blaine rushed in and caught his limp body, and he and Ward lowered him to the ground.

"How far has he ridden like this?" asked Captain Blaine.

"At least five miles," answered Ward.

Captain Blaine's trained eye caught something frightening in Nate's appearance and he grabbed Nate's chin and shook him. "Don't go to sleep, Nate!" he gruffly ordered.

Nate blinked a couple of times and focused his eyes on the captain.

"I'll get the doctor," said Captain Blaine. "Ward, you go get Colonel O'Brien, and Julie, you stay here with Nate." He grasped her shoulder. "Keep talking to him. Don't let him go to sleep."

She nodded and the men left. When they were alone, Julie tried to quell the lump in her throat as she watched him lying so still. She took her handkerchief and wiped his forehead. "Nate, what happened?"

"We were ambushed," he weakly replied between breaths, "in the woods west of here."

"Oh, how awful."

"Would you do something for me?"

"Of course."

"Inside my shirt is a message... . It's for Colonel O'Brien... . Make sure he gets it."

She reached inside his shirt and brought out the birch bark and eagle feather. "He'll get them," she assured.

"Is Tara here?"

"Yes. We arrived yesterday. I'll get her as soon as the doctor comes."

"No," he quickly replied. "Please don't tell her I'm here, or about what happened."

Julie fought to resist crying in front of him, but her efforts failed. "Nate, if... if something happened she'd never forgive me."

"I'll be fine... . Please don't tell her."

Julie regained her composure and her confidence in him. "All right, I won't."

Captain Blaine returned with the post doctor, and together they carefully lifted Nate onto a stretcher and carried him to the doctor's office. Julie followed and, once inside, stood out of the way while the two men, aided by a nurse who had been awakened and was attired in a nightgown and robe, placed Nate in a bed and removed his shirt.

Ward entered with Colonel O'Brien. "He was shot by a Cheyenne Indian," explained Ward, for the first time sounding miffed about the incident.

The colonel went to Nate's side. "I never thought the Cheyenne would do this to you, Nate. Honestly I didn't."

Julie was reminded of the message. "Here, Colonel," she said, giving him the birch bark and eagle feather. "He wanted you to get these."

The colonel read the message, then looked around the room at everyone, his face registering triumph. "The Cheyenne are willing to talk to us." He leaned over Nate and grasped his shoulder. "I promise you, this is not in vain. You got our foot in the door. It's a good start."

Nate's lips moved, but his voice was inaudible. Colonel O'Brien leaned down and heard his whisper. "Don't you try me for murder."

"I won't. You have my word."

202

"Your word's no good," he replied, louder this time.

Reluctantly the colonel answered, "I'll put it in writing. I'll have a witness." He went to the short, whiskered Dr. Bramer, who was readying his operating instruments, and eyed him gravely. "You take good care of him, Doctor. We need him alive."

"Yes, sir," replied Dr. Bramer. He turned to the nurse. "I'm ready to operate. Get the anesthesia."

The nurse took a small, clear bottle from a cabinet and poured a few drops of the liquid inside onto a clean white cloth. This she held down snugly over Nate's mouth and nose and told him, "Just relax and breathe deeply."

He did as she said and seconds later lapsed into a deep, painless sleep.

*　　*　　*

Out in the once-again still night Julie and the captain silently walked across the grounds to the cabin where Julie was staying, each absorbed in their thoughts. They reached the doorstep and Julie put forth a hand to open the door, but Captain Blaine caught it and pulled it towards him. Julie looked down at the ground, afraid that if he saw her eyes he would know the mass of confused feelings that filled her heart.

"Don't worry about him, Julie," he said. "He'll be fine. Just think about us being at peace with the Indians. Isn't it marvelous?"

"Yes, of course. It's been a long time coming. But I won't be here to enjoy it." And then as an afterthought, "I wonder what the Indians are like in California."

"I've been meaning to talk to you about that."

"About the Indians in California?"

"No. About your going to California. I don't want you to go and leave me."

"We already talked about that, Josh."

"No, we didn't talk about it. You told me you were going and that was it. Your mind was made up."

"But my family's going. What else would I do?"

"You could marry me."

Julie stared at him wide-eyed.

"I can provide for you," he went on. "I have acceptable officer's quarters here. I may even be up for a promotion soon and—"

"Josh, are you only suggesting that to keep me from going?"

"No." He took off his hat and looked down at it resting in his hands. "I had thought about it before, and then when you showed up here yesterday and gave me the news, I thought about it again. I love you, Julie, and I want you to be my wife."

"Oh, Josh, I don't know. This is all so sudden. I mean Nate's shot, and Tara doesn't know, and I feel terrible about it and—"

"I know maybe tonight wasn't the best time to bring this up." He remembered their first dinner together shortly after Mark's death. "I seem to be the master of bad timing. But I have to seize opportunities when they come, and in a few days you'd be gone and I'd never see you again. Is it really that easy for you to just pick up and go? Don't you feel anything for me that would make you think twice?"

"It's not that. It's..." She searched for the right words. "Well, I've been around the cavalry before, in Oregon. I've seen them killed and I've seen their loved ones devastated. You're a soldier, Josh. I don't want anything to happen to you."

Captain Blaine took her into his arms. "Nothing's going to happen to me."

Julie laid her head against the dark blue flannel of his coat. "I do love you, Josh."

He gently placed a hand under her chin and raised her head to meet his waiting lips. She was accepting of his kiss, a warm and tender expression that came closer than anything to breaking the barrier she had built around her heart.

"Does this mean you'll marry me?" he asked.

"I can't answer that now. Let me think about it a little while, okay?"

Captain Blaine lowered his eyes, disheartened at her response. "All right." Julie reached for the cabin door but his voice halted her. "I know you've been hurt before." Julie looked back at him, surprised at his perception. "I can tell," he said. "Julie, if you'll just accept me I won't let you down. But whatever you do, don't let my job as a soldier come between us."

Julie smiled and gave him another kiss before saying good night. Inside the cabin she found Tara in the front room by herself, trying to crochet lace.

"You know how old-fashioned Mother is," Tara said with a smile. "She says I have to get better at this. How was your walk? You were gone a long time."

Julie thought about Nate and covered her eyes.

"What's the matter?" Tara inquired, dropping the lace and going to her.

"Well, it's Josh. He—he asked me..."

"To marry him?" Tara finished for her. Julie nodded and Tara clapped her hands exuberantly. "What did you tell him?"

"I said I'd think about it." She smiled through tears. "And I think I already have."

"That's wonderful!" Tara threw her arms around Julie and hugged her. "You won't have to go away!"

"No, I won't." Julie searched for her handkerchief, remembered that she had used it on Nate and left it outside, and wiped her eyes with the back of her hand. When her eyes had cleared she saw her father had come in from the back room.

"Is this what you really want?" asked Hiram Curtis.

"Yes, I do. But I'm going to miss you and Ma." She broke into tears again as she rushed into his waiting arms.

"Your ma's not gonna like you staying behind," said Hiram. "But he's a good man."

* * *

The following morning found Julie and Captain Blaine in the doctor's office, where Dr. Bramer met them. "Good morning to you, Captain, ma'am. I know what you came for, and yes, he's going to be all right."

Julie slipped her arm into the captain's and smiled up at him.

"Mr. Taylor got him here just in time last night," Dr. Bramer went on. "I was able to get all the pieces of the bullet out. There are a couple of broken ribs and he'll be laid up awhile, but I dare say not as long as most people in his condition would be. He's very strong."

"Can we see him?" asked Julie.

"For a few minutes. He just woke up and he's very drowsy." He held back the curtain over the doorway to the room where Nate was and the couple entered.

Ward was sitting beside Nate's bed and looked up at the visitors.

"You look tired, Ward," said the captain.

"And hungry," added Ward. "But I'm told that Mrs. Bramer makes the best biscuits this side of some river I've never heard of. That could be good or bad." He stood and beckoned Julie to sit in his chair.

When Ward had gone, the captain pulled up a chair for himself, and Nate turned his head to look at his new visitors through half-closed eyes. The blanket was drawn up around his bandaged chest with his bare shoulders showing above it, and his face had lost its color.

"How do you feel, Nate?" asked Julie.

"Awful," he whispered. But he managed a smile to let her know that things could be worse.

"Well, you'll mend in no time. Guess what. I came here to say goodbye to Captain Blaine before my family moved to California. However, there's been a change of plans and I'm not going. We are engaged."

"You and the captain? Well, I guess since I wasn't available you had to settle for someone else." He gave her a teasing wink.

"Nate Hunter, you're incorrigible." She laughed and continued, "And he told me this morning that they need a schoolteacher here at the fort. I'm going to study to get my teacher's certificate."

"That's great, Julie. Congratulations. You treat her right, Captain, or I'll have to hurt you."

"I certainly will."

"So, Captain, when are we going back to the Cheyenne camp?"

"Not you, Hunter, you're staying here to recover. The rest of us are leaving Thursday morning."

"No, Captain, I have to go. My sister's down there waiting for us. Besides, I got other business to attend to."

"No, Nate, this is not a mission of revenge. I know how you feel, but please let it go."

"That's like asking the moon not to rise. Don't worry, I won't jeopardize the treaty."

"You won't jeopardize yourself either. With a couple of broken ribs you're not going anywhere."

"You misjudge me. Four days'll do wonders for me."

"Not enough to make the trip. You're not going and that's final."

Nate simply smiled. There would be more time for arguing Thursday morning.

Captain Blaine squeezed Julie's hand. "Would you leave us alone for a minute, dear?"

"Yes. I need to help Pa with the wagon. Take care of yourself, Nate."

When she had left, Captain Blaine turned very somber. Nate noticed that it seemed difficult for the captain to make eye contact with him, and he had a pretty good idea of what the reason was.

"I owe you a very big apology," the captain began. "That day, in Colonel O'Brien's office, you were right. It was an immoral order and I did nothing. I have felt guilty ever since, and then when you showed up last night and you'd been shot, I was so ashamed of myself."

He paused, but Nate said nothing, allowing him to feel the guilt a while longer.

"I have no right to expect your friendship. But anyway, I have written a letter to the proper authorities telling them of the situation."

Nate raised an eyebrow. "Is that what the book says to do?"

"What?" asked Captain Blaine, his train of thought broken by Nate's irreverent question.

Nate chuckled, then grimaced from the pain it caused him. "I'm just kidding, Captain. Don't worry about it. Everyone's going to get what they want. We will likely have a peace treaty; if the colonel's yanked out of here you maybe get to move up the ladder; and I don't have to get hung. And I'll even give you my friendship. With us getting married to women who are best friends, I expect we'll be seeing each other from time to time."

Captain Blaine smiled. "Well, I'm grateful that you've taken it so well."

Chapter 27

By the time the cavalry's departure day came, Nate was tired of the prescribed bed rest. He had never stayed in one place for so long in his life and it was driving him mad. And anyway, they needed him along, he thought. Red Feather would probably be more cooperative in Nate's presence. So at daybreak Thursday he began getting dressed, his movement hampered by the tight bandage around his chest.

Captain Blaine walked in as Nate was buttoning his shirt. "What do you think you're doing?"

"I'm dead and this is my ghost, and I'm going to haunt you all the way to the Cheyenne camp."

The captain wasn't impressed. "Get back in that bed."

Nate cast him a sidewise glance and the corner of his lips turned up in a sly smile. "I'm not under your command, Captain." Gritting his teeth to conceal the jabs of pain that accompanied every movement, he donned his jacket and knife belt. "Now would you get me my gun?"

"Absolutely not," replied Captain Blaine. Nate slowly shuffled past him, took his holster from the wall hook, and strapped it on. Captain Blaine could almost feel his pain. "All right then," he conceded. "But don't try to saddle your horse. I'll arrange for a bed for you in one of the supply wagons."

"That sounds very comfortable," said Nate, half-joking.

An hour later as Nate was being mercilessly bounced and jolted in a particularly rickety wagon, he was cursing the captain something fierce. He could see his appaloosa tethered to the back of the wagon. He would slip out of the back of the wagon, untie the horse, and ride him bareback. Anything had to be better than the wagon. But just as he sat up and started to move towards the back, the wagon hit a rock and the resulting bump landed him back on the bed with a yell of pain. He promptly changed his mind about being friends with the captain.

* * *

Early in the fourth day of travel Colonel O'Brien, Captain Blaine, Ward, Nate, and the small contingent of soldiers entered the valley where the Cheyenne were camped. Nate climbed from his wagon and accompanied Ward into the camp to locate Lena. Inquiring after her, they were told she was at the far end of the camp. There they found her carrying an armload of firewood.

"Lena," Nate called.

She turned, and when her eyes met Nate's, her arms went limp and the wood fell to the ground. She stared trancelike, and Ward and Nate were puzzled at her reaction.

"What's the matter?" asked Nate. "We weren't gone that long."

A tear slipped down her cheek as she ran to embrace him. "They told me you were dead."

"Oh, no," whispered Nate. He clasped his arms around her.

"Beartooth came back and said he'd found your body after you'd been attacked by bandits. I believed him. I knew Ward would be coming back here, and I decided to wait here for him."

"I am so sorry, Lena. I'm fine. I'm here now."

"Why did he do that, Nate?"

"Because he really thought I was dead. But thanks to Ward here, I'm okay." He pulled away from her and urged her in the direction of her husband.

"I'm sorry Beartooth put you through that, dear," said Ward as he hugged and kissed her.

"Is Beartooth here now?" asked Nate, looking around him.

As if he'd heard his name, Beartooth appeared from behind a tepee. If he was surprised to see Nate he didn't let it show. "You think the Wise One Above smiles on you, Eagle Shadow," he said in disgust. "But you are not one of us any more than you were before."

"Well, maybe that makes two of us," replied Nate. "A true brave wouldn't disobey his own chief and ignore the best interests of his people for his own satisfaction and then come back and lie about it. You're no brave."

"I will kill you for that."

"You will never! I'll get my revenge on you, Beartooth, and I won't even fire a shot. And you'll wish you had killed me."

Beartooth strode away, not intimidated, and Lena was left bewildered. "What happened?"

"He headed up those bandits he told you about," answered Ward. "He put a bullet in Nate."

She clapped a hand to her mouth and beheld Nate sympathetically. "If I'd known that when he came back here..." She didn't finish the sentence.

*   *   *

Nate felt a measure of pride at the moment that he introduced Colonel O'Brien and Chief Red Feather to each other, and he was secretly surprised by it. He and the chief had not always seen eye to eye, but he had come to respect and even appreciate the noble leader for his calm candor and sincere desire to achieve fairness in all matters. He certainly took into account the fact that, as of late, Chief Red Feather had treated him better than Colonel O'Brien did.

The negotiations over land and hunting rights lasted for two whole days. Most of the time Nate translated for the chief. It seemed that Red Feather preferred to go through Nate rather than speak in English directly to the colonel. Nate also mediated the discussions to keep them from getting hostile, but to Colonel O'Brien's dismay, it became clear early on that one of his worst fears had materialized—Nate had taken the Indians' side, and it was going to cost the colonel dearly in the concessions he had to make.

Colonel O'Brien was feeling a sense of relief when it appeared that the time was drawing near to put together the finished treaty and sign it. But Chief Red Feather wasn't done just yet.

"There's one more thing," Nate translated from the chief's words. He waited for Red Feather to continue. "He says that if you try to do anything to me, ever, the treaty will have no effect."

Colonel O'Brien stared at Nate disapprovingly. "Well, it looks like between the Sinclairs and the Cheyenne, you've created a neat little barrier for yourself, haven't you?"

Nate maintained a steady, expressionless gaze at the colonel and made no reply. He was only here to mediate a treaty; he had nothing else to discuss with the colonel.

Colonel O'Brien's eyebrows knit together as he spoke. "Tell him you're safe as a bear cub, Mr. Hunter."

Nate assured the chief that he was free of the cavalry and Red Feather nodded. The deal was done.

Following the signing of the treaty when the soldiers had commenced striking camp, Nate, Lena, and Ward met with the chief's council in his tepee.

"Eagle Shadow is to be honored," said Red Feather. "You have the great gift of wisdom which was your grandfather's."

"As well as yours," replied Nate. "And I need to rely on your wisdom one more time. I vowed I would not fight against our people again, and I will not go back on my word, but I appeal to you for justice."

"Go ahead," said Red Feather.

"I would've come here a few days earlier but I was delayed at the fort because of someone who tried to kill Ward and me. He hired a band of men and ambushed us just west of the fort. I was shot by him."

A look of concern crossed the chief's face. "This person should be punished for such an evil deed. Where is he?"

"He sits in the tepee with us this minute."

When the chief had looked at everyone present, his eyes fell upon the brave sitting to his left. Beartooth was the only one who had been gone the same time as Nate and Ward.

"That's right," said Nate.

"I was not wrong!" erupted Beartooth. "I do not trust one who shares the white man's blood. He and his treaty will one day bring destruction to us all."

"Eagle Shadow is a Cheyenne," Red Feather firmly replied. "You have broken a trust. You have made bitter the Four Sacred Arrows." The chief hesitated to pronounce judgment. Beartooth had been his friend for as long as he could remember. But in his position he knew what he must do. Showing no trace of emotion he made his declaration. "If it is the will of Eagle Shadow, you must die."

Suddenly all eyes were on Nate. The warrior's life depended solely on his decision and it was more of a responsibility than he cared to have. But he knew that other braves would be angered by Beartooth's death, and this was supposed to be a peace mission. "I am still alive. Let him live. But let him forever remember what he did."

The chief nodded and turned to Beartooth. "My heart is sick because of what you've done. Eagle Shadow has shown mercy, and now I must use justice. Your life will not be taken but it will mean nothing to us. For as long as you live you will be banished from this people. No more will you ride with us to the hunt. You will not speak to us and we will not speak to you. To us you will be dead. Go now, take your bow, your arrows, and your horse, and leave this place."

Beartooth was shocked by this rejection from his own chief, but he made no attempt to argue the decision since he knew it would stand as it was. He hid his shame as he rose to his feet and started to leave. He stopped by Nate and beheld him with a malicious glare. "I would rather you had me put to death."

Judging by the way Beartooth eyed him, Nate knew that they would meet again someday in a deadly confrontation. The next encounter would not be affected in any way by soldiers or Indians; the next time would be personal.

After Beartooth was gone, Nate looked over at Lena and could tell that she was thinking the same thing he was. They had just witnessed a scene probably much like the one in which their grandfather had been given the same sentence over thirty years before. Now they had finally gained acceptance among their people, on their own terms, only to see one of their own cast out.

Ward was the only one not moved by what was happening. "Well, Lena, it looks like we're in need of foreman number five, unless I can convince Nate to stay on."

"Much as I like your company, Ward, I think I'll have to pass."

Outside near the officers' tent, while Ward and Lena stood by, Captain Blaine shook Nate's hand. "Colonel O'Brien asked me to relay his many thanks to you."

"I'm sure he did," Nate replied with a smirk.

The captain smiled awkwardly. "Well, he said some words to that effect. Seriously, Nate, you've done a great thing here. It couldn't have happened without you."

"I'm afraid I can't take all the credit. My sister played a part in this too."

Captain Blaine nodded to Lena. "You both are to be commended. Now, Nate, you are still under Dr. Bramer's care. He insisted I make sure you return to the fort so he can keep an eye on you as you recover there."

Nate straightened up and snapped his hand to his brow in a salute. "Yes, sir. Right away, sir."

While Captain Blaine walked away chuckling, Nate bent over with his hands on his knees, grimacing in pain.

"How do you like that?" muttered Ward. "He didn't say one word about my part in this."

"And without doubt, that was the most important part," Nate teased, taking a deep breath and straightening back up. "You were the perfect observer, always watching and listening. You're a master, Ward. Next time the cavalry has a mission for us, I'll insist on having you along."

"Well, it won't be anytime soon," said Lena, a gleam in her eye. "I'm going to have a baby."

Ward and Nate's mouths dropped open, then Ward let out a gleeful shout and hugged her tightly. "Darling, how long have you known?"

"Since before we left home, but I didn't want to distract you from the job you had to do."

Nate laughed as he threw an arm around Ward's shoulder. "How about that, Ward? It looks like there's two things you're good at."

Shelly Greenhalgh-Davis

Epilogue

The shadows were beginning to lengthen as twilight drew near on the Broken Bow. A few gray clouds hung over the land and the yellow grasses bent under the force of a chilly autumn wind. Tara stood alone at the top of a knoll beneath a solitary oak tree, enveloped in a haunting silence that matched her gray mood. It had been five weeks since she bade farewell to Nate, three weeks since she had returned from Fort Mason, and she had not heard any word of Nate, Lena, or Ward. Nate had always slipped through peril's grasp before, but this time she thought surely he'd walked into danger that was too much for even him to handle. She felt helpless as she endured the endless days and nights, lonely even when surrounded by people. She was beginning to lose hope, and when hope was gone, there would be nothing else to cling to.

The Curtises had departed for California within days of Tara, Julie, and Hiram's return from Fort Mason, and Julie was staying alone in their big house in town whose rooms used to ring lustily with the activity of a family of seven. Julie had hoped Captain Blaine could come to Timber Fork so they could be married before her family left but he'd had to leave on some mission. Her mother had wanted to wait until the marriage could take place before they left, but her father had insisted that with the season changing they could not delay. It had caused quite a heated debate within the family, and Julie and her mother were left devastated.

It all seemed rather trivial to Tara. At least Julie knew the captain was safe and wasn't doing anything risky. How could such details be so important? So to escape hearing about these petty concerns, Tara had taken to early evening rides to lonely places. She had left Molly at home and brought the pinto, the one Nate had gotten from the Arapaho for her to ride. She had ridden him bareback. Nate had tried to saddle train him for her but the feisty little thing had bucked him right off and he'd had a few choice words for the horse. So Tara had decided maybe saddle training wasn't really important.

"You lookin' for me?" a voice sounded from behind.

Tara whirled around to find Nate standing only yards away. She drew in a breath but no words would come out. She raised her arms and walked towards him. The last few steps were a run and he caught her up and swung her around. As she buried her face against his shoulder and smelled the familiar, rugged scent of the leather jacket, she couldn't prevent a tear from escaping and sliding down her cheek. She raised her head to meet his lips and he kissed her hard. "I missed you," she breathlessly whispered.

"I spent the last couple weeks at the fort recovering from a gunshot wound."

"Oh, Nate." Tara's eyebrows drew together in concern. His plan to bring peace must not have worked. "We can go away where the Indians won't bother us. I'll go with you anywhere you want to go, anywhere."

"How about right here?" A hint of a smile broke on his face.

"You mean..."

Nate nodded. "We have a signed treaty."

Her face lit up. "That's wonderful news. You did it!"

"Yep, and I was thinking, we could build our house on that rise right over there."

Tara looked at where he pointed but in her confusion she didn't see it. She looked back up at him. "What?"

"Well, if we're going to run the Broken Bow, we ought to live somewhere nearby, don't you think?"

Tara clapped a hand to her mouth as she burst into laughter, then she hugged him again. "You went behind my back and talked to Papa, didn't you?" She brought out his Cheyenne beads from the pocket of her riding skirt and reverently tied them around his neck. "I should never have doubted that you'd come back as you said you would."

"And I'm here to stay," he assured her.

"So when are we getting married, Eagle Shadow?"

"How about tomorrow? I don't have any plans, do you?"

Tara's mouth gaped. "We can't do that. I haven't gotten anything ready."

"You don't need to get anything ready."

"But we don't have a place to live."

With his arm around her waist, Nate began leading her back to their horses. "What? You mean we're the owners of the Broken Bow and we don't even have a roof over our heads?"

"Stop teasing, Nate. This is very serious."

"Hey, sweetheart, we're in debt up to our ears. You don't think I'm gonna worry about a place to live, do you? Remember, I'm the one who spent two years sleeping under the stars, and even enjoyed it."

Tara laughed at his carefree attitude, which always somehow made her not care either. "Tomorrow then."

About the Author

Shelly Greenhalgh-Davis, a native of Florida, now makes her home in Utah. Her professional experience includes eleven years as a network news editor with a national press clipping bureau and five years as a movie reviewer with a Tennessee newspaper. The story of *Eagle Shadow* is a reflection of her keen interest in Old West history and Native American culture. Married since 1994 to artist David Kimball Davis, they are the parents of two sons, and Shelly has embarked on a new career as a home school mom. She is currently writing a sequel to *Eagle Shadow*.

Printed in the United States
4738

9 780759 667884